336
W75
2004
C:2

ORIGIN STORIES IN POLITICAL THOUGHT:
DISCOURSES ON GENDER, POWER, AND CITIZENSHIP

*Joanne H. Wright*

# Origin Stories in Political Thought

Discourses on Gender, Power, and Citizenship

UNIVERSITY OF TORONTO PRESS
Toronto Buffalo London

© University of Toronto Press Incorporated 2004
Toronto Buffalo London
Printed in Canada

ISBN 0-8020-8812-0

Printed on acid-free paper

---

**National Library of Canada Cataloguing in Publication**

Wright, Joanne H. (Joanne Harriet), 1966–
Origin stories in political thought : discourses on gender, power, and
citizenship / Joanne H. Wright.

Includes bibliographical references and index.
ISBN 0-8020-8812-0

1. Political science – Philosophy.  2. State, The – Origin.  3. Patriarchy –
Philosophy.  I. Title.

JC336.W75 2004     320.1′1     C2003-904579-X

---

University of Toronto Press acknowledges the financial assistance to
its publishing program of the Canada Council for the Arts and the
Ontario Arts Council.

This book has been published with the help of a grant from the Canadian
Federation for the Humanities and Social Sciences, through the
Aid to Scholarly Publications Programme, using funds provided by the
Social Sciences and Humanities Research Council of Canada.

University of Toronto Press acknowledges the financial support for its
publishing activities of the Government of Canada through the
Book Publishing Industry Development Program (BPIDP).

*For Harriet and Frances*

# Contents

*Acknowledgments*    ix

1  The Origins Imperative in Political Theory:
An Introduction    3

2  The Birth of Philosophy:
Plato's Creation Politics    24

3  Hobbes and the Discourse on Origins    54

4  Gender in Hobbes's Origin Story:
The Case for Original Maternal Dominion    77

5  Pateman's Sexual Contract:
An Origin Story of Her Own    105

6  Getting to the Root of Patriarchy:
Radical Feminism's Quest for Origins    127

Conclusion    159

*Notes*    165

*Bibliography*    205

*Index*    221

# Acknowledgments

As this book began as my dissertation at York University, I wish to thank the members of my supervisory committee, all of whom have been, and continue to be, enormously supportive and helpful to me. Ross Rudolph, my dissertation supervisor, is the person to whom I owe my greatest debt of gratitude for his patience, encouragement, and insight. David Shugarman encouraged me in the development of this project and has consistently offered me excellent advice. Lorraine Code has been invaluable, not only for her feedback on this manuscript, but also for her supportive guidance through the various hoops of academia.

I completed this manuscript while a SSHRC postdoctoral fellow with Gordon Schochet at Rutger's University. My sincere thanks to him for the fruitful conversations about Hobbes and consent and for his always helpful counsel.

Throughout the process, I was assisted by the advice, criticism, and guidance of several other people, including Christine Saulnier, Leah Vosko, Gerald Kernerman, Pamela Leach, Barbara Falk, Peter Nyers, Linda McNutt, Patricia Hughes, Leah Bradshaw, Shannon Bell, Carman LeBel, Stephen Newman, David Johnston, and, most notably, David Bedford. My thanks also to the researchers and archivists who assisted me at the Canadian Women's Movement Archives, University of Ottawa; the Barnard Center for Research on Women, Barnard College, Columbia University; and the Tamiment Institute Library, New York University.

The research for this book was made possible through the generous financial assistance of the Social Sciences and Humanities Research Council of Canada, the New Brunswick Women's Doctoral Scholarship program, and the O'Brien Foundation. Publication was also facilitated by a Brock University Advancement Fund Subvention for Scholarly Books.

I also wish to acknowledge the support of my family, especially Janice Wright Cheney, whose work appears on the cover of this book, and Eric Wright. And, finally, thanks and appreciation go to Donald Wright for his years of reading and editing.

Earlier versions of this material have appeared elsewhere: 'Going Against the Grain: Hobbes's Case for Original Maternal Dominion,' *Journal of Women's History* 14:1 (Spring 2002): 123–48; and 'Birth and Reproduction as Perennial Feminist Issues: The Case of Plato and Mary O'Brien,' in Krista Hunt and Christine Saulnier, eds, *Feminism(s) on the Edge of the Millennium: Rethinking Foundations and Future Debates* (Toronto: Innana Publications and Education Inc./Canadian Woman Studies, 2001), 107–17. My sincere thanks to my editor at the University of Toronto Press, Jill McConkey, and to her predecessor, Kristen Pederson, for all of their assistance in making this project go forward; to Barb Porter for seeing the manuscript through its final stages; and to John St James for his careful copy-editing. A sincere thanks to Mary Newberry and Alex Campbell for preparing the index. I also wish to thank the anonymous reviewers of the manuscript for their suggestions for improvement. Any errors of fact or interpretation are mine alone.

ORIGIN STORIES IN POLITICAL THOUGHT:
DISCOURSES ON GENDER, POWER, AND CITIZENSHIP

*Chapter One*

# The Origins Imperative in Political Theory: An Introduction

Our origins preoccupy us. The desire to understand origins is as close to a universal phenomenon as might be imagined. There is, as Edward Said observes, 'an aboriginal human need to point to or locate a beginning.'[1] Fascination with and curiosity about origins in general, and an interest in the beginnings of human societies, human life, and indeed the cosmos itself, lie at the heart of religious, scientific, and philosophic inquiry. Although these fields of inquiry produce disparate answers to the question 'Where do we come from?', they share an impulse to both investigate and posit theories about origins.

For their part, religious creation stories claim the existence of a causal force that is responsible for the composition and ordering of all things from the cosmos to human relations. Forming the cornerstone of most religions, creation stories reconcile the relationship between that causal force and human beings. The scientific inquiry into origins aims at uncovering everything from the origins of the galaxy and the earth to the origins of the human species. It is evident in the disciplines of archaeology, anthropology, astrology, and chemistry, to name a few.

The tradition of political thought is not exempt from preoccupation with origins. Indeed, the question of the origins of politics and power is fundamental to political theory. Political theory shares with religious and scientific modes of thought the desire to uncover origins – in this case, the origins of political societies, the origins of power. This quest takes a variety of different forms in political theory, but its most compelling manifestation is in the telling of origin stories. Political origin stories are narratives about the beginnings of politics and power. While individual origin stories, like that concerning the social contract, have received a great deal of scholarly attention, the use of origin stories as a device in political theory has not. My purpose is to identify origin stories as a recurring motif in historical and contemporary political thought and to analyse the unique set of problems that they engender.

In this book, I examine three political origin stories in particular: Plato's *Timaeus*, Thomas Hobbes's social contract, and early Second Wave feminist stories about the beginnings of patriarchy. While these stories differ tremendously in their content and style – and I will elaborate on these differences throughout – it is clear that they share certain themes. In what follows, I will draw upon Plato's myth of the metals to introduce some of these themes and to highlight the politics inherent in the origins discourse.

### 1. Plato's Myth of the Metals: An Autochthonous Origin Story

Let us begin our inquiry into origin stories with one of the most famous examples from political theory: Plato's myth of the metals. In the *Republic*, Plato's main character, Socrates, expresses the need for an 'opportune falsehood' or a 'noble lie' to persuade the inhabitants of the city to accept the logic of its organization. According to the noble lie, the citizens of the city are to look upon one another as brethren, born from the same mother earth and nursed by her as well (414e).[2] The earth moulds its children carefully, fashioning each for a specific role in the city. Those who rule are composed primarily of gold, those who protect the city, silver, and the farmers and artisans have iron and brass in their constitution.

The myth of the metals is an autochthonous origin story. An idea deeply embedded in ancient Athenian consciousness, autochthony suggests that the origins of the human race and of entire cities is in the earth (khthōn) itself. Being born from the soil, or having ancestors who claimed to be, allows citizens to declare an original citizenship in that land – a 'natural' citizenship. Athenians asserted their autochthony, claiming ultimate title and authentic citizenship, thereby excluding immigrants, foreigners, and invaders from true membership. When Plato draws on the autochthonous myth to tell a noble lie about the origins of his city, he, too, asserts the authenticity of Athenian citizenship.

Yet perhaps more importantly in this instance, the autochthonous myth of the metals justifies and elicits consent to a hierarchical ordering of classes in the republic. Plato envisions a tightly organized hierarchy of specialization in the city, according to which only those with the proper breeding, intellect, and orientation of the soul will be admitted to the guardian class. Those who undergo similar training and are especially courageous will become protectors of the city, and the rest will constitute the common class. To guarantee that only those of a certain ability and upbringing become guardians, subsequent generations must be convinced that the state will be undermined if anyone but the 'gold race' rules. When sons are born their metal content will be assessed to ensure that they will be raised in the appropriate class.

Plato relies on the noble lie to quell uprisings and disorder, and to ensure conformity to his envisioned hierarchy. Simply put, the lie generates consent where there is none. It creates an artificial unity and harmony among the classes in a city that might otherwise be divided by class. Plato recognizes that creating such rigid class distinctions within the city has the potential to be highly divisive. Thus, he develops a mythical legitimation strategy – a sanction against farmers and artisans ruling – in order that they will consent to this hierarchical arrangement rather than resent it. The myth of the metals provides citizens with a script of citizenship; they need only believe the lie to accept their place in the city. Indeed, with this myth Plato opposes the democratic script of citizenship and its promise of the basic equality of citizens, and replaces it with his own script of natural hierarchy.

As an origin story, the myth of the metals is intriguing in that it is self-consciously political. In calling the myth an 'opportune falsehood' or a 'noble lie,' Plato is openly acknowledging that his political vision for the city needs some justification; it needs the solid foundation that only an origin story can provide. What is less clear, and remains a matter of debate, is whether or not Plato himself views his recommended hierarchy as entirely conventional, and thus in need of a story that will make it seem natural. Or does he believe the hierarchy to be grounded in nature, but recognize that not everyone will act according to nature? In the latter case, the noble lie explains and justifies the hierarchy to those who would not otherwise understand or accept its foundation in nature.

The myth of the metals shares with other political origin stories some key themes. Most political origin stories, for example, are concerned with the derivation of power relations in society and with the origin of society's political hierarchies. Again, Plato's myth is overtly political in its recognition of the need to provide a justification for these hierarchies. Moreover, whether directly or indirectly, origin stories must address the problematic of consent, as they all offer an interpretation of how things got to be as they are now. Are the hierarchies in political society a result of natural differences between citizens, for example, or did political society come into being through an act of consent or contract? These are the kinds of questions that most origin stories are written to address. The myth of the metals gives us a sharper sense than most of the contrived nature of origin stories as Plato is more explicit than many political theorists about the need to manufacture consent.

Most origin stories also at least hint at a theory of human nature and address the configuration of gender relations. Plato understands human beings to be divided into body and soul. In the *Republic*, he further divides the soul into three parts, the rational part, the spirited part, and the appetites. These three parts correspond to the three different metal compositions of human beings as specified in the noble lie. Those born with a predominance of gold are the ones whose soul is dominated by wisdom and reason. Those with the greatest amount of silver are the ones whose soul is dominated by courage. Finally, the commoners, whose composition is dominated by iron and brass, have imbalanced souls that are governed by the appetites. The myth of the metals, then, reinforces and mythologizes Plato's tripartite theory of the soul. Plato organizes his city on the premise that some are governed by the body, and are unable to rule as a result, while others – those who should rule – are able to subordinate bodily concerns to the faculty of reason.

The myth of the metals is ambiguous on the issue of gender relations. Part of the reason for this may be context: in the *Republic*, Plato is advancing a rather enigmatic and controversial plan for the inclusion of women in the guardian class. It is possible that he deliberately evades the question of the original arrangement of gender relations in this origin story so as to avoid any confusion regarding his controversial plan. Nevertheless, we should note that Socrates' tale makes mention only of sons who are born from the earth; women of different metal types are only added later. Socrates does refer to the earth as mother, which leads Arlene Saxonhouse to conclude that Plato acknowledges women's important contribution to reproduction.[3] Still, I suggest that an equally compelling interpretation of autochthonous origin stories is that they decontextualize the human species from actual reproduction. Rather than celebrating – or even acknowledging – women's reproductive capacity, autocthony elides women's roles in reproduction by focusing on the rise of human beings from the earth. Autochthony reflects not so much the 'misunderstanding of the laws of reproduction' as the 'desire of a city of men to deny the reality of reproduction.'[4] The advantage of such a move, according to Nicole Loraux, is that men 'rid themselves of the opposite sex and exclude all references to femininity from their discourse.'[5] A city that has autochthony built into its self-understandings is a city that is severed from its connection to the human cycles of birth, life, and death to which it is, in truth, inextricably attached.

## 2. Examining the Politics of Origin Stories

Plato's myth of the metals serves as a useful point of entry into the discussion of the politics of origin stories. I suggest that origin stories present us with an aporia. Political beginnings, the beginnings of politics and power, are elusive to us: we are unlikely to arrive at a truth about how things got to be as they are. Still, we are driven to tell these stories in spite of, and perhaps even in response to, the mystery that surrounds our political origins. The telling of political origin stories is an expression of the same 'aboriginal human need' that guides scientific and religious inquiry.

In an important sense, the value of origin myths lies partly in their telling. In other words, origin myths serve an important function in helping societies organize their ideas about themselves and about the universe. Myth can be thought of as a 'complex but revealing symbolism' that results from a society projecting its interests, beliefs, and fears onto a cultural narrative.[6] The creation myth, viewed through this lens, is a culture's means of making sense of itself; cultures create these myths because they 'feel better if [they] think in this manner.'[7] That these stories are fictional, and are often recognized as such, has little bearing on the cultural currency they achieve, as they become cultural symbols – and conceptual prisms – through which a society interprets the world.

In creating origin stories, political thinkers too 'make sense' of their society's history, its defining questions, and its very purpose. Political origin stories are a contentious and political means by which Western society organizes and represents its experience – both real and imagined. Furthermore, to delineate beginnings is to set the course for what is to follow; it is to carve out an identity for those who see their experience reflected in myth. Thus, when we read these stories we gain access to our society's perception of itself, as well as to some of our perennial political preoccupations.

As an interesting example, we might consider the story of Genesis in the Hebrew bible and what it reveals about the political preoccupations of its writers. Genesis can be read as, among many other things, an expression of social tension and ambivalence about gender. The ambivalence about gender emerges in the character of Eve, who is created second and punished by God for her 'sin.' The more interesting but lesser-known character in the story is Adam's first companion, Lilith. According to the original Jewish scripture, Lilith refused to submit to Adam, and was punished by God and banished to the Red Sea. Contemporary feminists show an interest in Genesis because of its status as the dominant creation myth in the Western tradition.[8] Its rendition of gender relations continues to hold sway over our own modern conceptions. Feminists have revived Lilith in an effort to reveal the deficiencies in Eve's character, and to valorize a sexually dominant woman in Judeo-Christian mythology.[9] In their view, the creation of Eve as a sexually submissive partner to Adam reveals the patriarchal subtext of the Judeo-Christian tradition.[10] At the same time, we need to remember that the tradition that reveres Eve is the same tradition responsible for Lilith's creation. In light of this fact, Deborah Sawyer suggests that the record of Lilith 'can be interpreted to mean that the notion of equality was an issue within ancient Judaism.'[11] The point here is simply that, no matter how hierarchical and patriarchal the system, equality is always at issue and all origin stories must grapple with the justification of its presence or absence. It would seem, then, that the banishment of Lilith to the Red Sea and her early extrusion from scripture indicates that, for the multiple writers of the Genesis origin myth – just as for their present-day readers – gender relations were unsettled and unresolved. This has immediate relevance for our interpretation of gender relations in political origin stories, as these stories also contend with the issues of equality and gender hierarchy.

All of this is to say that origin stories serve a heuristic purpose, allowing us both to explore our fundamental questions and problems and to assign meaning to our human existence. Our need to tell these stories, or to piece them together and fashion them from the disparate strands of our culture, is as universal as it is powerful. At the same time, however, origin stories are also infused with, and driven by, power. They are designed to authorize or confer authority on preconceived political solutions. Therefore, in accounting for the significance of origin stories, we need to be attentive to their relationship to politics and power.

For example, while origin stories satiate an ontological need, they are also mired in the politics of essentialism. Michel Foucault addresses this point in his work on genealogy and history. He suggests that the search for origins reflects a desire 'to capture the exact essence of things; their purest possibilities, and their carefully protected identities.'[12] However, this is a pointless search, simply because 'what is found at the historical beginning of things is not the inviolable identity of their origin; it is the dissension of other things. It is disparity.'[13] Foucault contrasts the origins theorist with the genealogist. The origins theorist thinks in terms of essences and teleology; the political origins discourse assumes that origins contain essential and indispensable data from which political solutions are moulded. The genealogist, by contrast, casts aside metaphysics and the faith in a 'primordial truth.' In so doing, the genealogist finds out that 'there is "something altogether different" behind things: not a timeless and essential secret, but the secret that they have no essence or that their essence was fabricated in a piecemeal fashion from alien forms.'[14]

Plato and feminist origins theorists imply the existence of a primordial truth and essence that need only be recovered and restored. We see this, not as much in Plato's myth of the metals as in the *Timaeus*, wherein he invokes an original truth about the beginnings of the world in order that it be recaptured in contemporary Athenian politics. For Plato, there is an original and true ordering of the natural world that ought to be reflected in the political sphere. Similarly in feminist origins discourse, while feminists have typically eschewed the idea of sexual essences, there are overt references to the natural superiority of the female sex and the loss of female power in an all-out prehistoric patriarchal conquest. Feminist origins theorists became entirely preoccupied with the desire to reconnect with their essential matriarchal identities.

In the case of Hobbes, the belief in essences is less obvious. In the story of the state of nature and the social contract we do not find the same evidence of the desire to uncover the human essence at its beginnings. At the same time, however, the state of nature does invoke the natural, and does suggest that pre-social human beings will be driven to behave competitively because of their nature. Hobbes also participates in the fantasy that it is possible to get back to origins – if not to the historical beginning of things, to use Foucault's phrase, then at least to our original nature.

Origin stories, then, are essentialist narratives that do more than simply uncover beginnings: they authorize implicitly particular solutions. 'Myth does not deny things,' Roland Barthes observes; 'on the contrary, its function is to talk about them; simply it purifies them, it makes them innocent, it gives them a natural and eternal justification.'[15] And, indeed, origin stories confer upon politics the permanence of nature. Contingent political arrangements, arrangements that are the result of accident and dissension, as Foucault posits, are invested with truth and essence in origin myths. Political origin stories are premised not only on the belief that origins can be revealed or at least hypothesized but on the notion that 'things are most precious and essential at the moment of birth.'[16] What they are at that moment determines and authorizes their subsequent configuration, hence the impulse to recover that moment of originality.

An additional problem with the use of origin stories in politics is the fact that they often do more to derail attempts to find political solutions to concrete problems than to solve these problems. It remains unclear why political solutions hinge on political origins, for rather than opening us up to innovative political solutions, political origin stories construct an imaginary political scenario that restricts our thinking to its narrow parameters. Origin stories tend toward oversimplification, for they are abstracted from the messiness and complexity of actual politics. Indeed, to be persuasive as stories they must be simple. Moreover, in constantly invoking origins, such stories redirect our energies from politics, avert them from real conflicts, and refocus them on questions to which there might never be satisfactory answers. In the myth of the metals, Plato's choice to invoke origins as a means to justify his arrangement of hierarchical specialization avoids contemporary Athenian politics altogether. The origin story, in this instance, is told as an attempt to rise above internal tension and strife between the different classes of the city. In telling the story, Plato is both recognizing the challenges of class strife and circumventing the politics that accompany and might resolve it.[17] Ultimately, however, avoidance of such tensions can only be temporary, and evading the problem through the use of an origin narrative only postpones serious attempts to find a solution.

If Plato is avoiding the morass of politics, he may also be trying to avoid recognition of the violence of beginnings. Hannah Arendt has argued that beginnings 'must be intimately connected with violence,' and that 'no beginning could be made without using violence, without violating.'[18] Plato may be offering the myth of the metals to gloss over that violence, concealing it with a harmonious script of natural hierarchy, or as Bonnie Honig has put it, 'to prohibit further inquiry into the origins of the system and protect its center of illegitimacy from the scrutiny of prying eyes.'[19] Yet, in this instance, it is perhaps more likely that Plato uses the origin story to *forestall* violence, the violence that he anticipates will be the natural result of the agonistic, money-making behaviour that so dominates the society in which he lives.[20] Other origins theorists, by contrast, write origin stories to expose violence. Feminist origins theorists bring to the surface the violence of a patriarchal war, and of an original rape and/or matricide. They replace the myth of consent between the genders with the 'truth' of war and violence. Similarly, Hobbes's version of the social contract acknowledges the violence of beginnings. As Arendt points out, the social contract is nothing but a 'theoretically purified paraphrase' for the conviction that 'In the beginning was a crime.'[21]

Arendt's thesis about the violence of beginnings provides one possible answer to the question that lies at the heart of most origin stories, the question about the derivation of power and of political hierarchies in society. Yet it is only one of several possible answers, for it is not necessarily the case that violence marks the beginning of all societies. Perhaps more importantly, Arendt's thesis may lead us once again down the path of trying to uncover an elusive primordial truth – in this case, the truth that all human societies are born out of conflict. Rather than taking her assertion as a governing fact about origins, then, we might read it as an instructive caution about the political motivations of origins theorists and their desire to gloss over or purify politics.

In short, there is much to be critical of in the origins discourse. Deconstructing political origin stories requires that we acknowledge the connection between origins and essences, that we denaturalize politics and recognize the contingency of history. It requires, too, that we are attentive to the ways in which origin stories may suppress the violence of beginnings or evade politics altogether, even as they are, themselves, deeply political. In politics, there is more at stake in locating beginnings than satiating an ontological need. The desire to *know* origins constitutes only part of the fascination with the subject; this desire to *know* is, in fact, overshadowed by the desire to *make political use* of origins. The impetus to 'uncover' the origins of politics and power is never dissociated from the politics of the present. If origin stories did not serve multiple political purposes, that is, if they were not of value to their authors, it is unlikely that they would be as prevalent as they are in the history of political thought.

And so we have the origins aporia. The desire to create origin stories is an expression of our fundamental need to come to terms with our own beginnings, to make sense of our own experience. Yet this desire is not innocent. Its object – the primordial essence of things – is elusive and its driving force is political. As we proceed to the discussion of specific origin stories, we need to keep in mind this aporia and to explore the contradictions embedded in the origins discourse. Simply put, our purpose in this book is to examine the process by which political thinkers use origin stories normatively, to justify, not just the past, but the present and future. At the same time, we will want to think about some key questions: If origin stories are laden with these political difficulties, then what can serve as the foundation for our politics? Is it possible to avoid altogether the process of reasoning back to a single point of origin in our political thinking?

At this point, I want to posit historical inquiry as an alternative to origins thinking. That a proper understanding of politics requires knowledge of our history is axiomatic. But the inquiry into our past need not be preoccupied with a relentless (and fruitless) search for origins. Turning to history can help us avoid many of the problems that inhere in the origins discourse; history can potentially provide a better, more solid foundation for politics. 'History should be studied because it is an absolutely necessary enlargement of human experience,' writes historian Bernard Bailyn; 'it is the necessary, unique way of orienting the present moment, so that you know where you are and where you have come from.'[22] Without making contentious claims about the objectivity of history, it is necessary to commit ourselves to avoiding potentially harmful distortions of the past. Indeed, as Bailyn testifies, accumulating knowledge of historical experience works against the competing inclination to 'fantasize about the past and make up myths to justify some immediate purpose.'[23]

It is at this very juncture that historical study and the investigation into political origins necessarily part company. The origin story's point of departure from historical narrative is precisely its willingness to knowingly distort history. Those who search for origins through the origin story are led to hypothesize, to engage in conjecture where there is no evidence, or where history leaves off. While the study of history has the potential, as Bailyn suggests, to *enlarge* human experience, and to orient the present moment, origin stories *delimit* the range of political solutions by presenting a purified and often a reductionist view of our nature and our origins. Feminists learned quickly, for example, the need to move from quasi-historical speculation toward a historical understanding of the operation of gender hierarchies in specific contexts, on the one hand, and toward an analysis of feminist political goals, on the other. In short, the essentially fanciful exercise of justifying political proposals with the aid of origin stories must give way to legitimate discussion of the political problems facing us.

Again, to be clear, the point is not to place historical investigation on a pedestal high above politics. Foucault warns about this as well. The historical project 'does not resemble the evolution of a species' nor does it 'restore an unbroken continuity that operates beyond the dispersion of forgotten things.'[24] While admitting the interconnection of history and politics, and recognizing the contingency of history (both as a form of inquiry and as a description of the past), I am nevertheless offering historical inquiry as both 'a necessary enlargement of human experience' and a meaningful substitute for the fallacious theorizing on origins that has so often served as the foundation for our politics.

## 3. Reading Origin Stories Historically

Deconstructing or demystifying origin stories in political thought entails more than simply asserting their untruth. We need to begin the process of uncovering their political motivations, motivations that are driven by a set of historical and political circumstances. The content of these stories is inevitably influenced by the context in which they are written and the author is a historically embedded subject. Origin stories offer political thinkers a means by which they can organize and interpret their immediate political experience. Therefore, they bear an intimate – but not a straightforward – relationship to the historical context from which they emerge. They provide a window into that historical epoch, revealing to present-day observers aspects about the period in which they were composed. Given the relationship between origin stories and their specific historical and political context, I argue that a historical approach is required to understand them.

Quentin Skinner is the most notable authority for developing and utilizing an intention-oriented historical method – often referred to as the Cambridge approach – to reading political theory. In his study of Hobbes, *Reason and Rhetoric in the Philosophy of Hobbes*, Skinner asserts the necessity of reading Hobbes against the backdrop of the wider discourse from which his ideas emerge, of uncovering 'what traditions he reacts against, what lines of argument he takes up, what changes he introduces into existing debates.' Skinner's stated aim is 'to return to Hobbes's texts armed with the kind of historical information' that is 'indispensable for making sense of them.'[25] The basic premise underlying this method is that we will be better equipped to understand Hobbes's manipulation of gender relations – to take an example relevant to the present study – if we know how his contemporaries understood gender relations. An awareness of the actual configuration of gender relations, as well as the popular intellectual justifications for that configuration, illuminates both what Hobbes meant in his own usage and his similarity or difference from his peers. Similarly for Plato and for feminist origins theorists, an understanding of what they were reacting against, or what their defining political questions were, aids us in our interpretation of their origin stories. In each of these cases, historical research and inquiry produces a more well-rounded interpretation.

My desire to read these texts in light of their author's political and historical contexts does not mean that I share Skinner's contention that there are no perennial questions in the history of political thought. Skinner has gone so far as to argue that any statement made in political theory is 'inescapably the embodiment of a particular intention' and is 'thus specific to its situation in a way that it can only be naive to try to transcend.'[26] Put in other terms, 'classic texts cannot be concerned with our questions and answers ... only with their own.'[27] Avoidance of anachronism is undoubtedly essential, but Skinner takes the point unnecessarily far. The notion that there are 'only individual answers to individual questions' and no overarching political questions is too restrictive. This interpretive approach constrains inquiry and reduces the historical study of political texts to a matter of only historical – and not contemporary – interest.

The most obvious criticism that can be levelled at the Cambridge-Skinnerian approach is that it can, and often does, mean that critical analysis of issues such as gender relations are excluded from consideration on the basis that they could not have been relevant to the author in question. The exclusion of gender analysis is evident in the works of several historical-contextualist authors – although there are notable exceptions[28] – and in the recent series offered by Cambridge that includes *The Cambridge Companion to Locke* and *The Cambridge Companion to Hobbes*.[29] Despite volumes of work being done by scholars on these two seventeenth-century English thinkers – work oriented toward interpretation of the public/private division, the family, and the masculine meaning of politics – none of this work on gender is included, or even cited, in these volumes. The work of Carole Pateman is an obvious omission, given her focus on seventeenth-century thought.[30] The assumption seems to be that, since gender was not of primary concern to Hobbes or Locke, to discuss their interpretations of gender is to read our political concerns and problematics into the past.

Yet, there is no reason to assume that, because gender was not of *primary* concern to Hobbes, or to Plato, gender divisions and dynamics did not occupy part of the backdrop against which they wrote. Gender is as relevant historically as it is in the present day: no society in which hierarchical gender relations prevail can possibly escape the tensions that accompany them. That gender was less contested in ancient Greece or seventeenth-century England than in 1960s North America does not legitimate its exclusion from scholarly analysis. Indeed, the Skinnerian constraint to account only for what could have been of relevance to Hobbes can be used to show the *need* to include gender as a factor to be considered. The very fact that both Plato and Hobbes use and manipulate gender within their political theory is evidence enough that the subject merits further investigation. Even utter silence on gender would beg inquiry: what sorts of gendered assumptions are embedded in this text? In what ways does this political argument presuppose the existence of gender hierarchy? In the cases of Plato and Hobbes, our analysis will be enhanced by drawing upon the historical context of gender relations and the intellectual history of gender in their respective periods to understand their politics.

This justification for studying gender in the history of political thought leads to a final methodological point about feminist interpretation. Recognizing the importance of historical perspective in interpretation of political texts has relevance for feminist political theory as well. The prevailing – if unacknowledged – approach in feminist political theory is to concentrate attention on the significance and implications of political arguments in historical texts, or to confine the scope of inquiry to the texts themselves, rather than position these political texts in context.[31] Again, my point is not to suggest that all feminist inquiry should be historical, only that the lack of attention to the historical dimensions of a text *can* produce less-than-adequate results. Carole Pateman's *The Sexual Contract*, which I examine at length in chapter 5, is a case in point, although her findings are not in any way 'more skewed' than those of other feminists who have treated Hobbes.

Although her motivating question is 'What are the implications of social contract theory for women and feminism?' – that is, not a historical question – her conclusions are marred by her undifferentiated treatment of the social contract thinkers. While the sexual contract as an idea is provocative for understanding modern liberal societies in general, I am not convinced it helps us to understand Hobbes specifically. In my view, she assumes Hobbes to be arguing points that, in all likelihood, he was not, and she misses some of the significance of Hobbes's argument regarding gender. Part of the purpose of this book is to point to the necessity of increasing the historical perspective in feminist political theory. The method I am recommending combines the critical perspective of feminism with the historical sensitivity of contextualist interpretation. These two approaches are not immiscible; they are, in fact, highly compatible.

An increased historical sensitivity is useful, not only for the interpretation of texts in the history of political thought, but also for analysing the history of the women's movement in North America. It has become commonplace to dismiss the claims of radical feminism, to point to its essentializing tendencies and its creation of a 'victim' culture for feminists and women.[32] Moreover, radical feminism is reproached for being responsive only to the experiences and needs of white, middle-class women. However, an examination of the early phase of the Second Wave of feminism reveals a far more complex picture. The strong political claims made about women's oppression, its severity and longevity in history, had an immediate political purpose in the early movement: to achieve recognition of feminism as an independent and legitimate political movement. The telling of origin stories formed part of this effort. The intent was neither to essentialize women nor to paint them as helpless victims, but to unify them in a political struggle against a system of oppression that had heretofore received only scant recognition as a problem. The drive to create a movement for women emerged from women's experiences in other movements such as the civil rights movement and the New Left – movements that had not addressed women's specific concerns. This is not to suggest that the Women's Liberation Movement did not evolve into a class- and race-specific movement but that, at its inception, exclusion was not the issue that it became later. The lack of clear perspective on early feminist politics signifies a lack of attention to the historical development, and to the political complexity, of the rise of the Second Wave of feminism.

In the final analysis, a measure of historical sensitivity will aid the interpretation of the origin stories under consideration here. Each of these stories served as a focal point for their authors to address specific political tensions. They also offer a means by which we can interpret the *dominant* as well as the *latent* concerns of these thinkers.

### 4. Origin Stories as Compensatory Masculine Narratives

Feminists have a particular interest in origin stories insofar as these stories often attempt to legitimate a patriarchal configuration of gender relations. Just as the function of myth is, as Barthes observes, to talk about things and to purify them, origin myths talk about gender hierarchies, purifying them with the language of nature. The extent to which the stories selected here (feminist stories excepted) perform this particular function is one of the subjects under investigation in this book. Yet feminists, most notably Mary O'Brien, have also turned their attention to origin stories for another, tangentially related reason. In O'Brien's view, origin stories serve a crucial function for the men who narrate them: they compensate for men's reproductive envy of women by appropriating the language and power of reproduction for the sphere of politics.

O'Brien articulates with clarity and theoretical rigour the highly persuasive view that the roots of patriarchal social relations lie within the '*total process of human reproduction.*'[33] Feminism, then, ought to begin its struggle, and feminist theory its theorizing, with the process of human reproduction. Indeed, it is O'Brien's stated intent to formulate a theory of birth, a neglected and essential human process that philosophy has yet to come to terms with. Having spent the first part of her adult life as a practising midwife, O'Brien's choice to focus on reproduction and birth seems logical. According to her argument, men are forced by biological necessity to create and generate in the only way that they can: politically, intellectually, and philosophically. 'For women, anatomy is creativity,' such that women are not in need of filling the creative-generative void. But nature is not so kind to men, in O'Brien's view of the sexes. The only relevant and awe-inspiring form of creation in the masculine world of politics becomes the creation of cities and nations. These entities emerge from the creativity of men, who neither honour nor require women for their contributions to reproduction. Men 'must resist the alienation from nature ... which is inherent in their reproductive praxis,' O'Brien argues; they must 'heal the discontinuous sense of man the uncertain father.'[34] Men must find a way to make up for their biological shortcoming of not being able to gestate a child; and investing intellectual activity and political creation with awe-inspiring significance is part of that compensatory process.

The compensatory process involves an inversion of reality: women's actual procreativity is portrayed as imitative and passive while men's creative potency is empowered and valorized. Birth is reduced to a biological event, base and unthinking, while creation in the intellectual-political realm is elevated above, and transcendent of, biological imperatives. This portrayal inverts what O'Brien takes to be reality: it is women who possess an awe-inspiring power to create, gestate, and give birth to new life. The goal of feminism must be to uncover and reclaim that power, to reconnect the intellectual with the physical process of reproduction for women, and to engage with the new politics of reproduction. There is a practical purpose here, as O'Brien sees enormous potential for women in their newly acquired ability to control their fertility; at the same time, she sees new reproductive technologies as a further dimension of men's desire to appropriate control of reproduction from women.[35]

The envy-appropriation thesis constitutes a central theme of my investigation of origin stories. It will surface in the discussion of Plato and the treatment of Hobbes, and is central to the radical feminist origin stories of the Second Wave. The question that we must face in each context is, why is it necessary to invest women's reproductive role with awe-inspiring significance? Can we not argue that women's role is unique without either investing it with fabricated importance, on the one hand, or comparing it to men's role and designating it as aberrant or anomalous on the other? To acknowledge women's reproductive significance without falsely elevating it or comparing it to male experience requires an altogether different language, a language that is not readily available. Even those scholars who attempt to think differently about reproduction fall short. For example, feminist bioethicist Laura Purdy writes that 'fetuses are dependent on women in an unusually fundamental and continuous way.'[36] The sentiment is right, and yet the use of the term 'unusually' connotes women's difference – and difference always means difference from some objective and universal standard, that is, the male.

There is an additional problem with O'Brien's thesis in that it is contradictory. On the one hand, reproductive biology structures social relations insofar as alienation from the process is thought to be the root of patriarchy. On the other hand, birth is theorized as a unity between the intellectual and the material. In other words, by the latter theory, birth would change and evolve historically and culturally precisely because it is a product of our consciousness. Indeed, cultures value and interpret reproductive processes differently.[37] Yet O'Brien's explanation for the rise of patriarchy is at odds with the recognition of historical and cultural variability in birth experiences. The idea that reproduction means something inherent (and inherently the same) simply does not correspond with the idea that reproduction changes with consciousness. While O'Brien acknowledges the historical changes in reproductive practice, her tendency toward biological determinism, toward grounding her theory in essences, undermines this recognition and the strength of her argument.[38]

In the end, the envy-appropriation thesis put forth by O'Brien as an explanation for the prevalence of masculine origin stories offers us a way into the discussion of origins, reproduction, and gender, but – as persuasive as her thesis is – it can not provide the key to this discussion. While Plato in particular has invested male creativity with a potency that is obviously derived from parturition, I will argue that he does not simply appropriate woman's power in the way that O'Brien suggests. Moreover, the feminist origins theorists invert Plato's line on reproduction, *reclaiming* but at the same time *inventing* woman's power. Feminists, too, find origins a useful and convenient tool in politics. This fact alone would seem to disprove the thesis that origin stories are driven exclusively by a masculine ontological or biological need. Origin stories are driven by politics, and to ignore radical feminism's participation in this drive would be naive.

### 5. Origin Stories as Scripts of Citizenship

Just as origin stories structure and legitimate the hierarchical relationship between men and women, they also function as scripts of citizenship, structuring the hierarchy of relations between citizens themselves and between citizens and non-citizens. Indeed, as political myths, origin stories are discourses on the subject of citizenship, broadly conceived. Every society and culture has its own foundation myths, its stories about the beginnings of the nation or city-state. Origin stories in political theory function similarly, although they are not usually meant to account for the origins of a specific nation or city-state, but rather to address the generation of politics and power in general. Nevertheless, like the foundation myths of cities and nations, origin stories provide a context for citizenship, a narrative by which citizens are to understand, and consent to, their place in society.

Foundation myths are the primary organizing myths of nations: they establish a common history, a common origin, and a national identity. Their significance stems from the idea that '[t]he sense of "whence we came" is central to the definition of "who we are."'[39] Foundation myths often assert the glory and prominence of the nation and justify its rightful place internationally. They mythologize and sanctify an imaginary beginning to the nation,[40] or take the historical "facts" of the nation's origins and legitimate them from a particular political perspective.

For example, the nations that constitute North and South America take the arrival of Christopher Columbus to signify the 'discovery' of the continents. The effect is to rewrite and mythologize history in favour of European immigrants at the expense of the Aboriginal peoples who inhabited these continents. This process has an obvious effect on the construction of citizenship in the North American context, for to suggest that this continent was 'discovered' is to imply that no one – at least no one significant – was here upon the arrival of Columbus. If no one of significance was here, then only those who arrive are given a rung on the citizenship ladder. Foundation myths account for who belongs and who does not, who is a proper citizen and who is rightfully excluded from full citizenship.

The example of the Americas points to some of the problems with foundation myths in general. True, founding stories provide a sense of common purpose, a common ancestry, a national identity. Yet myths that attempt to manufacture a national identity must inevitably come up against the charge that they are based not on historical truth but on historical white-washing, if not outright fabrication. As Eric Hobsbawm aptly states, 'nationalism requires too much belief in what is patently not so.' Furthermore, he argues, 'getting history wrong is part of being a nation.'[41] In Canada, for instance, it has traditionally been the norm to refer to two founding nations, English and French. It is not part of Canadian foundational mythology to address the First Nations' experiences of Confederation, and indeed to do so would be to fundamentally disrupt the Canadian self-image.

Origin stories in political theory are distinct from, yet perform many of the same functions as, foundation stories.[42] Origin stories are not nationalist myths in that they are often not territorially specific.

Indeed, the origin narratives of Plato and Hobbes were written in pre-nationalist epochs. There was, in the period when Plato wrote, no Greek nation per se, only competitive, individual city-states, each with a strong sense of city loyalty and patriotism (meaning, in this context, a loyalty to one's own and a strong sense that whatever beneftis the polis will also benefit oneself). However, Plato's autochthonous myth of the metals is an explicit attempt to manufacture a communal feeling and citizen attachment to the polis in the face of potential class conflict. Likewise, the *Timaeus*, while not a true nationalist foundation story, is a patriotic myth written with the intent of glorifying the birth and natural order of Athens.

As I have suggested, Plato's myths serve the important function of legitimizing his political order and the hierarchy within it. By using an autochthonous narrative to explain and justify the existence of classes in the polis he addresses the problem of citizen unrest and discontent. If citizens of the polis understand themselves as having common ancestry, and as being part of a functioning whole that has an ultimate purpose, they are thought to be less inclined to object to their specific place and role in the city. Similarly, the *Timaeus* is a script for citizens that justifies the ordering of the whole through the use of a natural cosmogony. Plato's narratives carve out the identities of members of the polis; citizens ought to think of themselves as 'true' Athenians in a rejuvenated, revitalized, and post-democratic Athens and against the backdrop of barbarians and non-citizens alike.

Hobbes also wrote in an era prior to the development of the modern nation, and thus nationalism. Moreover, his origin story does not dwell, as Plato's does, on the glorification of the political entity of which he is a part. Rather, Hobbes's conclusions have a broader applicability: they could refer to, and be useful for, understanding any nation in a state of internal strife or civil war. Hobbes is less determined to show the glory of the English nation than to achieve the basis for English stability and order. Nevertheless, from his origin story – the state of nature and the social contract – a script of citizenship can be recovered. On the one hand, Hobbes infers an equality of subjection to absolute authority as the sovereign assumed his place of authority over citizens who have mutually contracted to establish his power. The identity of citizens, in this script, is exemplified in their being named *subjects*; these subjects are not empowered or free in any liberal sense, but are instead radically constrained by the agreement they have just entered. On the other hand, within this political configuration the patriarchal family assumes its traditional place, such that there is no sense in which women are to view themselves as equal subjects, or as fellow-contractors in the new social pact. Women and servants, embedded in the patriarchal family unit, are equally obliged but doubly subjected.

Written in the 1960s and 1970s, feminist origin stories are influenced by nationalist drives but are not nationalist in a spatially or temporally specific way. The feminists who tell stories about the beginning of patriarchy and the original, prehistorical matriarchal society to legitimate their politics do not explicitly acknowledge the desire for a feminist state or a matriarchal nation. Nevertheless, these feminists (with the possible exclusion of Pateman who, as we will see, moves beyond some of the more obviously naive aspects of the feminist origins tradition) imply that the (re)creation of matriarchy would solve many of the problems of dominance associated with patriarchy. They adopt many of the traits of true nationalists in that they use history to suit their political objectives, and they advocate a separation from the excluded (men) in some extreme cases. They, too, use an origin narrative to elicit consent to their political goals, to generate unity and conformity to the goals of the Women's Liberation Movement, all the while inviting 'belief in what is patently not so,' to use Hobsbawm's phrase. Like the other varieties of origin stories, the feminist stories also offer their subscribers ready-made identities.

In providing the context for citizenship, do foundation stories and origin stories perform a beneficial political function? I have outlined the negative implications of these myths, particularly their manipulation of history, their naturalization of conventional political relations, and their function as justificatory scripts of citizenship. But does my critique overlook the value of these stories in generating a common language, a basis for shared understanding about citizenship and politics? Is it possible that some form of shared narrative is a prerequisite to citizenship precisely because it establishes a foundation?

Martha Nussbaum, in writing on the twentieth-century imperatives of multicultural citizenship, highlights the importance of literature, visual art, film, and dance to citizenship. Literature, in particular, develops 'a citizen's imagination'; it has an 'ability to represent the specific circumstances and problems of people of many different sorts.'[43] The arts, Nussbaum argues, play a crucial role in 'cultivating the powers of imagination that are essential to citizenship.'[44] In this view, the citizen needs more than a knowledge of history and social fact; he or she requires a deeper understanding of the nation, of other citizens and their unique experiences, than can be gathered from history. Here the role of fictitious narrative performs an essential function: it enlarges citizen awareness and empathy at the same time as it establishes the framework within which citizen debate and dialogue can take place.

Nussbaum's analysis is insightful. The ability to understand our present situation in an abstracted and reflective way is facilitated by the arts, by political theory, by narratives of all kinds. Our interactions with each other as citizens are necessarily guided by a variety of (sometimes competing) narratives. Still, I am not convinced that the recognition of the significance of our narrative imagination ought to lead us to an uncritical acceptance of the origin story as one more aspect of our narrative imagination, necessary and benign in its contribution to our self-understandings. Rather than increasing mutual citizen understanding, Western origin narratives tend to forestall such understanding, and thus delay the possibility of achieving real political solutions by attempting to gloss over the problems of hierarchy and power relations. They unquestionably tell us something about ourselves as citizens, but their content is not usually conducive to achieving deeper political awareness. We might also query whether the required precepts to citizen dialogue must be of a mythical nature. Could not the premises of the society, the shared narrative, be drawn from historical reality rather than from outright fabrication? Here I think it is important to make a distinction between artistic cultural production, on the one hand, and the fabricated origin narrative, on the other.

All of this is not to say that, because origin stories are problematic, they can simply be eradicated. As we proceed through the various origin stories, the persistence and longevity of the origins impulse – and its manifestation in origin stories – become apparent. Perhaps origin stories will remain a permanent feature of the political landscape. However, our goal of achieving deeper awareness and enlarged mutual understandings, of finding political solutions to ongoing and historically based problems, is achieved not in the telling of fictional origin stories but in exposing the flaws embedded in them. Thus, my purpose in this book is to cast a critical eye on the origins motif as it surfaces in the tradition of political thought. This study is not offered as a means of extending origins-thinking, nor as an origin story of origins, but as an exploration of this significant political discourse.

*Chapter Two*

# The Birth of Philosophy: Plato's Creation Politics

The process of examining ancient Greek origin stories might easily begin with any of a number of Greek texts or thinkers. Hesiod's *Theogony*, written in the eighth century BCE, gives a poetic and mythical account of the origins of the universe, the anthropomorphic gods, and human beings. The quest for beginnings also dominates the fragmented writings of the Ionian or Milesian philosophers, who replaced Hesiod's poetic accounts with physical, proto-scientific ones. The origin stories of Hesiod and of the natural philosophers remain integral to the Western philosophical and mythical heritage. However, Plato is the starting point of a new kind of origin story. He is the foundational *political philosopher*, who at one and the same time transcended the natural philosophers and poets with rationality and synthesized their findings to create a new political and cosmogonical origin story.

Plato's political theory combines the quest for natural origins with a desire for rational political *cosmos* (order). While this double desire for natural and political order is evident in several Platonic dialogues, it emerges clearly in his *Timaeus*, Plato's central story of origins in which he attempts to reconcile his political theory with the debates of the preceding natural philosophers. Unlike the myth of the metals, which is an autochthonous origin story primarily intended to create harmony in the *polis*, the *Timaeus* is a cosmogony: a narrative about the creation of the universe. One of Plato's incentives to write a cosmogony is to reveal the correlation between the rationality and order that lies behind the natural world and that which informs the well-conceived and just polis.

In the reading of the *Timaeus* that I am offering, particular attention is focused on the reproductive metaphors used to describe creation.

The *Timaeus* is rife with metaphors of pregnancy, birth, maternity, and paternity, metaphors that perform important political and philosophical work in the dialogue but which have been all but ignored. In using patrogenic – or male-led – reproductive metaphors, Plato is not merely engaging in myth-making; he is tapping into an important Athenian discourse about the primacy of the male sex in reproduction and politics. While it is probably impossible to arrive at a final meaning of these metaphors,[1] or a causal explanation for Plato's use of them, I suggest that Plato finds the fantasy of male self-reproduction useful in his attempts to empower and refashion Athenian masculinity from its democratic instantiation to an idealized, philosophic model.[2]

## 1. The Origin Story of the *Timaeus*

The *Timaeus* is a metaphorically rich, poetic, and philosophic description of the beginnings of the world through to the creation of human beings. It is the first dialogue of an incomplete trilogy; the second dialogue, *Critias*, was interrupted before completion and the third dialogue was never written. It begins with a reiteration of some of the main conclusions of the *Republic*, as though Socrates had been explaining his theory of the just city to this new group of interlocutors on the previous day. During this brief recounting, Socrates takes the time to criticize the poets and the Sophists, both of whom he finds inadequate to the task of celebrating and honouring the goddess and the city itself. From the initial conversation between Timaeus, Critias, and Socrates, we understand that this is a day of honouring the goddess and, moreover, that since Socrates has entertained his friends on the day previous, it is their turn to entertain him today with a 'feast of discourse' (20c).[3]

Critias then offers an abbreviated, preliminary foundation story to Socrates as a kind of introduction to the larger origin story in the *Timaeus*. In this preliminary story – which he claims as historically true – Critias gives expression for the first time to the myth of Atlantis. Critias's version of the myth glorifies the ancient city of Athens. He tells his listeners that Athens was once a great city whose 'marvellous actions' had 'passed into oblivion through lapse of time and the destruction of mankind' (21a). The people who once dwelt in this ancient city 'were the fairest and noblest race of men which ever lived,' from whom the current inhabitants of Athens descended. Rivalling the great city of Athens was an ancient empire centred on the island of

Atlantis. In an imperialist bid, Atlantis attempted to conquer the ancient city of Athens and the surrounding region. Athens was 'pre-eminent in courage and military skill,' and thus soundly defeated the Atlantean empire. However, following its victory came 'violent earthquakes and floods,' as a result of which all of Athens's 'warlike men in a body sank into the earth.' The island of Atlantis 'in like manner disappeared in the depths of the sea' (25d).

Although Critias's tale of Atlantis is not the mainstay of the dialogue, it is not without political significance either. The ancient Athenian city to which Critias refers bears striking resemblance to Socrates' just city of the *Republic*. The Atlantis story, located at the outset of the dialogue, reminds the reader that Plato's imperative in the creation narrative is not exclusively philosophic; it is also political. Plato's aim is to restore virtue and justice to the Athenian regime, principles that had been lacking since the creation of Athenian democracy. It is the ancient, pre-democratic Athens that is glorified in the Atlantis tale, described therein as a great sea power, a moral empire, 'first in war' and possessing 'the fairest constitution of any of which tradition tells' (23c–d). Ancient Athens, by virtue and skill, is able to conquer even the imperialist Atlantis and thus to free the enslaved. R.B. Rutherford suggests that this must have served as a message to an Athens in decline. While the degenerate and decadent empire of Atlantis is destroyed, Athens survives, and can in fact be 'regenerated' if it listens to the lessons of history.[4]

As the dialogue proceeds, Critias explains to Socrates that the duties of entertainment will be shared between himself and Timaeus. A more elaborate version of the tale of Atlantis will follow, but only after Timaeus has outlined the generation of the world up to the creation of man. So the origin story begins in earnest with Timaeus, who offers an account of creation and cosmogony, and it continues with Critias, who is 'to receive the men whom he [Timaeus] has created, and of whom some will have profited by the excellent education which you [Socrates] have given them' (27b). In choosing to review the primary recommendations of the *Republic* at the outset of the *Timaeus*, and in situating the incomplete trilogy on a continuum with the recommendations of the *Republic*, Plato is making an important political connection between the origin story of the *Timaeus* and the ideal city of the *Republic*.

We might wonder why Timaeus, rather than Socrates, is chosen to expound Plato's theory of creation in this dialogue. In fact, we know very little about Timaeus as a character, only that he is from Locri in Italy, and has made 'the nature of the universe his special study' (27a). There is some debate about whether he is an actual historical figure – perhaps a Pythagorean – but if he is, there is no historical evidence to document it.[5] Socrates speaks favourably of him as having held 'the most important and honourable offices in his own state,' as well as having 'scaled the heights of all philosophy' (20a). From this description we know that he was up to the task of philosophizing the origins of the universe and the creation of man. In the absence of any final conclusions as to why Timaeus is chosen for the role, I can only surmise that it may be related to the fact that Socrates plays a less significant part in the later Platonic dialogues. Indeed, in *Timaeus* and *Critias*, both among Plato's last works, Socrates is only a minor character, and by the time Plato writes the *Laws* he is absent altogether. Perhaps Plato no longer needs Socrates to expound his views or perhaps his own interpretations have broken off so completely from those of the historical Socrates that he chooses not to rely on him.

Timaeus begins his monologue by rehearsing the Platonic ontology. 'What is that,' asks Timaeus, 'which always is and has no becoming, and what is that which is always becoming and never is?' (27d). He draws a contrast between two realms, or two states of existence. There is a state of Being, which can be 'apprehended by intelligence and reason' and is always the same; and there is a state of becoming, which is 'conceived by opinion with the help of sensation' and 'never really is' (27d–28a). The created world, as a physical and visible body, is in the realm of becoming: it has been generated, created. In this statement, Timaeus reveals that his origin story will be creationist as opposed to evolutionary. That is, the world did not *evolve* from matter, but was *created* from matter, having a beginning, 'being visible and tangible and having a body' (28c). If indeed it is created, it must have a cause, some force that brings it into existence and that cause is the creator god, 'the father and maker of all of this universe' (28c).[6]

The creator bases the world, his creation, on the unchanging and perfect models of the Forms. To do otherwise, to use created matter as the model, would preclude the world from being 'the fairest of creations' (29a). Plato, of course, wants to deny that the world as we know it is the product of pure chance, one of the grand chaotic, schemeless aspects of the universe. Rather, Plato envisions the world as having a *telos*, as partaking in goodness because it is made by the creator. He sees the world as 'a living creature truly endowed with soul and intelligence by the providence of God' (30c). 'Finding the whole visible sphere not at rest, but moving in an irregular and disorderly fashion, out of disorder he brought order' (30a). Out of random motion and pre-existing, disordered matter, the intelligent designer imposes a pattern on the universe.

Timaeus's narrative continues with the creation of the four elements – fire, earth, water, and air; the creation of the planets, stars, and the sun; the creation of time; and the creation of a second tier of gods whom he asks to create mortal beings. Much of the narrative consists of what we would now see as fantastic science and does not have particular political significance; it provides an obscure account of the generation of the elements using geometric shapes and means and mathematical formulae. We ought to recognize, however, that for Plato, the *Timaeus* was an attempt at a scientific understanding of creation that was influenced greatly by the Presocractic thinkers.

Indeed, even Plato's decision to write a cosmogony at this late stage in his career is attributable to his desire to respond to the ideas of the Presocratics. The Presocratics represent the beginnings of natural philosophy in Greece; they were the first to attempt to replace mythical and anthropomorphic thought with scientific ideas about cosmogony. They sought a causal explanation for the existence of the world, and found the answers more in physical substances than in male and female gods, or a mating heaven and earth. The Ionians, or Presocratics, generally held the view that behind the chaos of change there must be some permanence or unity, an idea of obvious significance for Plato.[7] Plato does not entirely agree with any one of them, and he uses the *Timaeus* as an opportunity to both synthesize their ideas and correct those by whom he is most influenced, including Heraclitus, Parmenides, and Pythagoras. The way in which Plato absorbs and reinterprets their thought is key to understanding his own ontology and epistemology.

From Heraclitus Plato takes the idea that the physical world is unstable, constantly in strife, and thus unsuitable as an object of knowledge. Since the senses portray to each person a different reality, nothing perceived merely by the senses is truly knowable. As Plato summarizes Heraclitus: '[A]ll things are in process and nothing stays still, and likening things to the stream of a river he [Heraclitus] says that you would not step twice into the same river.'[8] As a result, Heraclitus '[looks] within himself' to find the Logos that is behind everything. It is perhaps for this reason that Plato is drawn to his ideas, in particular the idea that there must be a hidden meaning or truth behind the surface of change and discontinuity. Plato's innovation on Heraclitus is epistemological, for while he would have been loathe to suggest that nothing *at all* is knowable, he could agree that the instability of the physical world prevents it from being an object of knowledge.[9]

While Parmenides of Elea would have seen his ideas as the antithesis of Heraclitus's philosophy, Plato was able to take something important from them both. For Parmenides, a thing either exists or it does not, and we cannot say anything of value, *we cannot say anything at all*, about that which does not exist. Moreover, and this is important for understanding Plato's creation myth, that which *is* is uncreated. The implication is that change does not occur, that Being is ever-present (and thus timeless), indivisible, and motionless (recall Timaeus's question about that 'which always is and has no becoming'). Parmenides, trained as a Pythagorean, incorporates the ideas of Unity and Limit from the Pythagorean Table of Opposites, but abandons their negative complements.[10] The things that can be perceived with the senses are not considered to be in the realm of reality. Parmenides' conclusion was counterintuitive to his contemporaries, as it elided the flux and change of nature around them. Of course Plato, by the very fact that he writes a cosmogony at all, escapes Parmenides' abstract and monist conclusion, but he does not dismiss its value out of hand. Onto Parmenides' permanent Being Plato inscribes his patterns of reality, the permanent Forms or Ideas.

Plato is also influenced by Pythagorean thought, although his philosophical system is undoubtedly more sophisticated and complex than theirs.[11] Unlike Heraclitus and Parmenides, who tend toward monism, Pythagoreans are dualists. They developed a Table of Opposites, a double list of the characteristics of reality, or of the principles of things, each principle having a complementary opposite: Limited/Unlimited, odd/even, one/plurality, right/left, male/female, resting/moving, straight/curved, light/darkness, good/bad, and square/oblong. Limit is associated with unity, goodness, light, and the male, and the Unlimited with plurality, badness, darkness, and the female. While Plato does not simply adopt the Pythagorean Table of Opposites, he does accept many of its terms, making reference in the *Timaeus* to the principles of Limit and Unlimited, and he too equates the Unlimited with the female. He also agrees with their theory that numbers are 'the first things in the whole of nature,' and that 'almost all other things [are] numerically expressible.'[12]

When we read the *Timaeus*, the traces of Plato's Presocratic influences are unmistakable. If not in all of his dialogues, in the *Timaeus* Plato reveals an ontological dualism in which Being is contrasted with becoming. Being can be 'apprehended by intelligence and reason' and is always the same, whereas becoming is 'conceived by opinion with the help of sensation' and 'never really is' (27d–28a). The influences of Heraclitus, with his description of ceaseless flux, and Parmenides, with his state of timeless Being, are evident. Nevertheless, just as the Presocratics remain important for their attempts to transcend the mythopoetic cosmogonies, so too is Plato important for the leap he makes over the Presocratics. Plato inscribes in his rational advance an entirely new ontological and epistemological system that leaves the formative interpretations of the Presocratics behind. Moreover, where the Presocratics fail to make a connection between the physical and metaphysical realms, Plato wants to show the rationality in the ordering of the universe *as well as* in moral, human affairs. Above all, Plato wants to demonstrate that there is a rational pattern underlying the physical universe that is also connected to the ethical and moral affairs of human beings. Here we see the key relationship for Plato between macrocosm and microcosm. Up to this point in his political theory he has demonstrated the relationship between the microcosm of the human soul and the macrocosm of the city; in the *Timaeus* he takes a further step by revealing the macrocosmic patterns of reality in the universe.[13]

In this overview of the dialogue, I have concentrated primarily on the significance of the story of Atlantis and the intellectual heritage of Plato's ontological theory as it is revealed in the *Timaeus*. But there is still more to the dialogue than this. For instance, the *Timaeus* contains more than one passage about the creation of human beings in which men are depicted as the primary human beings and women as a secondary, punitive creation. Another significant passage, which I will refer to as the receptacle passage, describes the creation of a third order of existence, a maternal receptacle. It is in these sections of the dialogue that we see Plato's suggestive use of reproductive metaphor and the gendered dimension of his creation story. While these passages have not received a great deal of attention from Platonic or feminist scholars, they are relevant to his ontology and epistemology and they reveal important clues about Plato's political purpose in the origin story.

## 2. The Gendered Creation

To see the gendered dimensions of the story requires that we look closely at the final act of creation. As Timaeus explains, the final act of creation involves the development of a heavenly race of gods, birds for the air, watery species, and pedestrian and land creatures (40a).[14] The external god, or Demiurge, himself designs the race of gods, saying to them: 'Gods, children of gods, who are my works and of whom I am the artificer and father, my creations are indissoluble if so I will.' He explains that, as gods, they are composed of strong materials at their birth, and will not be 'liable to the fate of death' because the Demiurge has the will to maintain them. It is the task of the race of gods to design the mortal beings who will occupy the air, earth, and sea. The fact that these lesser gods create the animals and birds means that these beings will not be immortal. The part of these mortal beings that is *immortal* is of divine origin, and the Demiurge tells them, 'of that divine part I will myself sow the seed' (41c). And so he instructs the gods to 'beget' the creatures, make them grow, and receive them again in death (41d). Timaeus then describes how the Demiurge mingles the remains of the soul of the universe and the elements, divides the whole mixture into souls, and distributes them to the stars. From here, although the description is sketchy, it seems as though the animals come forth from the stars (41e).

What is noteworthy about Timaeus's account of the final act of creation is that it is patrogenic. That is, the male creator god is the sole author of the race of gods. The male god is the *creator* of the gods beneath him; he is empowered to *bring them forth*. Similarly, the new race of gods will go on to beget living creatures. Although there are female gods in this second tier, there is no mention of a fertilization process, or of a combining of two types of seed, or of the female's distinct capacity, even where birth itself is concerned. Plato demonstrates here, for the first time in this dialogue, that he is conversant in the language of patrogenesis, and that he sees a value in utilizing this particular idea about reproduction and birth common in ancient Greece.

Compatible with patrogenesis and the ideal of masculine self-reproduction is Plato's story of the all-male race of human beings. Timaeus proposes that men are born alone on the earth, unaccompanied at first by their female counterparts. These men are given sensations and feelings that must be conquered. Invoking the Platonic ontology of soul before body, Timaeus states that if men look after, and are attentive to, the needs and health of the soul, they will return to a 'blessed and congenial existence' (42b). Alternatively, if men misbehave and take inadequate care of their souls, they are reborn as women. This unrighteous man 'at second birth would pass into a woman,' and 'if he did not desist from evil he would continually be changed into a brute' (42c). Women are a secondary and, clearly, impure creation; existence as a woman represents a punishment for intemperate men. Women reside on a scale somewhere between men and brute animals. 'Human nature was of two kinds,' according to Timaeus; 'the superior race was of such and such a character, and would be hereafter called man' (42a). The creator has imagined that there are two 'kinds' of human beings, but the male is the originary sex, the norm. He not only comes first as a creation but has no need whatsoever for the female. Thus, a further dimension of the patrogenic view is male self-sufficiency: men are self-sufficient in life *and* in reproduction. Men's souls, at least, are created independently of women, of their mothers, and they are able to regenerate themselves independently.

The parallels to the Hebrew bible are striking, as Eve too is a secondary creation to Adam. In contrast to Plato's story, Eve is not a punishment but a helpmeet to Adam (although Eve's status as a helpmeet by no means indicates equality). Just as Timaeus does, however, the first story of Genesis identifies woman as a source of shame. After the Fall, that shame comes to Eve as a punishment of pain in childbirth and subordination to Adam. In the *Timaeus*, the very existence of woman is a sign of shame, for if man had not acted intemperately, she would not have been born in the first place. One of the differences between Genesis and the *Timaeus* is that, in the former, there is a struggle over the subordination of woman – as I have discussed, Lilith is banished to the Red Sea for her refusal to submit. Even in the figure Eve, however, there is room for interpretation: true, she is subordinate, but at the same time we can interpret her as curious and independent in her choice to sample the forbidden fruit. In this particular Platonic dialogue, the inferiority of woman is presented as part of the natural ordering of the cosmos; it is not a point of struggle.

The other area of the dialogue in which Plato experiments with a patrogenic theme is in the receptacle passage. This passage commences with Timaeus announcing a new beginning to the dialogue, explaining that, while two 'categories' sufficed in the first part, he now requires a third class of being (48e). The first class has always been the intelligible

Forms, permanent and unchanging; the second is that which imitated the pattern, and was 'generated and visible.' These are the two categories to which Timaeus has already referred. The third category, he tells us, is 'difficult of explanation and dimly seen'; it is 'the receptacle, and in a manner the nurse, of all generation' (49b). This receptacle

> must always be called the same, for, inasmuch as she always receives all things, she never departs from her own nature and never, in any way or at any time, assumes a form like that of any of the things which enter into her; she is the natural recipient of all impressions, and is stirred and informed by them, and appears different from time to time by reason of them. (50b–c)

Timaeus seems to contradict himself, for if the receptacle never adheres to the form of that which enters her, how can she change her appearance 'by reason of them'? The description of the receptacle, like the receptacle herself, is ambiguous. Timaeus employs a reproductive metaphor to elucidate this obscure concept: the receiving principle, in which generation takes place, can be likened to a mother; the 'source or spring' is the father; and 'the intermediate nature' that is in the process of generation is the child (50d). To emphasize further that the receptacle is passive and inert and shall have no form of her own, Timaeus compares her to a liquid that 'shall be as inodorous as possible' in order to receive a scent of perfume (50e).

A truly mysterious and elusive concept, the receptacle is sometimes thought to be space, sometimes matter. To house all that is generated, it must occupy a space. Yet, that which is perpetually to receive, the mother and receptacle of all created and visible, 'is not to be termed earth or air or fire or water ... but is an invisible and formless being which receives all things and in some mysterious way partakes of the intelligible, and is most incomprehensible' (51b). She partakes of the intelligible, the highest order of being, but is simultaneously apprehended only by a 'kind of spurious reason' (52b). She is a fleeting shadow, hardly real. Moreover, we can have, according to Timaeus, only a 'dreamlike sense' of her as 'we are unable to cast off sleep and determine the truth' about this being or space (52c).

Plato has chosen some highly suggestive metaphors with which to expound his creation story. How have Plato's interpreters read and responded to these patrogenic images? Let us begin to answer this question by assessing how the classic and most influential readings of the dialogue treat the issue of the hierarchical creation of the sexes. W.K.C. Guthrie, for one, states that neither in the *Phaedo* nor elsewhere 'does Plato repeat this insult to women as originating from morally defective souls (90c), which is scarcely compatible with their role in the *Republic* (though that has actually been recalled at the beginning, 18c), or the *Laws*.'[15] He also argues that Plato obviously accepts that women are present in the beginning because otherwise he would not present human nature as consisting in two 'kinds.' Guthrie proposes two possible solutions to this conundrum. The first is that Plato might, at this one stage in the dialogue, be making Timaeus's character speak as a Pythagorean. Since the Pythagoreans place women on the negative side of the Table of Opposites, Timaeus too speaks of women as inferior. Guthrie credits David Krell as his source for this idea. Briefly, Krell makes the argument in his article 'Female Parts in *Timaeus*' that Timaeus is a historical figure, a Pythagorean, who, because of his blatant degradation of 'female parts,' causes the dialogue to be a 'resounding, if instructive, failure.'[16] In Krell's words, 'There is something altogether uncanny about Timaeus' view of women. In my opinion Plato does not share it and takes sufficient steps in his dialogue to make manifest the perversity of the Locrian's view.'[17]

Not only is it an enigmatic, and possibly mistaken, assumption that Timaeus was a real historical figure, it is difficult to see in the dialogue any point at which Plato tries to distance himself from the ideas of his own (probably fictitious) main character.[18] It is more likely that Timaeus gives voice to Plato's own creation myth, as Guthrie himself suggests; there is nothing in the dialogue that tells us otherwise. And indeed, why would Plato have Timaeus expound his (Plato's) views on the origins of the earth, but insert the Pythagorean view of women? Moreover, why Guthrie accepts Krell's argument on this one point even as he dismisses Krell's larger argument is not altogether clear. The problem in Krell's, and hence Guthrie's, formulation is that it attributes to Plato a positive, proto-feminist view of women. And yet Plato demonstrates in numerous instances in *Timaeus* his acceptance of certain misogynist views prevalent in ancient Greece; moreover, his political theory often establishes the male as the universal sex, as the paradigmatic human being, and as the primary actor in generation. If there *is* similarity between the Pythagorean and Platonic views of women, it is most likely a legitimate sharing, not an appropriation by Plato of the Pythagorean view where it is convenient.

Guthrie's second and related explanation for the 'inconsistency' is that 'the Orphic and Empedoclean doctrine of the cycle of births' held 'a strong attraction for Plato.'[19] While it is certainly the case that the cycle of birth, life, death, and rebirth is of central concern to Plato, it is difficult to discern how this would lead him to make the argument that he does about women coming last in creation. Plato demonstrates his fascination with the cycle of life and death most clearly in the *Phaedo*, where he describes the soul's afterlife and the happiness with which a true philosopher should greet death. Yet this does not explain Plato's gender-infused description of the cycle. If we are to understand how this cycle is gendered for Plato, we need to recognize first and foremost that he connects women with the body (his description of the elusive feminine receptacle notwithstanding).[20] Being so identified with the body, moreover, women are completely incapable of the sort of transcendence that Plato argues is necessary to do philosophy. This is why, in the *Phaedo*, Xanthippe is sent away from the death scene for, as a woman, she can understand death only as the death of the body, whereas Socrates views death as a sort of new beginning, something worth celebrating. Socrates further chastises his male companions for their emotional displays, and reminds them that they must not carry on as women do or they will have to leave. In the *Phaedo* Plato imposes a hierarchical view of the sexes onto a cyclical theory of life and death. In *Timaeus* he graphs this same dualistic ontology of soul/body and man/woman onto a cyclical theory of life and death.

Guthrie is not the only Platonic scholar who offers an inadequate analysis of the gendered creation in *Timaeus*.[21] A.E. Taylor warns interpreters not to take this passage as anything but straight humour:

> We must not moralize here on the 'inadequate ideal of womanhood' in the ancient world. That women are more timid than men and less scrupulously fair in their dealings may or may not be true, but it is the average man's opinion all the world over as the modern novel and comic paper are enough to prove. As such, the assumption is good enough to build a humorous fairy-tale on.[22]

The question should be not whether Plato was joking, or whether he should be taken seriously, but *why* he finds it useful or attractive to characterize men as autonomous, self-sufficient, and self-reproducing beings.

The first step to answering this question is to begin to draw together the various strands of Plato's cosmogony. We know from his description of Atlantis that he has in mind to revitalize ancient Athens. We should also note that Plato's intent is not simply to preach to the converted: Athenian democrats, the chief obstacle to a revitalized Athens, constitute at least part of his audience. In a sense, Plato is offering a critique of the democratic model of masculinity and he is being anything but funny. Under the democratic regime, masculinity is a display of dangerous characteristics – intemperance, immersion in the basest of pleasures, excess, and love of wealth. If we are to understand why men are born first and women are born only as a punishment to intemperate men, we need to understand not just that Plato, in this instance at least, reflects his society's dismissal of women as weak and bodily, but that, in his view, the democratic model of masculinity poses a serious threat to the future of Athens. If male citizens want to stop the decline of Athens, then they must act, they must alter their way of being. It is the normative dimension of this part of the dialogue – and the significance of the gendered metaphor Plato uses – that is absent from the existing interpretations of *Timaeus*.

In the traditional commentaries on the dialogue, then, the dimensions of the *Timaeus* with which I am most interested are either ignored or treated insufficiently. Significantly, feminist literature on Plato does not address this gap, as it is confined to dialogues such as the *Republic*, the *Symposium*, and the *Laws*. The most extensive feminist treatment is offered in Nancy Tuana's *The Less Noble Sex*, which analyses a series of creation myths in brief. Tuana does not, however, tackle the provocative maternal receptacle.[23] Luce Irigaray provides a philosophical interpretation of familial and reproductive imagery in *Timaeus*, in which she elaborates on the insufficiency of language to capture the maternal receptacle as Plato defines her – she is inexpressible, eclipsed. The 'non-representation or even disavowal' of the mother 'upholds the absolute being attributed to the father.'[24] While the father in Plato's imagery lies 'beyond all beginnings,' the mother is 'always a clean state ready for the father's impressions.'

As Irigaray argues, Plato needs the maternal receptacle as a means of defining the father, the Forms. 'Needed to define essences, her function requires that she herself have no definition.'[25] She does not even really mimic other things, 'for that would suppose a certain intention, a project, a minimum of consciousness.' From Irigaray's reading, we develop a sense of how elusive the receptacle is, but also of the ways in which Plato successfully uses the idea of the receptacle to enhance the essence of the father. If we recall that one of the features of origin stories is their tendency to invoke originary essences, we see that Plato's receptacle passage enables him to place the essence of Being, and the essence of the father, in sharp relief with the indefinite, the undefinable, the female.

Where other commentators have been silent, Irigaray helps us think about the meaning and significance of Plato's receptacle. As eloquent as her reading of the *Timaeus* is, however, her project is purely philosophical and thus brings a different set of questions to the text. What is missing from the feminist analyses in general is any sense of the historical context in which Plato used his patrogenic metaphor. What are the historical and political roots of this metaphor? How does it assist Plato in his larger political project? Situating the text historically allows us to see how Plato's use of patrogenic metaphors plays into a whole discourse about woman and the body that presupposes woman's 'lack.' Indeed, when we survey Plato's historical context, and the embryological literature of the period, we see that Plato does not stand apart from the popular discourses on reproduction and women, but rather, like many other Athenian thinkers and poets, he finds it politically useful to imagine men as autonomous, self-generating beings.

### 3. The Athenian Context for Patrogenesis

Significantly, Plato's patrogenic story of creation is developed and entertained against the backdrop of a masculinist political configuration and a phallocentric understanding of reproduction. It is entertained at a time in which women themselves are almost entirely excluded from participation in many aspects of Athenian public life. In this brief overview, my aim is to place the gendered images that Plato uses in the *Timaeus* in the gendered context in which they were written. I am most interested in how the hierarchical ordering of the sexes in creation reflects the hierarchical gender configuration in ancient Athens, on the one hand, and how the patrogenic aspects of creation coincide with a patrogenic embryological discourse prevalent in ancient Greece, on the other.

The gendered political backdrop to the *Timaeus* is characterized by the absence of women from political activity in the Athenian city-state. This does not mean women took no interest in politics, as there are references to them influencing and counselling their husbands on matters of state. Still, men alone, and only free men, were citizens (*politai*) in the true sense. The word used to describe women's relationship to the state was *astai*, which has been translated as 'citizen,' but connotes only their ability to 'share in the religious, legal and economic order of the Athenian community.'[26] Of course, women who were slaves or metics (foreign residents) did not even have that extensive a relationship to the state. In a city-state that put such a premium on public identity and the participation of its citizens, it is significant that women of all classes were excluded from political activity. Not only did women not speak publicly, women were ideally not even spoken *about* publicly. According to Pericles' famous funeral oration,

> If I am to speak of womanly virtues, referring to those of you who will henceforth be in widowhood, I will sum up all in a brief admonition: Great is your glory if you fall not below the standard which nature has set for your sex, and great also is hers, of whom there is the least talk among men whether in praise or in blame.[27]

In other words, as Aristotle puts it, 'A modest silence is a woman's crown.'[28] Indeed, to be spoken about in public signified disrespect for a higher-class woman. With such constraints on their public life, women clearly could not participate in the activity of politics that so much defined the citizen of Athens.

Women's lack of participation in the public realm implies their location in the private, but the question remains as to what the separation between the *oikos* (household) and the public realm connotes in the broad sense. The public realm in ancient Greece was primarily a realm of politics, the polis, and every citizen was thought to be, at least in part, publicly oriented. In the public sphere, citizen-men, making up only a portion of the total Athenian population, conducted the affairs of the state. Opposed to this dimension of life, and sometimes even a threat to it, was the private life of the citizen. Each citizen was entitled to exercise freedom in his choice of how to live his private life, and this freedom was extended to metics and slaves as well.[29] Private life included the life of the family in the *oikos*, economic affairs, and some religious ceremonies; it also encompassed symposia, as Plato's dialogues often describe gatherings of men engaged in a private philosophical discourse. The public and private lives of male citizens were characterized by a freedom to move from one sphere to the other; indeed, these citizens not only had private lives, but were mandated by social convention to participate publicly in politics. Pericles captures the scorn saved for private men thus, 'For we alone regard the man who takes no part in public affairs, not as one who minds his own business, but as good for nothing.'[30]

The meaning of the public/private dichotomy was obviously quite different for women.[31] It manifested itself as a protective ideal, which may have only been enforced among the higher classes and in the city, an ideal whereby women were most appropriately located in the *oikos*. The presence of the ideal does not mean that women in fact never physically left the domestic realm, for poorer women especially would have had to travel to work as midwives or washerwomen, and to shop in the market. As well, women saw each other in Greek society and as a result this ideal did not prevent female friendships from developing. Often when women did leave their private quarters, they kept separate from male company and thus maintained the imperative of segregation. Significantly, the division between public and private also prevailed inside the upper-class *oikos*, in which men and women maintained separate living quarters. When other men were present in the house, the women remained segregated so as to prevent any interchange between male company and female occupants.

The notion of a gendered public/private divide was defended as a means to protect women's honour. This leads us to question why women needed protection at all, and protection from what? Codes of honour such as this are laden with political meaning, and the choice to regard women as in need of a special kind of protection indicates that certain assumptions are being made about women in general: that is, that they are vulnerable and weak by nature, that their sexuality is untamed and must be controlled, or that they pose a threat to political order. Indeed, all of these themes emerge in the literary and philosophical works of ancient Athens. Plato is one of the few writers who entertains the idea of eliminating the public/private divide, at least in the ruling class, and to this extent one might assume that his theory transcends the concern with women's shame. However, Plato's elimination of the public/private divide is more likely motivated by the drive for citizen unity; and it should be noted that women's admission to the guardian class is contingent on their already having fought and won the battle between the lower and higher dimensions of the soul. Women guardians, then, have learned to suppress bodily desire (and to deal expeditiously with the process of reproduction) to conform with the strictures of Plato's masculine ideal.

Nevertheless, it remains significant that at the same time as women were excluded from much of Greek cultural and political life, cultural and political life appears on the surface to be feminocentric, to borrow David Halperin's term. That is, Greek culture abounded with images in plays, poetry, and philosophy of women and reproduction, with stories of female goddesses and female characters. Halperin advises that the presence of such a feminocentrism is not at all contradictory to the actual absence of women from public life. Rather, the two go together, for Greek men 'required the silence of women in public in order to employ this mode of displaced speech,' in order that they might speak *for* women.[32] Moreover, the public absence and silence of *women* permitted men to use 'woman,' her body, and her 'difference' to investigate 'the male imaginary, the poetics of male identity and self-definition.'[33]

Similarly, in Plato, images of birth and reproduction appear, *not as subjects for investigation in and of themselves*, but as tools in the pursuit of philosophic understanding about origins, and about masculine roles in the created universe. Recall that, in the Platonic corpus, the man, the masculine philosopher, is always the person to whom the monologue is addressed. Therefore, the 'questioning and manipulation of what a woman is like, how like a man she is, are aimed above all at the promotion of a particular sort of male virtue.'[34] It is no doubt true that in ancient Greece, as in any context, gender symbolism and discourses are varied and often competing, which means that it is impossible to draw final conclusions about their significance. Nonetheless, it is likely mistaken to see the emphasis on women within cultural works as a sign that women were highly valued, that they were valued for what they did well, or that Greek men were weighing the benefits of gender parity.

Certainly it follows from the gendered separation of the *oikos* and the polis that the primary contribution that citizen-women could make to ancient Athens was reproductive. This works in reverse as well, as their reproductive capacities are often used as a justification for why women cannot have public roles. Significantly, even in Sparta, where women gained more political rights than did women in Athens, women were still primarily valued for child bearing and rearing.[35] Women's lives in the *oikos* were generally centred around the maintenance and care of the next generation, whether that care was for their own children or the children of others. It was permissible, also, for women to be midwives, and there was a network of women who would attend to a woman as she entered the phase of childbirth and confinement.

Through child bearing and rearing, women contributed to the creation of the next generation of Athenian citizens. Athenian law stated that it was through both parents that citizenship was conveyed to the next generation.[36] That both women and men were assumed to contribute to the production of citizens would seem to indicate that Athenian lawmakers believed women to contribute something important to the reproductive process in addition to the gestation of the child. However, this may not actually have been the case, since this law served the political purpose of limiting the numbers of new citizens by delegitimizing children brought forth from male-citizen relationships with non-citizen females.

The question of how the Greeks assessed women's contribution to generation is, in the end, not a straightforward one. Halperin cites recent work in Greek embryology as proof that 'a major, if not the dominant, theme in ancient thinking on this topic emphasized the contribution which the female makes to conception.'[37] It is true that a number of sources identify women as contributing something important to the reproductive process beyond gestation, most notable among them being the Hippocratic writers. Yet there are also some key figures in ancient Greece who use patrogenesis as a metaphor or even offer it as scientific truth. Moreover, where women's contribution is taken seriously, the male is, at the same time, offered as the biological standard against which the female's contribution is assessed.

Patrogenesis had some currency among playwrights, poets, and philosophers, and even, as we have seen, among the Presocratics. The Pythagorean cosmology describes the male as the creator and the female as the passive receptor. Of the playwrights, Aeschylus is most famous for employing a patrogenic theme. In *Eumenides*, the last play of his Orestcian trilogy, Orestes, with the assistance of Apollo, defends his vengeful killing of his own mother on the basis that she had murdered Orestes' father, her husband, Agamemnon. The Eumenides, or Furies, who typically exact revenge on those who commit crimes against their blood relatives, demand punishment of Orestes for shedding 'the blood of (his) mother, from whence he derived his own.'[38] Orestes, however, is acquitted in a trial largely on the basis of Apollo's defence:

> The bearer of the so-called offspring is not the mother of it, but only the nurse of the newly-conceived fetus. It is the male who is the author of its being; while she, as a stranger for a stranger, preserves the young plant

for those for whom the god has not blighted it in the bud. And I will show you proof of this assertion: one *may* become a father without a mother: there stands by a witness of this in the daughter of Olympian Zeus, who was not even nursed in the darkness of the womb ...[39]

In other words, because his mother is not the true parent but only a receptacle, Orestes is justified in killing her to avenge the death of his true parent, Agamemnon. So Aeschylus depicts a battle between two opposed understandings of parenthood; one that values the maternal role as essential and another that denigrates the mother and elevates the importance of the paternal contribution. From Apollo's speech it is evident that the latter vision wins. Orestes asks the Furies whether they even consider him related by blood to his mother.[40] Despite interjections from the Furies that his mother nursed him with their shared blood,[41] and despite the fact that, in Apollo's terms, Orestes' mother 'is that body which gave him birth,' the father in this case assumes the status of generative parent, while the mother is a mere stranger, providing only soil in which the young plant may grow.

Apart from Plato, the philosopher who has gained the most notoriety for patrogenesis is Aristotle. *On the Generation of Animals* details Aristotle's thesis on reproduction, including the idea that men contribute the form and women the matter to reproduction. He believed menstrual fluid, as the female variant of sperm or seed, to be the matter from which the child was formed. Aristotle's theory of reproduction needs to be understood in the context of his theory of form and matter. While matter is inseparable from form, and while form does not have an autonomous existence outside its material instantiation, the form of a thing is nevertheless its essence. Although male and female each contribute something to the reproductive process, what they contribute and the importance of their contribution is quite distinct. This is not straight patrogenesis, as we find in Aeschylus, but here the male is still the primary generative parent: 'the male is the active partner, the one which originates the movement,' according to Aristotle, 'and the female *qua* female is the passive one.' As he puts it, 'the physical part, the body, comes from the female, and the Soul from the male, since the Soul is the essence of a particular body.'[42] Part of woman's deficiency in reproduction stems from her coldness, which in turn means that she 'lacks the power to concoct semen' from her menstrual fluid, and it also means that the child gestates very slowly in the mother's womb. That Aristotle had not discovered the existence of the egg is of little consequence to the quality of his theory, for many of his biological differentiations between male and female are not based on empirical observation, but on politics. Most significant is his universalization of male reproductive processes, leading him to conclude that '[a] woman is as it were an infertile male; the female, in fact, is female on account of inability of a sort,'[43] that is, woman is defined by her lack of male properties. Indeed, 'the female is as it were a deformed male';[44] the male is the universal, biological standard, the prototype of the human being, compared to which the female can only fail to measure up because of her difference.[45]

The Hippocratic treatises, most likely written by various authors, perhaps none of whom were the historical Hippocrates, generally assert a female seed as contributing to the make-up of the child. The treatises make reference to the fact that 'growth belongs, not only to the man's secretion, but also to that of the woman.'[46] In addition, however, there is the use of the plant analogy, whereby the author states that 'from beginning to end the process of growth in plants and in humans is exactly the same.'[47] As Helen King explains, the identification of woman with nurturing soil is a common one in Greek literature and embryology,[48] and Plato himself makes such a reference. The idea presented in the Hippocratic writings is that just as the health of the plant depends upon the soil in which it grows, so too does the health of the mother determine the health of the fetus. This is not, in itself, incorrect, provided that the imagery does not transform into that of the male farmer sowing his seed in the inert soil, which is exactly how Aeschylus describes generation. While the Hippocratic treatises are generally positive in their assessment of the female role in reproduction, they remain firmly within a masculinist model in their use of the male as the prototypical human specimen. Normal bodily processes in the female are enumerated at length, cast as different, and ultimately pathologized. Of course, they can only be pathologized on the basis that they do not conform to what is normal for human beings (read: the male).

Timaeus too makes use of the seed-in-soil analogy toward the conclusion of the dialogue and within the larger context of pathologizing the female body. After reasserting the true role of man – to exercise his intellect, show a love of wisdom, and learn the 'harmonies and revolutions of the universe' (90d) – and after reminding his listeners that the punishment for a man who does not follow such a course is rebirth as a woman, Timaeus describes the process of reproduction. The male 'organ of generation' has a natural lust, a lust that is masterful and does not obey reason; women have a womb or matrix that is essentially an animal living inside them, anxious to procreate. Lust and a desire for mastery on the part of the male is considered normal. Alternatively, the womb-animal can behave quite abnormally, for

> when remaining unfruitful long beyond its proper time, [it] gets discontented and angry, and wandering in every direction through the body, closes up the passages of the breath, and, by obstructing respiration, drives them to extremity, causing all varieties of disease ... (91c)

Plato's solution for such illness in women is sexual intercourse and procreation, and in this recommendation he sounds much like the Hippocratic writers who prescribe intercourse and pregnancy for just about every 'disease' of the female body.[49] Hippocratic writers also share this belief that the womb can wander in the woman's body and cause her to suffocate.[50] The procreation that Timaeus recommends to this suffocating woman and desirous man is akin to 'plucking the fruit from the tree.' The man 'sow[s] in the womb, as in a field, animals unseen by reason of their smallness and without form' (91d). These animals are 'separated and matured within,' and brought into light, thus completing the generation of animals. Plato, like many of his predecessors, relies here on the analogy of woman as inert soil in which the animal derived from the male seed is grown and developed. He also seems to be implying that the fetus is entirely formed before making contact with the female.

These passages reinforce what Plato has already outlined in the receptacle passage, that is, that he is preoccupied with images of patrogenesis, but simply relies on a different metaphor for its transmission. Plato's failure to acknowledge here that the womb has a unique capacity, distinct from the male's reproductive organs, mirrors the tension that generally surrounds Plato's discussions of difference of any sort. He can include women's reproductive organs only to the extent that he can describe them as sources of illness and disease. Natural differences, then, between men and women cannot be acknowledged in a neutral fashion, but need to be ordered hierarchically: one natural trait is universalized (the masculine); one trait is pathologized or elided altogether (the feminine).

In a persuasive interpretation of ancient Greek science, Thomas

Laqueur argues that a 'one-sex' model informed the embryological literature and understandings of reproduction right up until the end of the seventeenth century. Rather than viewing male and female as essentially and biologically opposed, and rather than reading sexual difference as ontological difference, the Greeks understood male and female as variants of the same sex – variants, Laqueur assures us, that were hierarchically ordered. One of the benefits of reading sex as Laqueur does is that it helps us make sense of the repeated suggestions, from Plato and Aristotle to the Hippocratic writers, that the female is but a deformed male. In asserting this idea, these writers meant, literally, that the female is the inverse of the male, that all of the reproductive organs found in the female correlate to those of the male. As Laqueur summarizes this view, 'Women ... are inverted, and hence less perfect, men. They have exactly the same organs but in exactly the wrong places.'[51] The only difference between them stems from the female's lack of heat; and heat is what makes the male the superior instantiation of the human being.

Laqueur's account is also useful in its clear articulation of the link between scientific interpretations of sex, on the one hand, and the social and political quest for masculine empowerment, on the other. 'In a public world that was overwhelmingly male,' writes Laqueur, 'the one-sex model displayed what was already massively evident in culture more generally: man is the measure of all things, and woman does not exist as an ontologically distinct category.'[52] Whether or not we accept the intricacies of Laqueur's one-sex thesis, I want to suggest that the effect is the same. There may, in fact, be some slippage between the one-sex and two-sex understandings of the human species, but both models are phallocentric; both models set the male as the standard and that they do so is an expression of ancient Greek masculinist power dynamics.

It is quite clear that the ancient Greeks were far from a scientific understanding of the beginnings of the human race and of reproduction itself. In my reading, however, patrogenesis is not just one theory among others that tries to make sense of the mysteries of creation and reproduction. It is of a piece with an important trend in ancient Athens that posits the male as the paradigmatic being of the human species. In this important sense, patrogenesis is infused with phallocentric politics; it is imbued with prior notions of women's 'lack' and is therefore far from being a benign scientific theory.

## 4. The Political Value of Patrogenesis

Plato shares with his contemporaries an affinity for depicting natural phenomena as well as social relationships using a patrogenic metaphor. Just what Plato finds attractive and useful in this metaphor needs to be considered. Some may find it tempting to surmise that Plato deliberately uses patrogenesis to further the ideological cause of women's seclusion in ancient Athens, but in fact his use of the metaphor may have more to do with a life that he desires for men, a life of masculine virtue, than with an *overt* project to subordinate women. Certainly there is a strong relationship between creation stories of the cosmogonical type and birth metaphors – how could this not be the case when cosmongonies are a quest to understand where we came from? Still, this is a complex connection and one that cannot easily be assessed.

One theory, advanced by Mary O'Brien and addressed briefly in chapter 1, is that male philosophers and politicians are drawn to origin stories because they are alienated from the material experience of reproduction.[53] It will be useful to examine this thesis further because of its relevance to Plato in particular. Men's reproductive alienation leads them to appropriate women's experiences of pregnancy and birth for the masculine realm of politics. According to this appropriation theory, male philosophers such as Plato would acknowledge female difference as a source of power and subsequently appropriate that difference and concomitant power. Also implicit in this appropriation thesis is the belief that women in fact have some mysterious creative potency that itself is a natural source of power. Robbie Kahn extends the appropriation thesis by claiming that origin myths 'attack' and 'dismember' the female body as they draw upon it for metaphors. Kahn asserts that the Western tradition is self-subverting, for in 'sacking birth for metaphors' this tradition acknowledges that 'no descriptions of commensurate power can be derived from male experience.'[54]

Although rhetorically appealing and provocative, the attempts to posit such a causal force behind Plato's patrogenesis, to identify a single reason for Plato's use of patrogenesis, are likely to be incomplete or reductionist. Furthermore, these causal connections are themselves related to, and often serve as the foundation for, a particular vision of feminist politics. Both O'Brien and Kahn imply that there is a deep cultural or philosophic truth about birth and reproduction that patriarchy has repressed, when in fact there may be no such deep truth or meaning. Birth and reproduction, as biological processes, have only the meaning and significance that we culturally and philosophically attach to them. To argue differently is, I believe, to commit two philosophic errors: the first is biological determinism (women give birth therefore they have a deep, creative power that is absent in men); the second, related to the first, is cultural universalism (positing birth and reproduction as having some pan-cultural meaning, when in fact we know that different cultures in different historical periods attach very different significance to these processes). The upshot of these criticisms is not that we should relegate birth back to being a strictly biological process, wherein it is devoid of meaning, for of course human beings are always engaged in the exercise of assigning meaning to the events we participate in. In this sense, human birth and reproduction have never been exclusively biological processes.[55] The point here is that the appropriation thesis, as a means to explain Plato, is itself political and may lead feminist theory into an unnecessary quagmire.

As an alternative to appropriation, I suggest that it may be more productive to think of Plato's use of patrogenesis in *Timaeus* as a theoretical fabrication. On this theory, Plato's use of birth and reproduction is entirely creative, and reflects no deep truth about the processes themselves. To be certain, he borrows the ideas of pregnancy and birth from woman, but patrogenesis reflects Plato's *wholly fabricated image of pregnancy and birth* rather than a patriarchal inversion of reality. This fabrication thesis is distinct from appropriation in a subtle but nonetheless vital way. Plato's patrogenesis is not appropriation from women precisely because appropriation requires that he acknowledge women's unique reproductive ability.[56] In the context of this dialogue at least, Plato underestimates and undervalues women's contribution. In this sense, Plato's reproductive metaphor appears to have little to do with his actual assessment of women, but rather has a lot to do with a masculine politics, even a masculine fantasy.

Just exactly why Plato appeals to patrogenesis may be impossible to uncover. Plato's image of reproduction, I am suggesting, is not the product of his own reproductive alienation, as O'Brien has posited. However, his masculine fantasy about reproduction may nonetheless be the result of a *perceived reproductive alienation* on his part. His perceived reproductive alienation may in turn lead him to inflate and glorify the male role at the expense of the female. It may also be a response to the fear that, if women were credited with a greater role in reproduction, or if their 'seed' was understood to be more potent than the male's, 'there would be no need for men at all.'[57] At the very least we can say that the images of reproduction that Plato does present, his characterization of reproduction as a masculine and awe-inspiring process, is not an inversion of nature but is itself a construction. As such it is of a piece with the patrogenic theme in ancient Greek writing. Plato is not robbing creative potency from woman as part of some biologically inspired compensatory act but rather he is *fabricating the very idea of creative potency.*

Consider Plato's *Symposium*, the dialogue on Eros in which Plato puts the metaphors of pregnancy and birth to work for his epistemology. In the *Symposium* Plato diminishes in significance women's pregnancy and birth experiences. Even in the discussion of the physical aspects of giving birth, men as well as women are depicted as pregnant and giving birth to human beings. Then, at the highest and most perfect level of Eros, *men alone* are pregnant and give birth to ideas in Beauty, the truly immortal progeny that so outshines its prototype. Plato can only simultaneously disparage all that is bodily and borrow birth for the masculine philosopher by transposing birth from the physical realm (where he thinks it is) to the metaphysical realm. In the *Symposium* Plato demonstrates both his *abhorrence* and his *fantasy-like image* of what pregnancy and birth are. In one sense, nothing is more base than human reproduction. Yet, at the same time, no bodily process holds as much theoretical appeal for Plato. The image of birth that he creates is a wholly fabricated, glorified one which he manipulates with such finesse that, in the end, the material experience of birth appears as a mere imitation of the birth of metaphysical ideas in Beauty. This philosophical manoeuvre is not strictly an appropriation because, again, appropriation implies recognition of *what women can do.* It is this recognition that Plato does not give. Instead he projects or transposes this image of a powerful, awe-inspiring process onto woman and simultaneously annexes it for the male for his philosophical journey of knowledge acquisition.

Patrogenesis in the *Timaeus* participates in a somewhat different Platonic reproductive fantasy. The image of the power of pregnancy and birth recedes, leaving behind only male gods, male human beings, and of course the paternal, life-giving Forms as the originary and generative beings in the universe. Plato does equip the maternal receptacle with gestative and birthing ability, but robs those two roles of any creative or intellectual dimensions. The receptacle is not powerful but is instead passive, dimly seen, neither space nor matter. She is mysterious and different from the paternal Forms, but not endowed with unique power comparable to the Forms. Moreover, since women are a secondary creation, and almost incidental to reproduction in this formulation, patrogenesis makes woman irrelevant, both politically and in terms of reproduction. Like the fantasy of pregnancy and birth in the *Symposium*, this cosmogonical fantasy depicts the incredible power of life-generation, the fabricated image of creative potency. The *Timaeus* is different from the *Symposium* in that the reproductive image has lost most of its feminine dimensions, and the great creative potency stems from the male act of seed generation. Here Plato is not 'sacking birth for metaphors'; rather, he taps into patrogenic embryology to depict an all-powerful process of male seed-generation. That the Greeks did not possess an advanced science of embryology in no way exculpates them for their theory of patrogenesis, as a lack of full knowledge would not necessarily lead them to conclude that women were incidental to reproduction.[58]

In the *Symposium*, as in the *Timaeus*, the male role is enhanced: in the former, males are empowered with gestational and birthing ability; in the latter, the female-associated aspects of reproduction are downplayed while the act of insemination is glorified. In both cases, male creative potency is fabricated, drawing on the *perceived* natural power of the female role in reproduction and subsequently transposing it to the male. Ontologically this projection of a male-empowered image of reproduction onto his cosmogony suggests Plato's uncomfortable philosophic relationship to the body, and in particular the female body. Plato demonstrates in this as in other dialogues his strong philosophical preference for the soul and the metaphysical as opposed to the body and the physical. The *Timaeus* affirms this soul/body dichotomy at every turn, as men are punished for improper care of the soul by being reborn as women. Again, this is Plato's warning to philosophic men of Athens; he is restating the importance of conforming to a particular virtuous code that abstains from bodily desire, pleasure, and trivial emotion, regularly called 'womanish.' Women, for Plato, are inextricably linked to the body, unable to escape its base processes and trappings. His characterization of the feminine receptacle as neither material nor ideal does nothing to undermine this philosophy of woman; the feminine, for Plato, is ambiguous, not fixed. The paternal Forms, by contrast, are entirely ideal by definition; they are empowered to beget with little female or bodily assistance. The *Timaeus* achieves patrogenesis in the realm of ideas. And insofar as phallocentrism is the universalization of the male and the relegation of the female to the status of perpetual analogue, patrogenesis is its ultimate act.

What remains to be considered, beyond the phallocentric implications of patrogenesis, is the political value of reproductive metaphors for Plato. What *is* the value of a reproductive metaphor? The political value of reproduction as a metaphor in the *Timaeus* stems partly from its status as a 'natural' event. Nature has many uses in political theory, including its ability to justify a preconceived political solution. In this sense, Plato's origin story carries with it that troublesome political baggage of essences and 'truth' that we identified in chapter 1. Plato repeatedly invokes the *natural* ordering – the *primordial* ordering – of reality as the *authoritative* ordering of reality. The philosopher, in understanding the Forms, apprehends the best, most natural pattern on which the actual polis should be based. Plato's cosmogony, his detection of order in the cosmos, is designed to reveal the correspondence between the polis and the cosmos. Such a correspondence legitimizes his political arrangement. Part and parcel of this legitimation exercise is the use of the natural metaphor of generation or reproduction. The political effect of the *Timaeus* is that it eliminates the need for public, political discussion of the best polis. If the true, essential polis is patterned on the cosmos then it needs only to be revealed. At the same time, Plato appears from this analysis to be an anti-political thinker, as he reveals his preference for a preconceived, 'natural' political solution over politics itself.[59]

Of course, it is essential to understand that, for Plato, democratic politics is inextricably linked with a deleterious love of money and money-making, the natural end of which could only be internal strife and war. In Plato's view, Athenian life as a whole was 'excessively given over to money-making, the social expression of an orientation to appetite and the body.'[60] This is one of the key reasons why, in the *Timaeus* as in the myth of the metals, Plato replaces the democratic script of citizenship, and its endorsement of a form of equality and political debate, with a script of natural hierarchy among citizens. Plato *is* anti-political, where politics is understood as being under the control of men whose souls are not properly oriented toward wisdom. Here we see the intimate connection for Plato between his disdain for the body and the appetites – the satisfaction of which requires immersion in a life of money-making – and his desire to posit a natural political order as revealed in his origin story.

Plato's use of a natural metaphor, his reliance on the idea that the polis has a natural ordering based on the patterns of the universe itself, serves him well in his battle against Athenian sophists. For the sophists, there are no absolute values or morals, no natural forms of justice. Truth itself is subjective; thus, one political arrangement is as legitimate and defensible as the next. Sophistic teachings not only legitimate democracy as a political configuration, they educate Athenian citizens on how to enhance their performance in a democratic forum. Democracy is anathema to Plato, as we have seen. Rather than being bound together by a love of reason and the proper temperance of the appetites, democratic citizens are bound together in the social relationship of money-making.[61]

Male potency as depicted through the reproductive metaphor serves another, related purpose for Plato: it augments his project to reshape and redefine masculinity.[62] Wendy Brown has made the argument that Plato removes the agonistic, wealth-seeking drive from Athenian masculinity, and replaces it with conventionally feminine traits. Plato, she suggests, attempts 'to relocate knowledge, knowing, and philosophy to a sphere less soaked by masculinist political power than the one it currently inhabits.'[63] Yet in his attempts to redefine masculinity, Plato also reaffirms what Brown identifies to be the 'traditional masculine virtues of the Greeks – temperance, courage, wisdom, and justice.'[64] Moreover, as she points out, his project neither demonstrates a concern for gender justice nor undertakes a 'defense of the feminine,' as Arlene Saxonhouse contends. Rather, Brown argues, 'Plato's subversion of conventional assumptions about gender is deployed to disturb a larger web of assumptions about political life and philosophic endeavor.'[65] So too, I argue, is Plato's use of reproductive metaphors in the *Timaeus* about redefining Athenian masculinity and reshaping the notion of politics. Plato is able to use femininity, by feminizing philosophy or empowering men with procreative potency, to accomplish his political ends. In my view, Plato has no quarrel with masculine power per se, only with its democratic instantiation.

In this reading, I want to suggest that Plato uses the *Timaeus* as a script of citizenship aimed specifically at male citizens. I have already posited natural hierarchy as the theme of Plato's script, but from the opening passages about the superiority of ancient Athens over Atlantis to the description of the primacy of men in creation, their autonomy, and their self-sufficiency, it is also apparent that the dialogue is offered specifically to summon men to action. Masculinity in Athenian democracy had been, as I have suggested, about excess, about the pursuit of wealth and status, and about the superficial practice of rhetoric. It embodied all of the human traits and pursuits that Plato found most repulsive, false, and petty. Thus, he urges in the *Republic* as elsewhere that young men take up the architectonic task of regenerating the polis in its pre-democratic configuration.[66] He implores men to resist the excesses and temptations of a democratic Athens, to rebuff the democratic model of masculinity. He envisions men's philosophic task to be nothing short of comprehending the order and workings of the universe itself. Such political and philosophical challenges require a heightened, finely tuned sort of masculinity, one suited to an oligarchic political configuration. This idealized masculinity, according to Plato, is epitomized in carefully controlled, wise, and virtuous philosophic behaviour.

The *Timaeus* can be understood as a rearticulation of this plea in mythical language. Here the language of patrogenesis is invaluable for describing the transformed masculine ideal. Only with the glorified power of self-reproduction – a power far above and beyond woman's capability – will Athenian men be able to rise to the philosophic and political challenges that Plato has articulated for them.

From this examination of the *Timaeus* as an origin story, it is evident that Plato had compelling philosophical and political reasons for turning to the origins discourse. The origins discourse allowed him to respond to his cosmogonical predecessors, the Presocratics, who so influenced his ontology and epistemology. Furthermore, it served a heuristic purpose in allowing him to imagine the birth of order in the universe and to imagine man's place in that order. It opened up a unique opportunity for Plato to recreate the city of Athens in its natural, pre-democratic form.

Of course, using the language of nature also led Plato into a deeply gendered, patrogenic political discourse. In this analysis, I have attempted to demonstrate that Plato's use of patrogenesis as a metaphor cannot simply be attributed to an overtly patriarchal project to appropriate reproduction from, and subordinate, woman. This suggestion about Plato relates to my larger view of origin stories – that it would be overly reductionist to assert that the masculine appropriation of reproduction is the primary ontological significance of origin stories. Nor, however, should the origin story be written off as mere myth. Plato's intent may be mythical, but myth, too, serves important political functions. It is able to render conventional human relationships natural and beyond question.

In the reading that I am offering, Plato's origin myth functions as a script of citizenship in two important ways. It posits the hierarchy in society as natural and fundamental; and it empowers Athenian males to act. Rather than simply appropriating reproduction from woman, Plato fabricates the notion of procreative potency to inspire Athenian men to shed the trappings of an indulgent, democratic masculinity and generate themselves and the polis anew.

*Chapter Three*

# Hobbes and the Discourse on Origins

As we turn our attention to the early modern period, and to the thinker often identified as the first modern, the focus on political origin stories must inevitably be drawn away from cosmogony in the broad sense and toward the practical politics of constitutional theory. That Thomas Hobbes was not a cosmogonist, that he did not ask in his political philosophy questions about the origins of the universe and humanity, in no way indicates a lesser concern with origins. Hobbes's concern was with the origins of power and politics, with the origins of political society. This is an interest that Plato and Hobbes share, as is evident in Plato's autochthonous metaphors. Although Hobbes's political theory is motivated by the study of the best possible constitutional arrangement for seventeenth-century England, it is nonetheless influenced by his deep commitment to the mechanistic, scientific world view. He still shares in the origins impulse, that drive to break down in a logical sequence the theoretical beginnings of any given phenomenon, such as political society. His origins impulse is evident in his development of the concepts state of nature and the social contract, the two components of his origin story, to explain the workings of the civil state.[1]

Hobbes's origin story makes an interesting study because he is not a thinker with whom we normally associate myth-making or storytelling. Hobbes is typically cast as the *opposite* of fanciful: as a rational, scientific thinker. So what, then, is the motivation and impetus behind his origin story? In this first chapter about Hobbes I explore the reasons why he finds the seemingly fanciful exercise of hypothesizing origins persuasive. To this end, I offer three suggestions.

The first suggestion is that Hobbes's contemporaries are themselves immersed in origins-thinking, and so for Hobbes to provide a sustained and consistent argument against the dominant constitutional theories of his epoch he must enter the origins discourse. After first outlining Hobbes's origin narrative in section 1, I situate his narrative in its political-constitutional context to demonstrate how the various theories of his era influence his own account in section 2. A contextual reading of Hobbes's story reveals the degree to which Hobbes is able to appropriate and transform elements of opposing theories for his own political purposes.

Second, I suggest that Hobbes's motivation for using an origin story in his political theory can be located in his fascination with geometric principles and mechanistic science and with their application to the problems of politics. Although his origin story may appear fanciful to modern readers, it constitutes part of his attempt to build a rational politics on the firmest scientific foundation possible. As we see in section 3, the device of the state of nature permits Hobbes to examine the basic 'units' of the state, while the leviathan is the rational, reassembled product of Hobbes's efforts. Hobbes's political philosophy is the direct result of his natural philosophy.

However, the scientific dimension is not the whole story. By the time Hobbes wrote the *Leviathan* he was aware that the problems of politics were becoming more complex and required corresponding innovations. He had observed that political success was contingent on people being convinced of the logic of one's arguments. For this reason, Hobbes began to frame his overall constitutional arguments in more deliberate, more convincing language. In the final section of this chapter, I offer my third suggestion as to why Hobbes finds the origins discourse compelling: because of its instrumental value as a device of persuasion. An origin story could terrify people – as the state of nature did – at the same time as it could provide a script of citizenship, encouraging citizens of England to behave as though they had entered into a social contract with one another. Although the origin story had been integral to his theory from the beginning, by the time Hobbes wrote the rhetorically enhanced origin story of the *Leviathan*, he was showing himself to be a strategic politician, drawing upon the most powerful and persuasive language for his purposes.

In the course of this examination of Hobbes, I demonstrate that Hobbes is not only an unconventional thinker in the context of his own times, but an unconventional origins theorist as well. Unlike those of Plato and the feminist origins theorists, Hobbes's origin story is not normative; it does not summon a golden age to which the citizens of

56  Origin Stories in Political Thought

England ought to return. Quite the opposite, Hobbes's story of the state of nature is framed as a warning about what might happen if the citizens of England do not restore order and obey the existing sovereign power of the Protectorate. It is this enigmatic usage of the origin story that sets Hobbes apart from the other origins thinkers and makes him a compelling choice for our study of origin narratives.

### 1. Hobbes's Two-part Origin Story

Hobbes's political theory is an attempt to justify the need for absolute power, invested in a sovereign authority and derived through consent. Hobbes might have simply asserted his belief in the benefits of absolute sovereignty for England by underscoring the destructive effects of faction and civil war. Yet rather than merely asserting his political opinions, he chose to tap into the prevailing origins discourse in order to reveal the derivation of the kind of rule he favoured. In this first section, it will be useful to review briefly the details of his two-part origin narrative.

To set the scene, Hobbes begins his origin story with a state-of-nature device, a story of an anarchic and presocial state that is ultimately transcended by a social contract. In part I of the *Leviathan*, Hobbes has already outlined his philosophical understanding of the nature of man and of motion. Considering now the natural condition of mankind, he wants us to think about what men would look like with no society, no laws, and no 'visible Power to keep them in awe.'[2] As Hobbes describes it, the state of nature would be a state of rough equality, for whatever their differences in body and mind, 'when all is reckoned together, the difference between man, and man, is not so considerable, as that one man can thereupon claim himselfe any benefit, to which another may not pretend, as well as he.'[3] The signficance of equality is, for Hobbes, profound. To claim the natural *equality* of human beings is to confront head-on and destroy the patriarchalist and divine-right understandings of natural *inequality* and hierarchy. Moreover, the significance of equality for Hobbes lies in its potential to create war. He argues that 'this equality of ability' generates an 'equality of hope in the attaining of our Ends.' Since nature has not laid out a hierarchy that determines who gets what, men have no choice but to become enemies to satisfy their desires; they must 'endeavour to destroy, or subdue one an other.'[4]

This state of nature, then, is actually a state of perpetual war or threat of war – and the two are equally unstable and intolerable. Here Hobbes confronts explicitly the fact that civil society has its origins in violence, as Arendt posits. Hobbes proclaims: 'Hereby it is manifest, that during the time men live without a common Power to keep them all in awe, they are in that condition which is called Warre; and such a warre, as is of every man, against every man.'[5] Men are in constant competition for what they want. At the same time, they are loathe to keep their contracts with one another for fear that the other contracting party might gain advantage by failing to keep their end of the bargain. The right of nature prevails – in other words, men will naturally do that which is self-preserving. There is nothing a man cannot or will not do, even to someone else's body, in order to protect himself. As long as the right of nature governs the behaviour of the inhabitants of the state of nature, battle will prevail. There are no such things as justice or morality, for these are purely conventional and are thus the attributes of society only. Where there is no common power, human beings live in a state that is famously 'solitary, poore, nasty, brutish and short.'[6]

The state of nature is only the first component of Hobbes's two-part origin story and it is not a normative model of society. Nor does Hobbes's state of nature represent a glance into the forgotten, idealized past. Indeed, it serves the opposite function; it is a foil, a circumstance to be avoided. As such, it is highly effective, for all rational individuals would want to put an end to this condition of brutality. In the natural condition, there are no markers of 'commodious living'; there is neither property nor security. This first part of the origin story is, then, far from being a script of citizenship and serves as a caution about what circumstances might look like if order is not established.

The second component to the origin story is the social contract. The social contract signifies the birth of civil society – a peaceful and orderly state governed by the leviathan – out of the morass of conflict and war. The social contract is Hobbes's script of citizenship, for Hobbes wants the citizens of England to behave as though they had come together and consented to the creation of the leviathan. The social contract is made possible both by the fear that all state-of-nature inhabitants rationally have of one another and by the existence of the immutable laws of nature. A law of nature is a general rule that we understand through our use of reason, a law that forbids a man to do that which is destructive to his own life. While the laws of nature have no coercive force behind them, men will be inclined to obey them in their desire for security. Indeed, the fundamental law of nature is to seek peace, and the second is '[t]hat a man be willing, when others are so too ... to lay down this right to all things; and be contented with so much liberty against other men, as he would allow other men against himself.'[7] This laying down, or mutual transferring, of rights is what constitutes a contract in Hobbes's theory. And in this case, when all state-of-nature inhabitants transfer their right to one man, or one assembly of men, the social contract is formed. Rational inhabitants of the state of nature will follow their own best interests and authorize one man or body of men to represent them all so they can 'live peaceably amongst themselves, and be protected against other men.'[8]

The second component of Hobbes's origin story also provides the script for the relations between the new sovereign authority and the new subjects of the commonwealth. Although a social contract might bring into existence almost any form of rule or government, Hobbes chooses absolute rule for the sovereign and absolute deference for his subjects. This new power is indivisible, that is, it cannot be shared by two bodies or more; it is irrevocable; and it is absolute. So while men in the natural state were essentially equal to each other in body and mind, they are now equal in their subjection to the sovereign.

The foundation of Hobbes's social contract is consent. Men make a choice to consent to absolute power rather than to continue to exist in an unlivably insecure condition of war. It is not, as Victoria Kahn has suggested, that Hobbes's individuals 'consent to fear,' but that they recognize the benefits of attaining some security over remaining in an anarchic state.[9] Putting Hobbes's troublesome understanding of what constitutes legitimate consent aside for the moment, we should note that his origin story is about conventional human associations rather than natural ones. This fact makes him an interesting point of contrast to Plato. In Plato's view, there exists a natural political order that needs only to be uncovered and re-established. Therein lies the utility of an origin story – to awaken Athenian citizens from their belief in conventionalism and relativism, to summon them from the excess associated with democratic politics, and to return them to a glorified, pre-democratic Athens. Alternatively, for Hobbes all human communities and associations are formed by consent – even marital and familial associations, as we will see in chapter 4. Unlike Plato, Hobbes appeals not to nature to construct his human association, but to a practical, scientific strategy. Justice and morality, conspicuously absent from Hobbes's state of nature, become agreed-upon conventions once civil society is in existence and the leviathan establishes their meaning.

Nonetheless, despite the metaphysical differences evident between Hobbes and Plato, both thinkers tell origin stories in an effort to create something new, or to create positive political change. The desire to spur action, to inspire change, is a feature that the three origin stories examined here have in common. Significantly, while both Plato and Hobbes would be considered conservative thinkers on the political spectrum of their respective periods, neither enters the origins discourse merely to justify the existing political regime. Their origin stories are meant to incite action, and in this sense they have what we would now call a radical rather than a conservative purpose.

Having briefly outlined Hobbes's two-part origin story, I will, over the next three sections, elaborate on my three suggestions about why Hobbes uses an origin narrative, beginning with his immersion in the origins discourse.

## 2. The Political-constitutional Origins Discourse

To understand why Hobbes tells an origin story it is essential to recognize that almost all the early seventeenth-century English writers used what Gordon Schochet labels a genetic strategy, that is, they believed that the beginnings of a phenomenon give insight into its present formation.[10] Patriarchalists relied on both the originary power of Adam and the grant of power from God to rulers to justify divine-right theory and absolute monarchy. Consent theorists believed that an original popular sovereignty determined the right of subjects to resist or limit monarchic power. The Levellers, to take one example, believed there had been an original contract that should be renewed through their Agreements of the People. Those who proffered the idea that England had been ruled under an ancient constitution based their view that power should be shared by king, lords, and commons on the belief that this reflected the ancient balance of the commonwealth. The origins of power, and the original political configuration of England, were understood to be all-significant to determining how things should be currently.

Hobbes also places a great deal of emphasis on 'how things began,' and in a very limited sense he, too, might be thought of as a genetic theorist. Often, when his critics take issue with his theory, they take issue with its foundations as well. Sir Robert Filmer expresses bewilderment at Hobbes's use of natural right and consent theory to sanction the royalist side, but he also sees dangerous implications in

Hobbes's origins narrative, not the least of which was the justification for Cromwell's rule. Responding to *De Cive* and *Leviathan* Filmer writes:

> I consent with him about the rights of exercising government, but I cannot agree to his means of acquiring it. It may seem strange I should praise his building and yet mislike his foundation, but so it is. His *jus naturae* [right of nature] and his *regnum institutivum* [kingdom by institution] will not down with me, they appear full of contradiction and impossibilities.[11]

Filmer's reaction to Hobbes typifies genetic thinking in seventeenth-century England. The conclusion is worthless if the method is wrong; the derivation of the source of power is almost as important as the constitutional theory itself.

The upshot of the pervasive emphasis on origins is that, in order to critique his opponents' political-constitutional theories, Hobbes must enter the origins discourse as well. He does so on two levels. First, he strategically counters the *content* of other theorists' origin narratives, poking holes in each theory from consent to patriarchalism. Indeed, Hobbes goes to great lengths to undermine the other arguments, appropriating aspects of each of them, but agreeing with not one of them completely.[12] Second, he calls into question the entire strategy or method of extrapolating political conclusions from origin stories. It is this latter point that renders Hobbes's status as a genetic thinker questionable and that sets him apart from the other origins theorists examined in this inquiry. Certainly 'how things began' impacts on 'how things should be at this time,' but the progress from beginnings to conclusions is not linear for Hobbes, as it is for his opponents. Hobbes's origin story in the state of nature does not prescribe any *particular* political solution. And neither the state of nature nor the social contract summons a golden age that the citizens of England ought to try to recover.

In Hobbes's view, among the most seditious of genetic constitutional theories circulating in the Civil War era is the widely held belief in England's ancient constitution. He credits the ancient constitution and the accompanying notion of a division of power in the realm for the Civil War:

> If there had not first been an opinion received of the greatest part of England, that these [political] powers were divided between the King,

and the Lords, and the House of Commons, the people had never been divided, and fallen into this Civill Warre.[13]

Theorists of the ancient constitution, in Alan Ryan's description, believed that 'England had a traditional structure: it was an organic community to be governed according to familiar principles,' that is, according to custom. As an origin story of seventeenth-century England, the ancient constitution paradoxically claimed that the English tradition had no identifiable beginning, but rather evolved out of the common traditions of the nation.[14] Indeed, to acknowledge an origin would be to envision a time *before* the ancient constitution.[15] Parliamentarians used the ancient constitution as a defence of their power against unlimited royal prerogative on the basis that the ancient balance between the original three parties of the constitution – King, Parliament, and people – ought to be restored.

Hobbes's opposition to the theory of the ancient constitution highlights his break with genetic theorizing in politics. To believe in the existence of an ancient constitution was to believe that 'the past and present existed in an evolutionary continuum,' and therefore that the past could offer moral lessons to the present.[16] Hobbes disagrees not only with the effect of the theory – that power ought to be divided between estates of the realm – but also with the belief that customary and habitual patterns should dictate the current order of things. As he states in the *Leviathan*:

> Ignorance of the causes, and originall constitution of Right, Equity, Law, and Justice, disposeth a man to make Custome and Example the rule of his actions; in such manner, as to think that Unjust which it hath been the custome to punish; and that Just, of the impunity and approbation whereof they can produce an Example, or ... a Precedent.[17]

The inquiry into causes, according to Hobbes, arises from the conviction that 'knowledge of them, maketh men the better able to order the present to their best advantage.'[18] The problem for Hobbes is that political inquiry often goes no further than the discovery of precedent, when, in fact, precedent or previous practice reveals nothing about the true cause or nature of the commonwealth.[19] And 'for though in all places of the world, men should lay the foundation of their houses on the sand,' writes Hobbes, 'it could not be thence inferred, that so it ought to be.'[20]

The origin of England's constitution, according to Hobbes, rests in popular consent. That Hobbes advocates a consensual origin theory of the constitution still places him at a considerable distance from typical consent theorists of seventeenth-century England and their origins discourse. Other consent theorists in that era posit the popular origins of political authority for the express purpose of justifying resistance to the king or, at the very least, limiting his powers. Perhaps the most popular proponents of consent theory during this period – although they were by no means a unified or coherent group – were the Levellers. The Levellers endorsed a two-pronged consent theory: the first to describe the political origins of legitimate government, and the second to allow for the renewal of that initial consent through the franchise. Consent, then, provides the initial foundation for rule and its ongoing legitimation; or alternatively, in the case of tyranny, consent can be withheld and the government resisted. Moreover, as Alan Craig Houston explains, the Levellers 'agreed that consent could not give rise to obligations that were self-destructive or to governments that violated the public interest.'[21] For the Levellers, however, it was not only royal prerogative that needed curtailing, it was also the authoritarian tendencies of the House of Commons.

The Agreements of the People are the Leveller examples of social contracts between individuals, contracts that establish a voluntary, civil association governed by mutual consent. Consent must be present in order for any government to be considered legitimate. 'Every man that is to live under a government,' asserts Colonel Rainborough in a famous exchange, 'ought first by his own consent to put himself under that government.'[22] In a similar spirit, John Wildman questions '[w]hether any person can justly be bound by law, who doth not give his consent that such persons shall make laws for him.'[23] On the one hand, such statements should not be romanticized and turned into the unlimited democratic advocacy that they are not. On the other hand, these statements do reveal a distinctly levelling approach to politics. Indeed, one of the premises of consent theory – which Hobbes shares – is that the hierarchies that exist in society are not the result of nature, as Aristotelians and patriarchalists would have it.

Hobbes's quarrel with consent theory stems, not from its conception of origins, for he accepts the idea of an original popular democracy and of a social contract. Rather, he takes issue with Leveller doctrine, with its justification of the resistance of subjects and its suggestion that limitations should be placed on the power of the sovereign. Furthermore, he rejects the notion that original popular democracy prescribes a similar distribution of power in the present. For Hobbes, resistance is justified only if the sovereign is no longer fulfilling his role of protecting his subjects. Hobbes employs consent theory to justify absolute, indivisible, and irrevocable power; he makes the act of consent a one-time event, never to be withdrawn unless the current sovereign fails to provide the requisite protection. However, he also makes consent an act that takes place between the people themselves and not between subjects and their ruler. That he does so has tremendous significance, because it shows Hobbes's ability to harness the most innovative and potentially radical aspects of consent theory for his own antidemocratic purpose. Consent is for Hobbes only an origin story; it is not a genetic theory and it is not the justification for resistance or sedition that it was for the Levellers. Hobbes was as opposed to, and as afraid of, popular sovereignty in England as any of the divine-right and patriarchalist thinkers.[24]

In fact, Hobbes's real political sympathies lie with absolutist theory of the kind advanced by James VI and I (and subsequently Charles I) and Filmer. Although a supporter of the royalist cause, he remained very critical of the arguments that royalist supporters chose to defend their cause, especially those of divine right and patriarchalism. Patriarchalism held the rule of fathers and of kings to be analogous, and derived the sovereign's power from God, who had originally granted Adam power over his progeny. According to divine-right theory, God mandated the monarch's rule directly; popular consent played no role in the creation of rule. Hobbes, like advocates of divine right, defends absolute, indivisible, and irrevocable rule for the peace and benefit of the commonweal. Theoretically, however, the seeds of disagreement lay in the idea of a divine sponsor of monarchic rule. To Hobbes, the original source of even absolute sovereign power had to be the people themselves. From his perspective, the danger in making a divine-right argument was evident in the power it accorded clerics to interpret the Bible and influence the rule of the commonwealth. Hobbes expressed similar reservations about patriarchalism. Any clerical interference with absolute rule had the potential to seriously subvert the order of the regime.[25] He feared the anarchic and dramatic response that divine right inspired in groups like the Levellers, who opposed both the origin story and the implications of divine right.

Hobbes was particularly inventive in his efforts to undermine the political theory of patriarchalism. Just as he enters the origins discourse in an effort to undermine the existing constitutional theories, he enters the debate about the family to critique the genetic foundation of patriarchal political theory. His innovations on the family and gender relations are the subject of chapter 4. At this point it will suffice to say that, from Hobbes's perspective, although royalist and patriarchalist writers were right about the kind of rule the sovereign exercises, they were entirely incorrect about the source of the sovereign's power. The distinction was a matter of crucial political significance to Hobbes.

Although enigmatic, Hobbes's origin story serves its intended purpose, which is to reveal the fallacious assumptions of the existing origins discourse. What seems fanciful to the modern reader of origin stories was for Hobbes and his contemporaries crucially important precisely because knowing the origins of the political community was thought to be the key to settling the dispute over how it should currently be organized. The origin narratives developed by these thinkers are first and foremost part of a justificatory strategy. From Hobbes's perspective, however, the origin narratives advanced simply *could not prescribe* a particular political arrangement. In his case, as we have seen, he participates in the origins discourse, not only to reveal the problematical assumptions embedded in opposing constitutional theories, but also to prove that origins are not prescriptive, that political solutions cannot be devised from past precedent. This stance sets Hobbes apart from his contemporaries and from the origins discourse in general. While the state-of-nature argument justifies and serves as the foundation for absolute government, it is a state to be avoided rather than recreated. Hobbes's use of the state of nature as a device in his political theory does not conform to the genetic approach. It is, however, broadly reflective of Hobbes's analytical philosophic method, according to which he needs to understand the causes of a phenomenon in order to understand the whole.

## 3. Hobbes's Scientific-origins Impulse

Given Hobbes's opposition to genetic theorizing, we might question why he chooses to use an origin device at all. Part of the answer to this question can be found in his definition of philosophy. For as much as Hobbes is led to the discourse on origins by his political-constitutional environment, his origins impulse is also the product of his philosophic method. Indeed, for Hobbes, first causes – the causes of the generation of a thing – represent essential knowledge about that thing. His relationship to mechanistic science is well documented; the purpose of revisiting that relationship here is to establish the fact that origins theorizing is entirely consistent with Hobbes's conversion to mechanistic scientific philosophy. This impetus to discover and posit first principles, and to derive conclusions based on first principles, he extends from his study of motion and endeavour to the study of human behaviour.

*De Corpore*, written and published in English translation in 1656, is an ideal place to begin analysing the scientific aspects of Hobbes's origins approach. In the first chapter, Hobbes defines philosophy as the knowledge of 'effects or appearances, as we acquire by true ratiocination from the knowledge we have first of their causes or generation.'[26] The logic of this method Hobbes explains in terms of geometry. If we are told that the figure before us that appears to be a circle was drawn in such a manner as to ensure a constant radius from the centre point, we would be confident in concluding that the figure is a circle. Conversely, 'by knowing what figure is set before us, we may come by ratiocination to some generation of the same.' So if it is a circle, we know it was drawn with a consistent radius from the centre point. Philosophy takes as its subject the things about which we can achieve some knowledge regarding their generation. By this definition, Hobbes explains, philosophy cannot undertake the study of the Divine, for we can never know its origins. God is explained as not only eternal but ingenerable by Hobbes.[27] Unlike theology, civil and moral philosophy are entirely open to such investigation. Given this general definition of philosophy, it is not surprising that civil philosophy investigates the origins of the commonwealth in order to better understand it. Indeed, in Hobbes's view, it is the search for true causes that the contemporary origins discourse lacks. Hobbes applies the logic of his scientific, philosophic methodology to his new science of politics. As his definition of philosophy shows, Hobbes detects a correspondence between a phenomenon as it currently exists and its origins.

He expounds his philosophic method with a different metaphor in *De Cive*:

> For as in a watch, or some such small engine, the matter, figure, and motion of the wheels cannot well be known, except it be taken insunder and viewed in parts; so to make a more curious search into the rights of states and duties of subjects, it is necessary, I say, not to take them insunder, but yet that they be so considered as if they were dissolved.[28]

Hobbes means to begin with 'the smallest and presumably least-contested bits of usable information, which are then logically combined into more complex formulas.'[29] In the case of the commonwealth, 'I took my beginning from the very matter of civil government,' he writes, 'and thence proceeded to its generation and form.'[30] Through this theoretical process of taking apart the commonwealth and speculating on its component parts at its origin, Hobbes ensures that the newly constructed state will be more secure and stable. The firmer the foundations, the more lasting and true the building.

The same logic applies to language and speech: Hobbes is often labelled a nominalist because of his belief that truth is a function of language. Assessing the truth of a statement involves assessing whether the words used correspond to their agreed-upon definitions, hence the lengthy textual passages he devotes to the proper definition of commonly used words.[31] Language has no value, and only obfuscates matters, if its basic units are not properly understood by all who use them.[32] Underlying Hobbes's fixation on definition is his conviction that to understand the whole, that is, language and speech, we must understand its basic components, words. Truth, for Hobbes, 'consisteth in the right ordering of names,' and therefore,

> a man that seeketh precise truth, had need to remember what every name he uses stands for; and to place it accordingly; or else he will find himself entangled in words, as a bird in lime-twiggs; the more he struggles, the more belimed.[33]

In fact, one of the sources of disorder in the state of nature about which Hobbes is most concerned is the relativism in people's use of language.[34] The use of words like justice or religion to signify all number of different things produces political and religious chaos. Nominalism, then, and the thorough treatment and redefinition of all contentious words, is Hobbes's solution to linguistic chaos; as such, it conforms with his general philosophic methodology. In his origin story, Hobbes enumerates and then defines the basic human passions as well as key political concepts such as justice as part of his rebuilding effort. Once the civil commonwealth is established, the sovereign is given the power to define words and even to be the sole interpreter of scripture, all toward the end of reducing linguistic and religious chaos.

The centrality of first causes to Hobbes's political philosophy is not accidental, but is rather reflective of his general interest in the causes of motion. Following in the intellectual path of contemporaries like Galileo and Descartes, Hobbes adopts the framework of the new mechanistic science, which is itself an intervention in the long-standing debate on the origination of motion. Mechanics is the study of motion, of the forces that affect physical bodies that are already in motion or at rest. Of course the study of mechanics is not unique to the seventeenth century, but the conclusions of the seventeenth-century scientists represent a significant break with the then prevailing Aristotelian and scholastic theories. Motion for Aristotle, and hence for his scholastic followers, began with a Prime Mover; it had a telos, and only ever occurred for some purpose. Once that purpose was achieved, motion ceased.[35] Now consider Hobbes's statement of the cause of motion: 'motion cannot be understood to have any other cause besides motion; nor has the variety of those things we perceive by sense, as of *colours, sounds, savours*, &c. any other cause than motion.'[36] Not only do objects have no essence, according to Hobbes, but their motion has no cause except other motion. All of the phenomena that had previously been treated as mysterious – and as reflecting an essential quality of the given object – are now explained by reference to motion itself. For Hobbes, a philosophical monist, all that exists is matter. Our senses may deceive us into believing that colour, for example, inheres in an object. Yet Hobbes is particularly concerned to demonstrate that the apparent qualities (what Aristotle termed essences) of bodies 'are merely sensations excited by bodies in motion impinging on the nerves.'[37] Moreover, the way in which our senses interpret this motion is subjective: 'the smell and taste of the same thing, are not the same to every man.'[38]

With the insights of Copernicus, and later Galileo and Descartes, geometry becomes the model through which motion is studied; and geometry is used to examine the motion both of celestial bodies and of terrestrial bodies.[39] Galileo's discovery is that neither motion nor rest requires a cause: if no friction were present, a body could continue to move indefinitely in a circle without some force acting upon it. Inertia dictates that only a *change* in the status of motion requires a cause, and that cause is mechanical, not teleological. The states of motion and rest, furthermore, say nothing about the essence or nature of a body; 'motion is merely a state in which a body finds itself,' and the body is indifferent to that motion.[40] Everything, then, has a simple, mechanical explanation; there is no need to resort to metaphysics or religion to explain the cause or purpose of motion. For Hobbes, everything is caused by physical motion, even the actions and thoughts of human beings. Inertia has such significance for Hobbes that he wastes no time in *Leviathan* before expressing his belief in it.[41] Man himself is simple matter in motion, nothing more, nothing less.

What is the political significance of Hobbes's theory of motion? Because Hobbes explains events with reference to motion, and considers all existing things to be matter, his philosophy, as one theorist describes it, 'transforms the categories of traditional metaphysics into categories of physics.'[42] In particular, Hobbes's theory of inertia in *Leviathan* does the political work of undermining those who adhere to a superstitious world view, who claim to see and feel the presence of spirits and ghosts, who succumb to the superstitious practices of witches, and who allow their fantasies to affect their perceptions of political reality. In turning to inertia to explain sensations, Hobbes effectively casts doubt on those so seduced by other-worldliness. Moreover, if everyone interprets the motion on their senses differently, the possibility of achieving peaceful coexistence without a state or leviathan is diminished severely. Finally, when man is understood to have no essence or telos, but only to be exhibiting random inertial behaviour, the idea that society is inevitable or natural is put to rest. If political society forms, and clearly it is a necessity if a state of war is to be avoided, it is entirely due to convention and consent, to an act of individual wills.

Hobbes's development of concepts of the state of nature and the social contract are the result of his resolutive-compositive method, in which the state is broken down into its basic units and subsequently reassembled on firmer foundations.[43] However, it remains important to point out that Hobbes's theory of inertia, used to depict the state in which people move like particles in random motion governed by nothing but the physical law of inertia, cannot entirely account for people's behaviour. Hobbes laments the fact that, rather than acting in their own self-interest, and thus following peace, people often do not. The state of nature, as a construct, allows Hobbes to explain people's basic nature, but it does not explain why people choose to create a civil society. The immutable and eternal laws of nature are what make civil society and peace possible. The laws of nature lead people to make a social contract with one another (but not with their sovereign) and it is from this social contact that the rights and obligations of subjects and sovereign are derived.

Hobbes's two-part origin narrative, then, conforms to, but cannot be entirely explained by, the scientific method he endorsed. At the very least, we can say that his use of an origin story is neither genetic nor entirely fanciful, but is in fact in keeping with his tendency to look for first causes, and to examine basic components in order to understand the nature of a thing itself. It is important to note that, while Hobbes avoids outright essentialism in his origins quest, he nevertheless falls into the trap of assuming an original or irreducible nature of things that largely governs their actions.

## 4. Rhetorical Appeals in the State of Nature

When Hobbes writes the *Leviathan*, he is responding to the eruption of political and religious chaos in England; he is frustrated by the apparent irrationality and superstition of his contemporaries, on the one hand, and by their inability to comprehend the true causes of war and peace in a commonwealth, on the other. While he continues to adhere to his analytic approach even in the later text *De Corpore*, on matters of politics Hobbes detects an increasing complexity and the need for new approaches and new methods to convince his audience. Indeed, a growing literature recognizes Hobbes's increased use of rhetoric, especially in the *Leviathan*.[44]

Hobbes's turn to rhetoric can be seen as an attempt to reach a wider audience with his later works.[45] As he writes later in *Behemoth*, 'the power of the mighty hath no foundation but in the opinion and belief of the people.'[46] Hobbes accepts that people must be convinced of the power and authority of the sovereign in order for that power to exist and survive. If people cannot calculate, and act according to, their own self-interest, Hobbes must intervene and convince them to do so. Here an origin narrative has a distinctive advantage over straightforward political theorizing: the power of persuasion. Therefore, Hobbes carefully selects the kind of narrative that will have maximum effect on his audience. It must be rhetorically convincing and speak to them in their own political and religious idiom to be persuasive. That Hobbes began to question the efficacy of elucidating straight scientific truth in his texts, that he saw the need to persuade his readership of the logic of his theory,[47] suggests that his origin story became more important to his political theory as his career progressed.

While Hobbes could have made his argument for indivisible and irrevocable sovereign authority without first tracing the hypothetical creation of civil society from the state of nature, the story of the state of nature is *invaluable* to the flow and plausibility of his argument. In Sheldon Wolin's view, the state of nature is Hobbes's 'supreme literary achievement'; it is 'a condition which had the same universal significance and dramatic intensity for the Hobbesian myth as man's fall from grace has for the Christian myth.'[48] In fact, for a theorist who abhorred 'insignificant speech' and metaphor, and who admired the 'austerity of geometry,' Hobbes's *Leviathan* is an unusually imaginative work.[49]

We ought to note here the apparent tension between Hobbes's scientific influences, including his nominalism, and his use of rhetoric and narrative. One might not expect a nominalist and someone opposed to the use of 'insignificant speech' to employ rhetoric and narrative, for the use of narrative implies that the explanation of mere facts and definitions is inadequate. Yet it must not be forgotten that Hobbes's whole purpose is to be heard and believed by his contemporaries. In spite of his commitment to nominalism, and because he was concerned about the linguistic chaos of the Civil War, the mere statement of facts and truths became inadequate for him. Any tension between Hobbes's nominalism and his rhetorical style fades when we recognize his purpose: to persuade his contemporaries of the dangers of the natural state and to encourage them to behave as though they had united in a social contract to obey the leviathan.

Integral to Hobbes's theory from the beginning, the story of the state of nature becomes more elaborate and rhetorically convincing as we move through his texts chronologically. To illustrate briefly, 'Of the state of men without civil society'[50] forms the first chapter of *De Cive*, published in 1642. This initial chapter details Hobbes's theory of presocial man, and contains most of the fundamental elements of the argument offered nine years later in *Leviathan*. However, one of the key differences between the two texts is stylistic. *De Cive* has a definitional style, conveying Hobbes's theories of natural equality, freedom, and mutual fear in straightforward terms. The chapter consists of one 'proof' after another, beginning with Hobbes's lengthy proof that the ancient Greeks misunderstood the reasons for the creation of society.

In subtle contrast to *De Cive*, *Leviathan* is a descriptive text. It has a narrative quality that is absent in the more definition-oriented *De Cive*. To take a brief example, in *De Cive* Hobbes provides a less-descriptive account of the condition of war; those nations inflicted with war were 'few, fierce, short-lived, poor, nasty, and deprived of all that pleasure and beauty of life, which peace and society are wont to bring with them.'[51] In the *Leviathan*, Hobbes devotes considerably more space to outlining the hazards and pitfalls of the natural state. Not only is it famously 'solitary, poore, nasty, brutish and short,' it is also devoid of industry, commodious building, and 'Culture of the Earth.' There is 'no Knowledge of the face of the Earth; no account of Time; no Arts; no Letters; no Society; and which is worst of all, continuall feare, and danger of violent death.'[52] By the time Hobbes writes the *Leviathan*, his account of the state of nature is elaborate and persuasive and, in that sense, not unlike the creation story of Genesis. Hobbes appears to have brought his realization of the import of rhetorical speech to bear on his story of the state of nature.

The increased use of rhetoric, including metaphor and analogy, is also evident in the addition of two stories to the *Leviathan* narrative of the natural state that were not present in *De Cive*. *Leviathan*'s 'Of the Natural Condition of Mankind, as concerning their Felicity, and Misery' contains two stories whose purpose is solely to convince and persuade the reader. The first is Hobbes's elaboration on men's tendency to 'invade, and destroy one another.' It is here that Hobbes asks his reader to consider his own actions if they doubt his conclusions. When 'he armes himselfe' to travel, or when he 'locks his dores' upon going to sleep at night, Hobbes queries, '[d]oes he not there as much accuse mankind of his actions, as I do by my words?'[53] Here Hobbes speaks to his audience in terms that will resonate with their own experience, and force them to examine the motivations behind their own actions.

The other story that Hobbes mentions only briefly in *De Cive* but elaborates upon in the *Leviathan* is that of American Aboriginal peoples. He mentions the 'brutish manner' of life of the 'savage people in many places of America' to enhance his state-of-nature argument. Aboriginals provide Hobbes with his only 'living example' of people in a state of nature. James Tully has shown that Hobbes and Locke effectively advanced the intellectual cause of European imperialism in America by writing of Aboriginals as though they lived in a state of nature. According to Tully's argument, if Aboriginals could be said to have no property conventions, no laws, and no 'state' by European standards, they could not be thought to own the land on which they were living. The appropriation of their land, then, was not articulated as a moral quandary but rather was justified away by the very idea of the state of nature.[54] I suggest as well that the American Aboriginals are an effective point of contrast for Hobbes: these 'savage people' illustrate by opposition the kind of civility and order that Hobbes envisions for England. In this sense, the state of nature is only partially hypothetical, as Charles Mills points out: it is hypothetical for European whites, but for the non-white populations of America it is literal.[55] With respect to origin stories, the example of the American 'savages' summons images of the wild – a Garden of Eden gone wrong. Hobbes implicitly ranks Aboriginals in the Americas at a lower level of modernity, where modernity is measured in exclusively Eurocentric terms.[56] Significantly, rather than turning away from or suppressing the violence at the origin, Hobbes records it with rhetorical flourish because it allows him to make the dangers of the state of nature more apparent to his readership.

Quite apart from its content, Hobbes's use of a creation story would have struck a resonant chord among his readers in seventeenth-century England – a society in which religion played such a constitutive part that it would be an anachronism to describe it as 'religious.'[57] This is an epoch in which the Bible was a widely read text, having been translated from Latin into English during the Reformation. It was the primary text from which political and intellectual life derived meaning, and biblical language and metaphor were in common currency. One strain of constitutional thinkers, of which Filmer is the most representative, derived the King's absolute power from Adam in the origin story of Genesis. Filmer was not alone in his use of Genesis: the political mythology of the Civil War period abounded with interpretation of, and debate on, the significance of the Garden, Adam, and Eve.[58] Therefore, while Hobbes's contemporaries disagreed with the political content of his theory, they would not have found his method, nor his several hundred biblical references, as 'innovative' or unusual as does his twentieth-century audience.[59]

The Garden of Eden is a useful point of reference for understanding Hobbes's origin story. There is more to the similarity between Genesis and the state of nature than the fact that they are both persuasive myths in the twenty-first century. Clearly, on one level, the state of nature and Eden are entirely dissimilar – the former being a condition of war, as I have mentioned, and the latter being an idyllic paradise. The Garden of Eden is normative for its creators, whereas the state of nature is evidently a state to be avoided at all costs. Nevertheless, on another level, the two origin stories display a functional similarity, including their shared attempts to provide justifications (or at least a foundation) for what is to follow – theologically and/or politically – on the basis of particular ontological assumptions.

The similarities between Genesis and Hobbes's origin story begin with their common and obvious etiologic intentions. While the Christian creation myth describes the origins of the earth, and of man and woman,[60] and corresponds more closely to Plato's cosmogony, the *Leviathan* describes the pre-social state of man and the origins of civil society and authority. At the time it was written, Genesis may have been intended as a historically accurate depiction of origins, whereas Hobbes's story is more of a thought experiment. Nevertheless, just as all authors of origin stories effectively separate themselves from their epoch, from the morass of its political and religious complications, Hobbes and the writers of Genesis alike clear an intellectual space within which they can posit the true nature of things. Of course, any such exercise is laden with ontological assumptions. Even the attempt to cut through history and politics in this way suggests an ontological commitment to order as the highest good. The authors of Genesis 1, during the sixth century BCE, were concerned with preserving the monotheistic tradition of the Israelite nation.[61] The result is the initial chapter of Genesis, which establishes God as the author of order. In Genesis 2,[62] even after Adam and Eve are banished from the Garden, order is not lost, but is continually sought after, promised, and re-established through successive covenants. The covenants in the Hebrew Bible signify the re-establishment of order. Similarly, in Hobbes, a high value is placed on establishing order, but in his case that order is the escape from the original state. Again, as in the Bible, it is the covenant, the social contract, that brings order to political affairs. The previous section outlined the kind of constitutional disorder that Hobbes is working against, and which he takes to be a perpetual threat to the English nation. As the moral arbiter on earth, the leviathan rules absolutely, ensures the observance of contracts (and hence justice), and maintains order. The disruption of this order, we are told, would effectively reintroduce this same 'condition of political nothingness' that was the creative impetus for this dramatic vision. In the *Leviathan*, order is achieved at the expense of politics, at the expense of any dissent from authority.

Another common function of these two origin stories is the legitimation of a particular view of human nature. As we have discussed, Genesis makes specific, if ambiguous, ontological claims. In *Adam, Eve, and the Serpent*, Elaine Pagels discusses the myriad ways in which Genesis has been deployed in Christian thought to reconcile the problems of sin, procreation, marriage, and the relationship between man and woman, and to justify conceptions of human nature more generally.[63] Certainly, Genesis invests Adam with the right and power to name what is around him, and suggests the centrality of human beings in the material world.[64] What is less certain, and highly contentious, is Genesis's statement regarding human nature. Does the act of eating the fruit of the forbidden tree symbolize humanity's licentiousness, the natural curiosity and quest for knowledge, or the subversive force of the female? There are also the problems of separation from the divine and human alienation, which are among the complex and challenging aspects of human life that Karen Armstrong sees reflected in Genesis. She contends that, in fact, this separation is present in the narrative of Genesis long before the Fall.[65] What is important to recognize, as Christopher Hill points out, is that almost any theory can be read into the Bible, that 'there are few ideas in whose support a Biblical text cannot be found.'[66] Given the potential for 'reading in,' perhaps the most that can be concluded is that Genesis exhibits the complexity of human life to the reader.

It is similarly difficult to interpret definitively Hobbes's theory of human nature.[67] Hobbes examines human nature in much the same way as he examines the civil state: by reducing it to its basic elements. With this approach, human beings can best be comprehended by stripping them of their socially acquired characteristics, by abstracting them from the complexity of social life. Yet the degree of abstraction that Hobbes has achieved is contestable, for his depiction of human behaviour appears to mirror the conflictual conditions of the Civil War. Moreover, the very suggestion that human beings *can* be stripped of their socially acquired characteristics and examined as 'natural' is problematic. Despite the overwhelming consensus that Hobbes depicts in a transparent fashion the rational, egoistic, self-centred man of modernity and liberalism, his understanding of human nature is actually more difficult to discern. True, Hobbes transports scientific theories into his political theory, describing men as being in perpetual motion, primarily self-interested, and as seeking to amass power and prevail in the competition that is life. Moreover, his autochthonous description of men in the state of nature as having 'sprung out of the earth, and suddenly, like mushrooms, come to full maturity, without any kind of engagement to each other,'[68] epitomizes a reductionist theory of human development. It has been taken for granted that a theorist who characterizes the life of natural man as 'solitary, poore, nasty, brutish, and short' must have a profoundly negative view of human nature.

Still, however negative Hobbes's depiction of the state of nature, it is not clear that he believes man to be inherently wicked. Hobbes also enumerates the positive attributes of men, including their capacity for benevolence and charity. The fear inherent in the state of nature comes not from the fact that all men are wicked, but from the fact that some men are. 'Though the wicked were fewer than the righteous, yet because we cannot distinguish them, there is a necessity of suspecting, heeding, anticipating, subjugating, (and) self-defending.'[69] While it is true that 'of the voluntary acts of every man, the object is some *Good to himselfe*,'[70] this theory does not indicate that man 'cannot be concerned with anything else.'[71] Man's greatest fault is his tendency to fall subject to his own senses and passions, and to miscalculate his own self-interest.[72] Conflict arises because men perceive their best interests differently, hence the benefit of an arbiter.

Hobbes's view of humanity may not be optimistic, but he did at least think that human nature is 'malleable, that one could train, educate, and discipline people into good citizens.'[73] To be fallen in the biblical sense, in Hobbes's theory, is not necessarily to be corrupt – it is to have lost immortality. In his reference to Christian creation, Hobbes states that when Adam ate the fruit from the 'tree of cognizance of Good and Evil ... his punishment was a privation of the estate of Eternall life, wherein God had at first created him.'[74] Eternal life would not be secured again until the Second Kingdom of God was established on earth. Hobbes's narrow reading of the Fall has implications for his assessment of the nature of woman, which will be the topic of the next chapter.

Hobbes's ability to harness religious language and metaphor, popular debate and literature, for his own purposes is evident. The *Leviathan* is a text that reveals great rhetorical flourish and ingenuity, as will be further evident in the subsequent examination of Hobbes's use of the Amazons to augment his case against patriarchalism. The examples of the Amazons, the American Aboriginals, the dangerous state of nature, and so on highlight his creativity, a feature of his thinking that is often underplayed in the categorization of Hobbes as a rationally oriented, scientific thinker.

Hobbes's origin story provides a script of citizenship to his fellow English citizens. It urges them to recognize and avoid the dangers of the natural state and behave as though they had united in a social contract to obey the leviathan. From Hobbes's description of the nature of sovereignty and citizenship, we get a clear picture, as his contemporaries were meant to, of the place of subjects relative to their sovereign in the newly formed commonwealth. Hobbes's script of citizenship presents a picture of a rigidly hierarchical relationship between sovereign and subjects – as connoted by his choice of the term subject over citizen. If Hobbes had viewed the natural inclinations of men differently, if he had been able to entertain a less grim scenario of political beginnings, his sense of possibility in politics might have been more expansive. While the subjects enjoy a degree of personal freedom, that freedom ends precisely where the sovereign decides. Moreover, there is no substantive discussion of equality after the social contract is instituted, so the theoretical equality that Hobbes entertains in the state of nature – including that between men and women, mothers and fathers – vanishes in the commonwealth. The origin story serves to legitimate, if not necessarily to explain, that reality. It is Hobbes's answer to the newly emerging Civil War discourses of resistance and revolt, neither of which are justified in Hobbes's calculus of absolute power and absolute subjection.

My purpose in this analysis of Hobbes has been to examine his origins impulse, to determine the sources of his attraction to the device of origin stories. In the end, the origin story proves useful to Hobbes for political, scientific, and creative reasons. It permits him to engage in, and dismantle, the contemporary political-constitutional debates; it reflects his drive to discover first causes and to understand the whole in terms of its parts; and it serves as a valuable device of political persuasion in the face of a charged and unstable political climate.

In the chapter that follows, I turn to discuss the gendered implications of Hobbes's political theory. We will see that, although Hobbes is not favourably received among feminist political theorists, his record on this front is again more complex than the surface might reveal. In addition to his provocative innovations on gender, I suggest, Hobbes's theory has important political implications – for origins theorists in general and for feminist origins theorists in particular. Hobbes's significant insight on the origins discourse is his recognition that political solutions cannot be found in the narratives of mythical, historical, or customary beginnings. More often than not, origins are used to come to terms with the present. The search for origins usually involves the creation of narratives that embody our present political concerns, narratives that can do more to limit, than to aid, our understanding of political problems and solutions. In spite of his recognition of the limitations of origins, Hobbes too is guilty of creating this kind of narrative. The lesson that he offers, finally, lies more in his critique of genetic theory than in his actual origin story.

*Chapter Four*

# Gender in Hobbes's Origin Story: The Case for Original Maternal Dominion

The preceding chapter having explored the philosophic impetus guiding Hobbes's origin story in *Leviathan*, my purpose in this chapter is to uncover what Hobbes's origin story reveals about gender relations. We have seen in the analysis of Plato that the constitution of normative gender relations is something with which origins theorists are often vitally concerned. Hobbes too discusses gender relations in his origin story, and while his concluding reliance on customary arguments about men's usual political rule is far from liberating for women, his depiction of women as independent contractors in the state of nature, contractors even with the children they bear, differs considerably from Plato's origins vision. While Plato sought a justification and rationalization for unequal gender relations, Hobbes effectively disrupted gender norms, opening a space in which gender relations could be dramatically – if briefly – reconceived.

Hobbes's narrative about the state of nature and the social contract has been the subject of a number of feminist treatments,[1] the most prominent belonging to Carole Pateman.[2] Pateman acknowledges Hobbes's unique interpretation of gender relations in the state of nature, but her primary focus is on his apparent exclusion of women from the all-important social contract that brings civil society into existence. Underlying the social contract, in Pateman's view, is a sexual contract that ensures women's subordination at the inception of civil society. In fact, Hobbes is not explicit about what happens to women: he does not expressly exclude them from the social contract, yet it is unlikely that he envisions them as contractors alongside men. Once the social contract is made, his provocative vision of gender relations recedes into the background, and he falls back on customary arguments about men being more suited than women to form a commonwealth. Pateman's conclusion is that Hobbes reaffirms modern (conjugal) patriarchy, even as he attempts to undermine political patriarchalism. Insofar as the ultimate *effect* of Hobbes's social contract is concerned, this basic judgment by Pateman is correct.

However, my reading of Hobbes differs from Pateman's in two respects.[3] First, it is my contention that there is more to Hobbes than his exclusion of women from the social contract. By examining Hobbes against the backdrop of the dominant gender ideology in seventeenth-century England, and by comparing his ideas to those of the female religious enthusiasts of the Civil War period, we can see that Hobbes's use of gender in his origin story was then, and indeed remains now, enormously significant. Second, whereas Pateman presumes that Hobbes can be made consistent on the question of gender relations – that he can be made to tell the whole story of women's subordination – I suggest that if Hobbes does not fully resolve the issue of gender relations in his theory, it is because he used gender instrumentally. Hobbes does not undertake the study of the family for its own sake, but is interested in families, and hence gender relations, only insofar as they reveal something important about the nature of political relationships.

Just as the feminist literature on Hobbes fails to situate his ideas on gender historically, political theorists and historians of political thought alike fail to account for the gendered dimensions of his theory.[4] And yet the dynamics of gender are key to understanding Hobbes's critique of patriarchalist political theory. Indeed, that Hobbes wrote in a period of increased female activism is significant – for this activism, and the contest over gender relations that accompanied it, set the stage for Hobbes's use of gender in his state-of-nature analysis. The purpose of this exercise, then, is to put aside existing feminist interpretations of Hobbes in order to employ a historically sensitive, feminist approach for understanding his social contract theory – in effect, to generate a conversation between feminist interpretations of Hobbes, on the one hand, and the intellectual history surrounding Hobbes, on the other.

To begin, section 1 situates Hobbes in the context of seventeenth-century gender ideology, comparing him to the two major theorists of patriarchalist political theory, James VI and I and Sir Robert Filmer. Here I demonstrate that Hobbes did not exhibit the same concern for maintaining the gender order as James and Filmer. Against this backdrop, section 2 examines Hobbes's arguments about women and consent and reveals the ways in which his ideas differ dramatically from the dominant contemporary political discourse. Finally, in section 3, I compare Hobbes's arguments to those of the female religious enthusiasts who created the public sense of confusion and contest over gender relations, but whose ideas on gender Hobbes effectively surpasses. Ultimately, what emerges through this analysis is a very different picture of Hobbes than has been typically presented in both feminist literature and in seventeenth-century intellectual history.

## 1. The Context: Gendered Power in Seventeenth-century England

To understand the significance of Hobbes's arguments about gender, it is first necessary to situate his ideas in their intellectual context. It is not the purpose here to summarize the social history of seventeenth-century gender relations,[5] but rather to provide a sketch of the gender ideology that permeates the public discourse as well as the political texts of the period. The gender order of the seventeenth century is premised on classical, Aristotelian, and biblical notions of women's inferiority in strength and reason;[6] an ideological (although certainly not actual) division between public and private spheres;[7] and a belief in the sanctity of marriage as the lynchpin of established order.[8] A brief look at the pamphlet literature as well as the political texts of the seventeenth century reveals a cultural preoccupation with appropriate roles and behaviour for women – and, indeed, for both sexes.[9] While women had many public roles and duties, and were by no means confined to a 'womanly' private sphere, public acts by women that did not have cultural acceptance were considered a threat to the patriarchal order. In this brief overview of seventeenth-century gender ideology, I will focus attention on the prevalence of a gendered public discourse, as well as on the central theorists of patriarchalism, James VI and I and Sir Robert Filmer, precisely because Hobbes's usage of gender is intended to undermine patriarchalism as a political theory.

To discuss gender ideology in seventeenth-century England properly we need to account for the ways in which gender became a powerful tool in the discourses about politics and the constitution. Mary Beth Norton develops the concept of gendered power to describe the system of seventeenth-century power relations in Anglo-America.[10] Gendered power refers not just to the prevalence of male political rule, but to the gendered terminology commonly used to understand power relations in and outside the household, in religion, and in politics. Gendered power points to the ways in which the contest for power and the discourse about the best constitution are infused with gendered metaphors, analogies, and language, language that has resonance only because of the unequal power relations that actually exist socially and politically. Among the constitutional discourses, patriarchalism is the most overt in employing gendered language and metaphor as a central pillar around which the rest of the theory unfolds. Patriarchalism as a constitutional theory can be understood as one of several possible *expressions* of gendered power; it is the political theory, most commonly associated with James VI and I and Sir Robert Filmer, that understands political right to originate in fathers, and which analogizes (or, in Filmer's case, equates)[11] the power of the King and that of the father.

Seventeenth-century England is characterized by a system of gendered power, which means that language about gender and the family works its way into the fabric of political and constitutional discourses. Gender was a key prism through which many other issues were debated and discussed. Gendered power can be detected not only in the works of men; women too make use of gendered language for their own purposes. Consider the example of the Baptist pamphleteer Elizabeth Poole and her comparison of the English nation during the Interregnum to a diseased female body, '*a woman crooked, sick, weak and imperfect in body,*' whom she (Poole) has the ability to cure with her 'gift of faith.'[12] Offering political advice, Poole may have deliberately sought the feminine analogy as a more permissible one through which to convey her message; that is, if the nation *is* a female body, Poole may be seen to have privileged access to 'her.' In her vision presented to the Army she goes on to suggest that a husband is the head of his wife's body, and also that the King is 'your Father and Husband, which you were to obey in the Lord.'[13] Here we see the familiar head-body hierarchy, used to capture the hierarchical ordering of God, kings, men, and women – a hierarchy that also appears in Hobbes's frontispiece to the *Leviathan*, wherein the King is the head and his subjects constitute his body.

Poole's *An Alarum of War* makes use of another common technique of this period, that is, the confusion or inversion of gender roles. If the Lord is husband to the members of the Army, the implication is that the Army is made up of wives. She states as much when she implores the Army not to hurt the King's person: 'now you were his Wife as offended by him ... Lift not your hand against him.'[14] The confusion of gender language in this case is meant to underscore the duty Poole believes the Army owes the King and God – how better to discuss duty than to analogize the Army to wives? Poole's choice of comparison is derived from the simple fact that the hierarchies that characterize familial and gender relations provide the richest source of analogies for any discussion of power, duty, and obligation. Again, the analogies are effective because of widespread acceptance of natural hierarchies and of order in the family and between the sexes. Of course, the use of familial and gendered images did not originate with Stuart rule, as Elizabeth I had also used and popularized them.[15]

Some of the male theorists and writers of the period who draw on the available gendered language reveal signs of what Mark Breitenberg has labelled anxious masculinity. Anxious masculinity describes the inevitable tensions that arise in 'any social system whose premise is the unequal distribution of power and authority.'[16] It is, in Breitenberg's own estimation, a redundant term because masculinity is inherently unstable and anxious. He argues that masculine anxiety functions in early modern England both to 'reveal the fissures and contradictions of patriarchal systems' and to enable the reproduction of patriarchy itself.[17] In other words, masculine anxiety is an *effect* of patriarchy and a *driving force* behind its self-reproduction. While the term gendered power describes the prevalence of gendered language in public and theoretical discourse, anxious masculinity refers specifically to the preoccupation with gender hierarchy, order, power, and privilege that is manifest in the writings of some of Hobbes's contemporaries. As an idea, anxious masculinity has its roots in psychoanalytic theory, but its use does not require that we read back into the seventeenth century the dynamics of 'Freud's family drama,' as Breitenberg explains. Rather it can simply help us to think about masculine subjectivity and to describe a cultural current in the early modern period.[18]

Breitenberg's concept serves as a reminder that, despite the entrenchment of male privilege, and often because of it, power relations are fraught with tension and instability. Indeed, in early modern England there exists a heightened awareness of, and concern about, potential disruptions to the gender order, as I will discuss further. Of course, gender relations themselves were not resolved or rigid during this, or any other, period. In the first half of the seventeenth century, the residual effects of a female monarch, contradictory though they were, together with the presence of women like Elizabeth Poole giving political advice to the nation's leaders, produced a public sense of gender confusion.[19] The 1640s in particular witnessed an unusually high rate of public religious activity on the part of women, activity that also led to political acts such as the petitioning of Parliament. As a result, we commonly witness in the writings of male theorists during this period a defensive attempt to reconsolidate 'natural' gender and familial relations along biblical and Aristotelian lines. In some writings, this defensive strategy assumes a more aggressive and misogynistic form: women who do not remain within the confines of the accepted gender order are singled out and targeted as Catholic sympathizers, as lustful, manly, or practitioners of the subversive art of witchcraft.[20] Overt misogyny does not set the tone, however. Far more common are expressions of anxiety, confusion, and fear regarding the perceived challenge to the patriarchal order.

As patriarchalists, James VI and I and Filmer exhibit signs of an anxious masculinity, working gender hierarchy into the core of their respective political theories. James and Filmer, while in basic agreement with Hobbes about the importance of absolute rule in England, provide useful counterpoints to Hobbes on the derivation of that rule as well as on the issue of gender. Both James and Filmer are advocates of political patriarchalism, the very theory that Hobbes's argument on the family is meant to defeat. While Hobbes's theory is by no means liberating for women, especially once the social contract has been made, I suggest that Hobbes exhibits far fewer symptoms of anxious masculinity than do many of his contemporaries with whom he would have been in basic political agreement; in particular, what is absent from his work is any sort of defensive attack aimed to shore up patriarchal social relations.

It is not an exaggeration to assert that, of all of the public figures and political theorists of early modern England, James proffered and acted upon some of the most misogynistic ideas and beliefs. He is among those who devote considerable attention to the duties and obligations assumed in marriage. On the subject of wives, James adheres to a combination of biblical and Aristotelian views, as he writes in his popular treatise *Basilicon Doron* of the 'godly and vertuous wife,' being '*Flesh of your flesh, and bone of your bone*, as *Adam* saide of *Henuah* [Eve].'[21] Just as women must maintain their bodily purity prior to marriage, so too does James recommend that husbands be chaste, and refrain from adultery once married. He urges his son, to whom the tract is written, to remember the three purposes of marriage: it is an outlet for sexual desire; it permits the procreation of (legitimate) children; and it exists so 'that man should by his Wife, get a helper like himselfe.' Employing all the familiar analogies, James commends to his son a hierarchical but loving relationship with his wife: 'command her as her Lord, cherish her as your helper, rule her as your pupill, and please her in all things reasonable; but teach her not to be curious in things that belong her not: Ye are the head, shee is your body.'[22] James summons on Aristotelian division of public from private when he advises that a woman is 'neuer to meddle with the Politicke gouernment of the Commonweale, but holde her at the Oeconomicke rule of the house: and yet all to be subject to your direction.'[23] James's passage on marriage, then, reflects accepted wisdom, combining the Christian notion of companionate, patriarchal marriage and the ideological division of roles limiting women's activity to the household because of her status as the 'frailest sexe.'

James is also a noted patriarchalist. While he may have thought that women properly belong in, and direct, the domestic sphere, as a patriarchalist he believed men ought to rule both the public and the private absolutely and by divine right from God. In addition to expounding on marriage and the proper rule of the household, James pronounced against the practice of witchcraft as well as masculine dress for women. In 1597 he wrote a tract on witchcraft entitled *Daemonlogie*,[24] and he is thought to be at least partly responsible for the high numbers of prosecutions in Scotland.[25] In 1620 he requested that the clergy in London 'inveigh vehemently and bitterly in theyre sermons against the insolencie of our women, and theyre wearing of brode brimd hats, pointed dublets, theyre haire cut short or shorne, and some of them stillettas or poniards.'[26] In James's view, women who dressed like men were a threat to the gender order of society. In his writings and public pronouncements, James seeks to maintain that order and exhibits signs of anxious masculinity.

Turning to Hobbes's political works, even a cursory comparison reveals sharp distinctions between Hobbes and James on gender. It is immediately evident that, compared to James, Hobbes invests little energy either in delineating the roles and duties of wives or in articulating the proper prosecution of witches. While he obviously discusses the family, most significantly in the state of nature, but also briefly in the context of discussing what is public and private in civil society, he does not elaborate on the position of wives with respect to their husbands. Nor does he even suggest that the private sphere is the female sphere. The most provocative statement Hobbes makes on the question of women is not a patriarchal one, but the opposite: it is an assertion of women's ability to decide whether or not to contract to have sole dominion over children. This comment will be examined in greater detail in section 2.

As for comments on witches, we might expect Hobbes, being versed in James's work, and no less a product of the early modern fervour over witches, to take up this topic with vigour. In fact, he does not, though he does associate witches with enthusiasm and the 'insignificant Speeches of Mad-men, supposed to be possessed with a divine Spirit.' He expresses obvious scepticism regarding the validity of witches' claims, calling witchcraft a 'pretended conference with the dead,' or Necromancy.[27] Nevertheless, Hobbes supports the punishment of witches, not because of some deep misogyny, but because of the threat witches pose to the social and political order.

> For as for Witches, I think not that their witchcraft is any reall power; but that yet that they are justly punished, for the false beliefe they have, that they can do such mischiefe, joyned with their purpose to do it if they can: their trade being nearer to a new Religion, than to a Craft or Science.[28]

It would appear, then, that Hobbes objects to witches for the same reason he objects to religious enthusiasts: for their potential to stimulate disorder among those who are too uneducated to know any better. It is primarily the 'rude' or uneducated, in his view, who are unable to differentiate 'Dreams, and other strong Fancies, from Vision and Sense,' and who believe that fairies, ghosts, and witches exist. Of course, we should not underestimate Hobbes's disdain for religious enthusiasts, but it is noteworthy that his disdain does not reveal any palpable misogyny. Rather, it is connected to his persistent drive to create an orderly commonwealth apart from any subversive religious forces.

Sir Robert Filmer is another important contemporary with whom Hobbes shares basic ideas on the nature of political rule. Filmer believed the rule of the commonwealth should be indivisible, and was as sceptical as Hobbes about the idea of power shared between the monarch and Parliament. Moreover, Filmer believed the King's power to be absolute and beyond judgment; for this reason he rejected the very thought of subjects' rights and liberties claimed in the *Petition of Right*. Any liberties possessed are 'the liberties of grace from the king, and not the liberties of nature to the people.' As a patriarchal political theorist, however,

Filmer relies on a similitude between Adam's God-given power, which is inherited by kings, and the power of fathers over families. As we will see, it is here, in the choice of similitude and the derivation of rule, that the divergence between Filmer and Hobbes is striking.

There are two related issues that bear examination in Filmer, the first being his reliance on the story of Genesis to ground his theory of politics. According to Filmer, Genesis tells the true story about the derivation of political and familial power in seventeenth-century England. If 'God gave to Adam not only the dominion over the woman and the children that should issue from them, but also over all the creatures on it,' then it was clear to Filmer that political power could not be held except 'by donation, assignation or permission from him.'[29] Although Filmer stretches the use of the story of Genesis to its extreme limits, he is not alone in reading the ancillary status of woman from the Fall; indeed, this was a commonplace in early modern England.[30]

Filmer's theory of patriarchalism eliminates any possibility of natural right, attributed by Hobbes and later Locke to human beings in the state of nature. In fact, Filmer expresses grave concern over the potentially subversive force of political consent. Consent and contract have no more place in the Commonwealth, according to Filmer, than they do in the relations between men and women in the family. The mere suggestion of consent breeds in Filmer a kind of masculine anxiety. He writes:

> [B]ut where there is equality by nature, there can be no superior power; there every infant at the hour it is born in, hath an interest with the greatest and wisest man in the world ... not to speak of women, especially virgins, who by birth have as much natural freedom as any other, and therefore ought not to lose their liberty without their own consent.[31]

Of course, in early modern England, wives and daughters were 'included' in their male counterparts and had no opportunity to express or refuse their consent. Legal consent was required of a woman only in marriage, in which her consent was as crucial as that of her husband-to-be to the legitimacy of the marriage contract.[32] Yet what we see in Filmer is a recognition of the power of consent theory and a defensive strategy designed to protect the privilege and right of fathers and kings in the face of their anarchic challengers.

The second and related issue that requires discussion in Filmer's thought is patrogenesis, or male-led procreation. While in the above instance he implies that any issue is the shared product of Adam and Eve, elsewhere he states that 'God at the creation gave sovereignty to the man over the woman, as being the nobler and principal agent in generation.'[33] Similarly, he suggests that 'all men came by succession and generation from one man. We must not deny the truth of the history of the creation.'[34] Adam came first, and from him the woman was made. Whether or not Filmer actually believed that men patrogenically created all other human beings is not the central issue; the point is that he propagates this idea because it augments his patriarchalist political theory.

Despite their shared premises, Hobbes and Filmer fundamentally disagree about the source of power in the Commonwealth and in the family. Hobbes nowhere implies a belief in patrogenesis of the kind propagated by Filmer, primarily because he does not read political right as having emerged from Adam's power in the Garden of Eden. Hobbes's argument about the family and gender relations is a direct outgrowth of his overall attack on patriarchalism. The origin of that constitutional attack lies in Hobbes's concern that the argument for divine right advanced the power of the clergy beyond what was safe for the commonwealth. Indeed, Hobbes's desire to limit the power of bishops for fear of their subversive potential in part accounts for his theory that the sovereign should have unlimited powers of biblical interpretation as well as the belief that power cannot be shared. Patriarchalists, by promoting the theory of divine right, further destabilize the order of the regime. By undermining the basis of their story about the origin of political right, Hobbes hopes to undermine their political argument as a whole.

To summarize our findings thus far, an examination of seventeenth-century political discourse reveals a preoccupation with gender hierarchy both as a metaphor for political rule and as an important indicator of order and stability in society. Threats to the gender order are met with fear and masculine anxiety on the part of the major theorists of political patriarchalism, James and Filmer. Yet, in his origin story, Hobbes not only fails to exhibit any comparable signs of anxious masculinity, he presents an argument about gender that attacks the foundation of the patriarchal order, if unwittingly.

## 2. Gender Relations in the Natural State: The Critique of Patriarchalism

In his description of the beginnings of politics and power in the state of nature, Hobbes is highly strategic. He carefully selects, to illustrate his points, examples that will have rhetorical appeal – indeed, his story abounds with the common analogies of family and state, and with images of powerful queens and Amazons. Hobbes's ingenuity, which distinguishes him from other political theorists and writers of the period, is found in the *substance* of what he says about the family, queens, and Amazons. His highly contentious reconfiguration of gender should be understood as centrally important to the justification of his political theory, for it is this argument that allows him to combat the theory that all political power is derived from Adam, and that both fatherly and kingly rule are natural and God-given. Moreover, this particular effort to undermine patriarchalist political theory is found not only in *Leviathan*, but in the earlier *Elements of Law* and *De Cive*. In the end, Hobbes posits the *consensual* nature of familial *and* political relations, and in the process presents a provocative account of original political right.

Hobbes fights his battle with patriarchalism in his state of nature, and it is here that we see his intriguing statements about women. Hobbes's quarrel with political patriarchalism is not based on a rejection of the analogy between family and political rule. In fact, he agrees with patriarchalists that the family can be a useful model for understanding the origin of the state and its relations with its subjects. At points he appears to accept Filmer's equation of familial and political rule; for example, in the *Leviathan* he suggests that cities and kingdoms 'are but greater Families.'[35] Hobbes participates in this analogical thinking that so dominates seventeenth-century political theory, but he depicts the family very differently than his contemporaries. Filmer's desire to prove the origination of political power in Adam is intertwined with his need for a justification of natural fatherly and kingly rule in England. In Filmer's case, the origin narrative prescribes that desired political end wherein the King is understood as a father and the father a king. Insofar as Hobbes's desired end is to conclude that sovereign power is derived from consent, he develops a model of the family that will match and serve as an appropriate justification for that end.

What is Hobbes's analogy for the state? It is a consensually created family, one that looks much different from the companionate-patriarchal arrangement recommended by James, and different again from the paternal dominion advocated by Filmer. As if to set the stage for his case, Hobbes asserts that,

> whereas some have attributed the Dominion to the Man onely, as being of the more excellent Sex; they misreckon in it. For there is not alwayes that

difference of strength, or prudence between the man and woman, as that the right can be determined without War.[36]

Certainly, this is not an explicit statement of the equality of men and women, but it accomplishes two important things for Hobbes. First, it disrupts the conventional view that women are the lesser sex as dictated by nature. Second, it implies that the power relationship of dominance and submission between men and women is one that must be decided by battle, which again bears the marks of a convention rather than nature.

Building on this preliminary assertion of a rough equality of men and women, Hobbes claims that primary authority over children lies with the mother if she chooses it. Going against the prevalent belief that parental authority resides in the father or that it should be shared by both parents, Hobbes claims that '[i]f there be no Contract, the Dominion is in the Mother.'[37] The state of nature, as Hobbes envisions it, is a state without laws of matrimony; there exist only the law of nature and the 'naturall inclination of the Sexes one to another, and to their children.'[38] Significantly, without matrimonial laws, there can be no certain knowledge of paternity, 'unless it be declared by the Mother.' Therefore, it is most logical that the mother is the first to have the opportunity to 'rule' the child, that is, raise and have dominion over it. As Hobbes explains in *De Cive*, '[A]mong men no less than other creatures, the birth follows the belly.'[39] Since no person can obey two masters, and authority is indivisible, women could not choose to rule the family jointly with men.

Hobbes's clear statement of 'original maternal dominion' is significant for its recognition of the simple fact of biological maternity. When this is considered in the light of Filmer's patrogenic theory of patriarchal dominion, it is evident that Hobbes does not import patrogenic or biblical theories of the Fall of woman into his political origin story. Rather, he fully recognizes the limitations on paternal certainty, and this leads him to question automatic paternal dominion. When Hobbes does invoke Genesis, it is to assert that God created one man and one woman – a defence of heterosexual monogamy, not patrogenesis. Even the reference to woman as Adam's helpmeet in *Leviathan* does not preclude Hobbes's more radical statements on maternal dominion. As previously discussed, Hobbes reads the Fall of humanity in Genesis in a limited manner; he expressly leaves out of the story of the Fall Eve's punishment, her 'sin,' and her subordination to Adam. As a result, the state of nature does not bear the marks of a defeated woman. This is significant because it leaves the door open for Hobbes to make his case about equality and consent – using the examples of powerful women – without contradiction.

What is also interesting in the analogy is Hobbes's understanding of the nature of the parent–child relation. In order to undermine patriarchalism, Hobbes claims that parental authority arises from consent, not from nature. This enigmatic assertion does not necessarily counteract his first statement that 'birth follows the belly': the original right to claim parental authority lies with the mother because of her immediate physical relationship to the child, but the actual bond itself, if it is formed at all, is conventional. It is entirely possible that the mother may choose not to nourish it, but rather 'expose it' or 'adventure him to fortune.' In the event that the mother does expose the child, the dominion over it falls to whomever does care for it. In either case, whether the mother or the father nurtures the child, it owes its complete obedience, because its life, to that person.[40] As Hobbes writes, '[E]very man is supposed to promise obedience, to him, in whose power it is to save, or destroy him.'[41] This relationship of dominion and obedience remains, however, one of at least *tacit consent*, the implication being that Hobbes understands the difficulty in achieving consent from an infant. In positing the parent–child relationship as one of mutual consent, his purpose is to demonstrate that parental power, like political rule over a commonwealth, is conventional and not natural.

To shore up his case for conventionalism against patriarchalism, Hobbes reverts to using historical and mythological examples of women who possessed such power. Here again we see Hobbes's deliberate rhetorical strategy at work. He uses the provocative myth of the Amazons – the women who selectively decided if, and under what conditions, they would mother a child, and who took up arms to fight for their own political predominance over nations of men – to cast doubt on the natural rule of men over women and children. Custom, writes Hobbes in *De Cive*, does not dictate against such a war, 'for women, namely Amazons, have in former times waged war against their adversaries, and disposed of their children at their own wills.'[42]

Hobbes's discussion of the Amazons is found in the midst of his analysis of the types of dominion over a commonwealth. Having already elaborated on the nature of sovereignty by institution – that is, sovereignty established through an agreement of the people – he introduces the subject of sovereignty by acquisition, or by force. He explains that sovereignty is acquired in two possible ways, by generation and by conquest. But his two central points are (1), that no matter how sovereignty is achieved, the rights and consequences of sovereignty are identical; and (2), that all rule is derived from consent. This is an important point in understanding Hobbes's use of gender. For when Hobbes posits sovereignty by generation, he is explicitly not saying that the power a parent has over a child is natural, or a result of the parent begetting the child. Even parental power is consensual, as we have noted already.

The mythological example of the Amazons is meant to prove the point that women and men are on a roughly equal plane; they are equally likely to predominate in a battle against one another. The Amazons corroborate Hobbes's theory that women can, and in many places do, have sole authority over children. As he argues in *Leviathan*:

[T]he Amazons Contracted with the Men of the neighbouring Countries, to whom they had recourse for issue, that the issue Male should be sent back, but the Female remain with themselves: so that the dominion of the Females was in the Mother.[43]

Amazonian motherhood is understood here as a contractual (and thus social) relation. Hobbes may have had the Amazons in mind when he opened the possibility that women may choose not to nourish and mother their infants, as the mythical tribe was infamous for abandonment.

In his particular deployment of the Amazons, Hobbes once again goes against the grain of his English and European contemporaries. It is true that Amazon mythology enjoyed renewed popularity in literary and political discourse during the Elizabethan and Stuart eras;[44] therefore, we should not be surprised by Hobbes's reference to them. Political theorists and writers alike debated the truth and practicality of the idea of an all-female community. Amazonian characters also appeared in drama; admired for their beauty, they were thought to be the embodiment of valour. However, Hobbes's contemporaries did not find in the Amazons a positive example for female authority, as he did. In fact, Amazonian treatment of children, including their recourse to infanticide and the refusal to suckle male children, was held in particular contempt. Also regarded as unnatural was the idea that women would take up arms or rule politically.

For the most part, the myth of the Amazons did the same cultural and political work in early modern England as it did in ancient Greece: it demonstrated the superior quality of more natural kinds of rule, that is, patriarchy. As Kathryn Schwarz points out, 'The authority of the Amazon myth might lie less in its truth-value than in its status as a story with a moral.'[45] Some contemporary examples illustrate the point. To Francis Bacon, the Amazons are an example of the 'preposterous government' of women, a government that contravenes nature.[46] In a similar vein, *A Parliament of Ladies*, a satirical tract that appeared in 1647, illustrates the scorn reserved for women who attempt to overturn the natural gender order. Its author (thought to be Henry Neville) recounts the story of a group of women who, upon hearing that the Parliament has passed a law permitting each man to have two wives, organize their own Parliament in a parlour. As an incitement to action, one of the ladies queries: 'Where be those magnanimous and Masculine Spirited Matrons? those valiant Viragoes? those lusty Ladies: those daring *Amazonian* Damsels' who are reputed to have turned princes into puppets, philosophers into fools, and their husbands into 'henchmen.' The conclusion of the women's Parliament is that the law should be reversed, allowing them two or three husbands who, incidentally, they should be able to torment and vex at will.[47] *A Parliament of Ladies* appeared at a time in which women were petitioning Parliament and demanding a voice. The transgressions of the gender order are ridiculed as lust in disguise, and the women themselves are characterized as manly and Amazonian.

The similarly satirical and tremendously popular *Hic Mulier: Or, The Man-Woman* also makes an interesting study, both for its allusion to the masculine Amazons and for its treatment of gender inversions. This short pamphlet was published as a commentary on James's criticisms of those who were inverting gender code by cross-dressing. Masculine are those women who 'have cast off the ornaments of your sexes to put on the garments of Shame,' harlots who have 'buried silence to revive slander.'[48] Women who speak too much, or who (appear to) fail to abide by the society's sexual standards are admonished for creating a mockery of the gender order.[49] Such women are 'man in body by attire ... man in action by pursuing revenge, man in wearing weapons ... and, in brief, so much man in all things that they are neither men nor women, but just good for nothing.'[50] The Amazons *epitomize* the masculine woman, and they rule not by God's sanction, as in the case of Elizabeth, but tyrannically, against nature, and in pursuit of a 'licentious liberty.'[51]

In a subsequent pamphlet, *Haec Vir: Or The Womanish Man*, the manwoman, Hic Mulier, and the womanish-man, Haec Vir, engage in a mock dialogue about their 'hermaphroditic' identities. (Hermaphrodite was used regularly to refer to individuals who take on the behaviour or dress of the opposite sex.) Hic Mulier is made to defend her choice to dress and behave like a man. She does this by claiming that women only became manly in response to men who had begun to dress and behave in effeminate ways first, robbing women of their distinctiveness. According to the laws of nature, of nations, and of religions, Hic Mulier states, 'it is necessary that there be a distinct and special difference between Man and Woman, both in their habit and behaviors.' Affirming the tradition of oppositional gender roles – and yet in a strange way admitting to the artificiality of gender distinctions – the two characters agree to restore order and resume their natural gender roles and identities. 'Henceforth we will live nobly like ourselves,' they agree, 'ever sober, ever discreet, ever worthy: true men and true women.'[52]

In this tract, as in the others, Amazonian rule and mannish women represent the complete and unnatural inversion of the proper hierarchy between men and women.[53] As Sara Mendelson and Patricia Crawford observe, '[T]he possibility of androgyny destabilizes the early modern classificatory system upon which the gender order rested.'[54] Thus, the restoration of order in *Haec Vir* necessitates the return to Aristotelian and biblical understandings of distinct and opposing gender roles.

The very things that his predecessors and contemporaries found ridiculous, even monstrous, in the Amazons, Hobbes uses for the purposes of proving the logic of his argument.[55] This goes against what we might expect from Hobbes. He, more than most, is a writer concerned with the preservation of order at all costs. Indeed, through his political solution, he sacrifices all public debate and discussion; he sacrifices all populist implications of his consent theory and opts instead for absolutism; and finally he sacrifices politics itself to public order in the state. Given his evident preoccupation with maintaining order, Hobbes is a likely candidate for a kind of masculine anxiety regarding any confusion of gender roles. Instead, he participates in this confusion, *skilfully utilizing* rather than *mocking* the Amazons. In this sustained argument about the Amazons, Hobbes creates a space in his political theory for an alternative conception of women, thereby disrupting conventional views.

The other image of powerful women that Hobbes summons to consolidate his point about maternal dominion is the female monarch. It is logical that he would theorize about female monarchy given the recent rule of Queen Elizabeth, but again the image he presents is enigmatic. It is important to consider, before turning to Hobbes's comments, the widespread ambivalence about female rule – even that of the Virgin Queen.[56] A direct challenge to Elizabeth's rule came in the form of John Knox's *First Blast of the Trumpet Against the Monstrous Regiment of Women*, published in 1558. Although intended to berate the Catholic and female monarchy of Elizabeth's sister, Mary I of England, as well as that of Mary Queen of Scots and her mother Mary of Guise, its publication coincided with Elizabeth's ascension. Knox later found himself in the awkward position of having to justify Elizabeth's rule, in spite of his stated fear that the whole world had been transformed into Amazons; he did so by claiming that Elizabeth was an *exception* to the general impropriety of women's rule because she was ordained by God himself.[57]

Although the severity of Knox's argument against female rule is not widely representative, but rather constitutes an extreme, the path he takes to defend Elizabeth as an exceptional woman is exactly that taken by most of her defenders.[58] This is important, for Elizabeth is 'never a mere woman'[59] in public discourse, but is always understood to be above the mark of most women. The implication is that the excellence of her rule and authority did not disrupt the established practice of male primogeniture. In fact, female monarchy could be defended within that very practice as a reflection of God's will. A key problem – to which Hobbes formulates an unusual response – remained, and that was the proper hierarchy within the monarch's marriage. The woman qua monarch ruled over every man in the Commonwealth, but was she subject qua wife within her marriage? Elizabeth's supporters worried that any husband she took might usurp her authority precisely because of his conjugal authority over her. A common solution to this problem was to differentiate conjugal and regal-political power. This would mean that even if a queen ruled a state, and ostensibly every male within it, she was still subject to her husband in marriage.[60] In this way, neither the sovereignty of the monarch nor that of the husband in marriage was compromised.

While his contemporaries struggle to find a justification for the legitimacy of female rule in the rare *exception* in which there exists no male heir, and while they search for a means to keep patriarchal authority in marriage intact, Hobbes goes characteristically against the grain by *generalizing* the case of female rule to discuss parental authority.[61] If a queen marries one of her subjects, 'the Child is subject to the Mother; because the Father also is her subject.'[62] Hobbes's statement is a two-pronged attack on patriarchalism: not only does the husband lose his conjugal authority over the queen in this case, but the child that they conceive is in the queen's dominion, not his. The reverse applies, of course, if the father happens to be the monarch. For Hobbes, conjugal power and parental power are intricately related: if one partner in the union is subject to the other, then their issue is also subject to the higher power. To give the monarch power over the commonwealth, but her husband power over her, would be to divide authority, thereby destabilizing the regime. Hobbes's maxims in this and all cases are, *power cannot be shared* and *right is determined by contract*. In political right as in conjugal right, parties must follow the dictates of the contracts made.

There are two essential and interrelated components to Hobbes's familial argument as I have presented it. The first is the theory of *original maternal dominion*, in which mothers are proposed to have the first opportunity for political right over the child. This political right is not automatic, as a woman may choose not to protect and parent the child. Motherhood is based on consent, and this forms the second component of the argument. *Consent* is, in point of fact, the basis for *all parental authority* over children. The question to be considered is why Hobbes would use both of the components of this argument. Is the suggestion that parental dominion is consensual not sufficient to undermine patriarchalism's belief in the God-given grant of political power to kings and fathers? Why does Hobbes posit original maternal dominion as well?

It is possible that once Hobbes transformed what others had thought were naturally mandated hierarchical familial relations into consenting ones, he recognized that it would make no logical sense for children always to consent to *paternal* rule and never to maternal rule. Arbitrary paternal rule would be especially unlikely when, as Hobbes puts it, 'birth follows the belly.' If the mother is the first adult with whom the child has an immediate physical relationship, then the mother–child relation should be understood as the first political right. Hobbes's suggestion to this effect has the increased likelihood of disarming his opponents who could not conceive of anything but patriarchal authority in the family. This is surely the point: to disrupt patriarchal authority in the family and hence in the political realm as well. Positing maternal dominion is the final step to *rationalizing every human relationship*, making every relationship the product of artifice not nature. By Hobbes's logic, if even the most 'natural' relation between mother and child is now understood as conventional, then surely it is evident that, by extension, the relationship between subjects and their sovereign is conventional.

If Hobbes had carried forth his suggestive images of Amazons, queens, and independent women from the state of nature into his social contract, his script of citizenship would read very differently. As it stands, women all but disappear from his story once the social contract is instituted, and thus his script for gender relations does not look all that different from the one that Plato offered. If, however, we were to extract Hobbes's insights on the conventional origins of gender hierarchies and the rough physical and political equality of men and women in the state of nature from the remainder of the text, we could fashion the beginnings of an egalitarian, feminist script.

## 3. Hobbes and Gender Confusion

Up to this point, this chapter has contrasted Hobbes's presentation of the family with that presented by his contemporaries. My argument has been that Hobbes consistently fails to conform to the dominant rhetoric about gender inversion, Amazons, masculine women, and witches. Rather than exhibiting signs of defensive and anxious masculinity, he creates spaces in his political theory that reflect the prevailing gender confusion. As we have seen, Hobbes opportunistically uses ideas about gender confusion and women's contractual abilities to make a more thoroughgoing and devastating argument against patriarchalism. In this final section, I consider Hobbes's attack on patriarchalism in relation to the women activists of the Civil War and Interregnum. Once equipped with a better understanding of the protests of the women activists, we will be able to assess the significance of Hobbes's argument against patriarchalism. An overview of the arguments put forth by the women activists reveals how Hobbes appears at times to play into, and at others times to surpass, their claims. Although women's public activism certainly increased during the Civil War and Interregnum, and although this activism stimulated concern over the preservation of the gender order, its ultimate effect was not devastating to the status quo. Indeed, the comparison of

Hobbes to the women activists yields a surprising result: his argument, although driven by opportunism, constitutes a more directly *political* critique of the political theory of patriarchalism than women themselves were formulating.

To say that Hobbes's epoch is one of contest and confusion over gender is to say that, despite the existence of a prevalent ideology dictating a hierarchical and oppositional gender code, the actual activities of people do not conform perfectly to this ideology. Certainly in all historical periods it remains important to distinguish between thought and practice as such, lest the ideology *about* women convince us – in the absence of evidence – that women abided by these strictures. In fact, as Laura Gowing observes, 'gender is always in contest.'[63] Yet in this particular historical period, the distinction between ideology and reality takes on additional importance, as there is an increasing gap between what is thought about women and what women themselves are actually doing.[64] This is not to imply, however, that gender relations were in 'crisis,' for, as Mendelson and Crawford, among others, conclude, there is a 'remarkable degree of stability' in the early modern gender order.[65] Still, 'stability here does not denote stasis,'[66] and particularly during the Civil War and Interregnum women engaged in religious debates, preaching, prophesying, speaking, and writing according to their consciences. Such acts were deliberately public, although they were not all directed toward the same goal. Not all religious women acted to free women from the constraints of subordination, and very few engaged in what would be defined as overtly political activity. Nevertheless, their activity disrupted the code of customary behaviour expected of women in a historical period still devoted to Aristotelian and biblical notions of male-female hierarchy.

Women's activism during the Civil War and Interregnum took various forms and defies simple categorization. Women's writing on all subjects rose markedly during this period, beginning in the 1640s, largely because of the breakdown in censorship. During the 1640s and 1650s women's publications constitute 1.2 per cent of all publications – still a small percentage – but this marks a substantial increase over the pre-war percentage of 0.5.[67] By far the bulk of their activity, however, is focused on religious issues as opposed to questions of politics or women's subordination in general. This is not to deny that the issues are, in practice, conflated whenever women enter the public, spiritual realm to speak. In an important sense, the very acts of preaching, prophesying, and publicly interpreting scripture allow women 'the only taste of public authority they would ever know,'[68] and constitute a challenge to the patriarchal order. This question of the political significance of women's activity is one to which we will return later.

Religious women, or at least those women who chose to speak publicly rather than continue their private religious practices, exploited an opening within the Christian concept of conscience to advance their public cause. Conscience, insofar as it was thought to be a human being's inner moral guide to, and judge of, outward behaviour, was universal and therefore ungendered.[69] Whatever their perceived deficiencies in other areas, women were expected to follow their consciences and choose their behaviour accordingly. Precisely because individual conscience was understood as the key to personal salvation, almost any act could be justified on the basis that conscience prescribed it. Acts of conscience by women took many different forms, ranging from the writing of religious tracts to fasting, to the dramatic demonstration by Lady Eleanor Davies in which she poured hot tar and wheat paste on the hangings of a church altar.[70] When we combine the universality of the concept of conscience with the fact that many women studied the Bible and held strong moral convictions about the practice of religious faith,[71] the potential for women's public religious activism is born.

Many of the women who challenged the patriarchal religious order were members of the newly emerging but as yet unconsolidated Protestant sects. They were, among other things, Quakers, Baptists, Independents, and Fifth Monarchist millenarians. Indeed, women predominated in the voluntary congregations of the sects, which they joined by their own free consent – sometimes against the will of their husbands – and in which they enjoyed voting privileges.[72] Those who preached had audiences of men and women alike, and some saw themselves as ministers rather than mere prophets.[73] Other women claimed to have been visited by God, or to have had prophetic visions, visions that left them no choice but to communicate to others their godly message. Mary Cary, a Fifth Monarchist millenarian, defends the act of female prophesy on the basis that she has not chosen, but is compelled by God, to speak. She has no more control over her behaviour, she writes, than a pencil 'when no hand guides it'; God alone is responsible, 'for I am a very weak, and unworthy instrument, and have not done this work by any strength of my own.'[74]

In a similar vein, Elizabeth Poole presented herself to the Army council as a conduit of God's word and 'Thy fellow sufferer in the Kingdome of the patience of Christ.'[75] She warned the Army of the treachery that would follow should they commit regicide and implored the members not to betray their trust by giving power over to the people. 'You justly blame the King for betraying his trust, and the Parliament for betraying theirs,' she writes. 'This is the great thing I have to say to you, Betray not you your trust.'[76] In the end, her moderate political message did not receive much support within the Army, but there is no question that she was perceived as a legitimate 'prophetess' whose message was taken seriously.[77] Indeed, in order to appear before the Army to express her religious vision, she would have to have received the support of Oliver Cromwell and Henry Ireton.[78] Poole is an example of a religious visionary who was able to use her religiosity to catapult herself into the political sphere.

It was not unusual for English women to have political causes alongside their religious ones. Leveller women remain the most prominent political women of the Civil War and Interregnum period; Elizabeth Lilburne, Katherine Chidley, and Mary Overton, and others, shared with the Leveller movement political beliefs that fell to the political left of many of their contemporaries. Because the Levellers accepted the spiritual equality of women and men, they showed a higher tolerance for women's participation in political activity than might have normally been accepted. Leveller women drew up and presented a number of petitions to Parliament, in which they presented themselves as 'honest' women who had no choice but to break convention and speak publicly to support their husbands and families.[79] Prior to 1649, these petitions had been accepted, as their tenor reflected the political sentiments of the majority of Parliament. However, in 1649 the women petitioned Parliament only to be rejected and told to return to their household duties.[80] The petition's authors claimed to be 'so overwhelmed in affliction' that they could not remain faithful to 'the custom of our Sex,' which was to keep silent on public matters.[81] Their petition was rejected – despite its submissive tone – because it argued for the release of Leveller men John Lilburne, William Walwyn, Richard Overton, and others, all of whom had been imprisoned. After being sent away from Parliament, the women returned not a month later to present a second petition; they demanded that the first be addressed properly and declared that they would not be satisfied 'except you free [the prisoners] from under their present extrajudicial imprisonment and...give them full Reparations for their forceable Attachment.'[82]

When the situation demanded it, Leveller women could employ strong language, that of rights and liberties, to defend their cause. In their follow-up petition of 1649, for instance, they ask:

## Gender in Hobbes's Origin Story 99

> Have we not an equal interest with the men of this Nation, in those liberties and securities, contained in the Petition of Right, and other the good Laws of the Land? are any of our lives, limbs, liberties or goods to be taken from us more than from Men, but by due processe of Law and conviction of twelve sworn men of the Neighbourhood?[83]

And further:

> Can you imagine us to be so sottish or stupid, as to not perceive, or not to be sensible when dayly those strong defences of our Peace and wellfare are broken down, and trod under-foot by force and arbitrary power.[84]

Consistently, the petitions based women's right to petition and be heard on the presumed spiritual equality of women. The outspoken Leveller Katherine Chidley, who was the likely author of a 1653 petition, derived women's 'undoubted right of petitioning' directly from God, who 'is ever willing and ready to receive the Petitions of all, making no difference of persons.'[85] Chidley had already registered her religious dissent from the Church of England when she refused to be churched and when she wrote a pamphlet justifying the Independents' separation from the national church.[86] She argued openly against clergy and male church members in a way that was considered beyond the pale for a woman.[87]

On the one hand, women's protests and petitions, like their public demonstrations of religious visions, created a powerful effect in public discourse. It was precisely these kinds of public acts, these attempts to voice their concerns, that stimulated masculine anxiety. As women transgressed the cultural and ideological boundaries that encouraged their silence, men's worst fears about women and the upset of the gender order were brought to the fore. Every time women speak publicly, 'every incident of verbal assertiveness,' represents the very real threat of 'the dissolution of the patriarchal order.'[88] Given early modern England's views on the sanctity of the patriarchal family, and given that the family is the symbol of order and stability, it is no wonder that women's attempts to speak outside the constraints of the patriarchal family represented the potential for social upheaval and collapse.

On the other hand, perception is not reality. Those who feared social collapse need not have. While there was a degree of gender contest and confusion, its magnitude was not nearly so great as the defenders of order imagined.[89] When women did enter the public sphere, whether it was to convey a godly message or to petition Parliament, their purpose was never to demand radical, sweeping change. Their very presence in the public debate signalled upheaval to many, but women's demands themselves were moderate. Their petitions and pamphlets tended to temper the radicalism of their demands with deference and humility. *A True Copie of the Petition of the Gentlewomen, and the Tradesmens-wives* illustrates the point well. 'We are imboldned to present our humble Petition,' the authors declare, 'not out of any felte conceit, or pride of heart, *as seeking to equal ourselves with Men, either in Authority or wisdome*: But according to our places to discharge that duty we owe to God, and the cause of the Church.'[90] True, women claimed to be 'sharers in the common Calamities that accompany both Church and Common-wealth,' but at the same time they placate their audience and reaffirm their inferior position.[91]

In short, the driving force behind women's increased public activism in the 1640s and 1650s is rarely politics per se, nor is it the desire to emancipate their sex. It is, of course, important to remember that there was no clear separation between religion and politics in seventeenth-century England, so to some extent women's religious concerns had obvious political implications. However, the driving force for women's activism was religion, or in some cases economic privation, rather than strict affairs of state. Certainly, women were led by their consciences to defy authority if it was necessary, and to this extent they challenged patriarchy. Yet as Patricia Crawford has written, 'women did not set out to defy fathers, husbands or ministers'; rather they were driven by the 'the intensity of their search for individual salvation, and their strong assurance of the authenticity of their own experiences.'[92] They sought salvation not emancipation. The submissive stance taken by the women who present themselves as mere vessels for God's word,[93] or of the women who admit to the impropriety of their petitioning Parliament, illustrates the dichotomous nature of female religious and political activity during this period. Although the acts themselves mount a challenge to the gender order, the content of the arguments they present is often ambiguous and occasionally even disempowering. Moreover, the radicalism of women like Chidley was never matched by the Leveller movement itself; nor did her radicalism lead her, or other Leveller women, to demand the extension of the franchise to women. More often than not, Leveller women were led to petition Parliament to proclaim the injustice against, and demand the release of, the imprisoned male leadership. In all of their acts these women did not challenge the very root of gendered power, the overarching political theory that regimented their silence and passivity: patriarchalism. In reality, then, the gender order continued to rest on firm foundations, despite the appearance and perception of an upheaval in gender relations.

Hobbes, being attuned to the many threats to order in the commonwealth, was undoubtedly aware of these religious and political activists, though he does not directly respond to their many pamphlets and public displays. In an unusual way, however, Hobbes invites and contributes to, rather than works against, this phenomenon of gender confusion and contest. In effect, Hobbes's origin story crystallizes the contest over gender relations. His political theory generates spaces for a different conceptualization of women than currently existed. To be sure, Hobbes seals over these spaces once the social contract is implemented, but his creation of these spaces remains nonetheless politically significant. Indeed, these fissures in Hobbes's political theory permit the reconfiguration of gender – from patriarchalism to a rough egalitarianism – in a way that the activity and discourse of women during this period does not.

In light of the scorn Hobbes reserves for those who advocate a freedom of conscience, especially Levellers and other Protestant sect members, it is that much more significant that he does not admonish women preachers, prophesiers, and pamphleteers specifically. There is no doubt that Hobbes would have held these women in low esteem, if for no other reason than he had a general low regard for all public biblical interpretation (with the convenient exclusion of his own) that was not pronounced by the sovereign. Being entirely displeased with both the religious enthusiasm of the Civil War period and the seditious potential of those claiming rights against reigning authority, he would not have been a supporter of female activists. Nevertheless, it is interesting to consider to what extent Hobbes absorbed, appropriated, and refashioned female enthusiasm for his own purposes. What enabled him, in the face of the disruptions to the gender order, to take women's arguments about consent one step further to undermine the political theory of patriarchalism?

The fact that Hobbes chose not to respond directly to the women activists limits our ability to arrive at any final conclusions regarding the above questions. Hobbes was in correspondence with very few women and none of them were of the levelling type. It would appear that the only woman with whom he had an intellectual exchange was Margaret Cavendish, Duchess of Newcastle, a conservative writer in her own right and the wife of Hobbes's friend, the Duke of Newcastle. From Hobbes's 1653 letter to her, we can gather that she had sent him a copy of her most recent publication; the most he expresses by way of response is gratitude.[94] Although Hobbes's influence on her writing is evident, as she too is motivated by his concern to create order in the commonwealth, Hobbes does not engage with her on the subject of her treatise, nor does he ever respond to the criticisms of his work that she makes in her *Philosophical Letters*. What is interesting about Margaret Cavendish is that she does engage Hobbes on the subject of his natural philosophy; and she asserts in the preface her profound love of reason and desire to be read, and if necessary criticized, seriously. However, she stops short of addressing Hobbes's political theory explicitly. In fact, she admits to not having *read* past part I of *Leviathan*; having given her opinion on the first part, she writes:

> I would go on; but seeing he treats in his following Parts of the Politicks, I was forced to stay my Pen, because of the following Reasons. First, That a Woman is not imployed in State Affairs, unles an absolute Queen. Next, That to study the Politicks, is but loss of Time...Thirdly, That it is but a deceiving profession, and requires more Craft than Wisdom.[95]

While the Marchioness did proceed in this text and elsewhere to voice her opinion on the politics of the day, her comments in the *Letters* confirm that the relationship of women to politics in the seventeenth century is a difficult and often remote one, such that she perceives her *philosophical* critique of Hobbes to be warranted and legitimate but the realm of politics to be off limits to (and perhaps even beneath) her because of her gender.

Had Margaret Cavendish considered it appropriate to both read and react to Hobbes's views of the family, the two might have had an interesting exchange. She too used gender relations as a similitude for political rule, and she depicted the Amazons positively in a drama about the recreation of order in a kingdom divided by faction.[96] Although an unreconstructed royalist (her husband was in the service of Charles I), and in likely disagreement with Hobbes about the Engagement controversy, she held views about the family, marriage, and motherhood that are as unsentimental as those held by Hobbes.[97] In her funeral oration for a newly married woman, she described marriage rather starkly: '[D]eath is by far the happier condition than marriage; and although marriage at first is pleasing, yet after a time it is displeasing, like meat which is sweet in the mouth, but proves bitter in the stomach.' Elsewhere she lamented the pain of woman in childbirth, and questioned how it was that women risked their lives giving birth only to have the children become the possessions of men. She concludes:

> I know of no good reason why she should be troubled for having no children, for though it be the part of every good wife to desire children to keep alive the memory of her husband's name and family by posterity, yet a woman has no such reason to desire children for her own sake.[98]

It seems that Cavendish's political conservatism did not prevent her from questioning deeply held beliefs on patriarchal marriage and father-right. On a purely rhetorical level, she presents the kernels of what would now be called a radical feminist critique of the family. Although devoted to her husband, Cavendish captures in her writing a desentimentalized view of the family. And it is this unsentimental view that she and Hobbes share, but probably did not discuss.[99]

Cavendish never articulated a coherent platform for change in the structure of gender relations, a failure that Anna Battigelli attributes to Cavendish's fear that her public words might spark political controversy and faction.[100] Still, this fear did not prevent her from publishing her dramatic and political works. Nor did the fear of sparking controversy deter Hobbes from publishing his controversial views on gender relations, views that were considered beyond the pale to his contemporaries and may indeed have increased his disfavour among them. As for the source of Hobbes's familial views, there is too little information on which to base any conclusion. As a tentative hypothesis, we can at least suggest that the Civil War climate of gender confusion along with the language of the prevailing system of gendered power – with its analogies and similitudes – created the conditions under which almost any argument could be made. It is perhaps this flurry of activity surrounding gender that enabled Hobbes to formulate his innovative theory. With this said, the exact cause for the disruptive substance of Hobbes's remarks, the cause of his divergence from his political contemporaries on the questions of gender and the family, must, in the absence of additional historical information, remain a mystery.

The point of this interpretive exercise has been to raise a different set of questions about the nature of Hobbes's gender arguments, in effect to cast his political theory in a different light by situating his thought in its intellectual context and by comparing and contrasting his ideas with those of his male and female contemporaries. My conclusion is that Hobbes's origin story had the potential, but not the intention, to unravel the core of patriarchalist political theory and, by extension, patriarchal social relations between men and women. Especially when viewed against the backdrop of other political thinkers of his period, even female religious activists, but also when compared to Plato, Hobbes emerges as an enigmatic but nevertheless important figure in the history of gender relations. My intention is not to convey the message that Hobbes is a proto-feminist, or that he qualifies as more of a proto-feminist than the women activists of the Civil War. Surely even the broadest definition of feminism would disqualify Hobbes, for he lacks the all-important intention to create progressive social change in the relationships between men and women. Like Cavendish, he does not make the leap from his provocative arguments in the state of nature to a coherent analysis of women's place in civil society. For Hobbes, gender is purely instrumental – and indeed, this fact may partially account for the boldness of his thinking.

What is most important, for our purposes, is to understand that as an origins theorist, Hobbes is not preoccupied with ensuring the correct, hierarchical ordering of gender relations in his origin story. In this sense, he differs from Plato. In the end, however, the implications for women in Hobbes's theory can only be bleak since, by the time the social contract is instituted, women are absent from the discussions of civil society and from descriptions of the family,[101] and Hobbes falls back on customary arguments about men being 'naturally fitter than women for actions of labour and danger.'[102] The rest of the argument about civil society proceeds as though Hobbes had never made his enigmatic assertions. As a script of citizenship, then, the Hobbesian social contract not only spells subordination for the subjects to their sovereign, but it also implicitly endorses the subjection of women to men. We might legitimately query why Hobbes falls back on such arguments about women when he has told us that they are no less capable of ruling than men. But it is essential to acknowledge, as Pateman does not, that for Hobbes, there would be no obvious inconsistency here, because he uses gender only as a means to another end. That he used gender instrumentally in his origin story, however, does not alter the fact that his ideas on women, consent, and the family were then, and remain now, provocative and unsettling.

Having deliberately set aside Pateman's interpretation of Hobbes up to this point, I turn now to focus attention on her elaborate origin story of the sexual contract.

*Chapter Five*

# Pateman's Sexual Contract: An Origin Story of Her Own

The most extensive and influential treatment of the consequences of Hobbes's origin story for women is Carole Pateman's *The Sexual Contract*. Pateman, whose work in contemporary democratic political theory is widely recognized in Europe, North America, and Australia, argues that Hobbes is ultimately a patriarchal thinker because he excludes women from participation in the social contract. Indeed, while Pateman's early work focused primarily on the tensions between obligation and consent in liberal democratic theory, her subsequent work extends her analysis to address the patriarchal subtext of both liberal democratic and radical political theory. Underlying the social contract, according to Pateman, is a sexual contract that ensures women's subordination at the inception of civil society. Moreover, social contract theory, in Pateman's assessment, is a story of masculine birth in which men 'generate political life' and women are rendered 'procreatively and politically irrelevant.'[1] Men consent to create civil society, giving birth to the public sphere of politics in which only they participate, and disregarding almost entirely the birth of the private sphere.

While *The Sexual Contract* offers a provocative reading of Hobbes, it is not without its problems. Some feminists, for example Nancy Fraser and Shannon Bell, have questioned the applicability of the sexual contract to gender relations within contemporary liberal societies.[2] Rather than entering into these debates here, I examine Pateman's theoretical formulation of the sexual contract from social contract theory. Revisiting Pateman's textual and historical interpretation of the social contract brings to light some difficulties embedded in the concept of the sexual contract itself. Moreover, Pateman supplements Hobbes's textual silences with conjecture, and in so doing develops her own origin story of the sexual contract. Thus, as much as Pateman criticizes the origins discourse, she also participates in it.

The purpose of this chapter, then, is twofold: to discuss the consequences of Hobbes's theory for women and to situate *The Sexual Contract* itself in the tradition of origins theorizing. In viewing the text as an origins narrative, it is important to consider the radical feminist politics informing Pateman's project, and to raise questions about the value of supplementing the hypothetical story of the social contract with further conjecture.

## 1. The Dichotomy of Public and Private

*The Sexual Contract* takes as its starting point the idea that male sex right, embodied in the sexual contract, undergirds the social contract. In Pateman's view, male sex right, or male sexual access to the female body, is the first political right, but its existence as a political right is suppressed by the contract that brings civil society into existence. The social contract is a 'sexual-social pact' about which we know only half the story; while political theorists devote ample attention to the social aspect, the sexual aspect of the pact is ignored. Yet it is that missing half that 'tells how a specifically modern form of patriarchy is established.'[3] Pateman's is an analytic – rather than a historical – exercise to expose the latent patriarchal assumptions of social contract theory, and to reveal the private sphere as the shadowy twin in the birth of civil society. That she uses an analytic approach is not in itself a problem – the problem stems, rather, from her use of history and historical political thought. In this introductory section it will be useful to examine Pateman's understanding of the public/private dichotomy, as it points to some persistent problems in her text.

The division between public and private is, to Pateman, fundamentally a division between what is thought to be natural and what civil. Women, while excluded from the social contract itself, 'are not left behind in the state of nature,' but are 'incorporated into a sphere that both is and is not in civil society.'[4] Here Pateman is correcting the oversights of political theorists who tend to dismiss the private realm as something altogether separate from the public sphere. The private is overlooked, in Pateman's view, because it is womanly and natural and thus remote from the masculine and civil sphere. 'The private, womanly sphere (natural) and the public, masculine sphere (civil) are opposed but gain their meaning from each other.'[5] She rightly suggests that the two must be understood to be in a dynamic and interdependent relationship, that to speak of the public without understanding the private is, once again, to miss half the story. The real meaning of 'civil freedom of public life is thrown into relief,' argues Pateman, 'when counterposed to the natural subjection that characterizes the private realm.'[6] The social contract reveals the story of how the civil realm came into being, but the origin of the private realm remains mysterious. This narrative of the sexual contract, then, reveals the private realm's previously hidden origins.

Pateman's analysis of the public/private division is designed to capture the theoretical and ideological essence of, rather than to describe, modern liberal society. In other words, Pateman knows that women are not, and never were, entirely segregated in the private realm. That is not her point. The benefit of her analysis of this crucial division stems from its incisive critique of the *ideology* that permeates liberal society, an ideology that perpetuates the symbolic association of women with the private realm even as they enter the public.[7] Aside from its practical application, of course, her general analysis is meant to capture the meaning of public and private *within* social contract theory. My purpose here is to determine how effectively this analysis describes Hobbes.

Hobbes devotes considerable attention to the division between public and private in his social contract theory, although as Pateman herself notes this division does not permeate his state of nature. Hobbes's state of nature, as we have seen, has no marital laws and no natural family, features that distinguish Hobbes from his successors. While Pateman is careful at points to show how Hobbes differs from the other classic contractarians, at other points, and especially in this analysis, she glosses over their differences in the interest of developing an all-encompassing theory of the sexual contract. The division between public and private for Hobbes is not premised on the fundamental split between the natural and civil in the way that it is for Locke and Rousseau. In Hobbes's analysis, no sphere in society is 'natural'; this is precisely the point of his argument about the family in the state of nature. All human associations are conventional.

In general, when Hobbes takes up the terms public and private it is to enter the religious and political fray surrounding the issue of private conscience. Hobbes was writing in a period during which the exact meanings of public and private were being hotly contested; this debate centred on the limits and liberties of private conscience. While Puritans upheld their right to judge the King according to their private consciences, James VI and I and others encouraged the view that public conscience obliged subjects to obey their monarch. Competing with the authority of individual conscience, then, was the idea that the Commonwealth shared a common conscience and formed a unified whole. As Kevin Sharpe points out, however, the notion of a common conscience was 'fraught with difficulties' precisely because God was believed to have put the 'light of conscience in all men' (*sic*).[8] How, then, could the autonomy of people's consciences be denied? Hobbes's answer to this question involved making a distinction between things indifferent and things necessary to salvation. His intent was to delineate the appropriate activities for subjects and sovereign once civil society had been created. To what extent could individuals follow the dictates of their consciences? Could they resist the King's orders? Could they rebel against the religious practices that they found inconsistent with their own beliefs? Hobbes answers a categorical no to the latter two questions and thereby severely limits the freedom of individuals to act in accordance with their consciences, for it is his contention that there is no greater threat to the order of the commonwealth than the belief that individual conscience should be the determinant of people's actions.[9] Among the diseases of the commonwealth, Hobbes counts the poison of seditious doctrines, including the idea that 'whatsoever a man does against his Conscience, is Sinne.' In a commonwealth, as opposed to the state of nature, 'the Law is the publique Conscience, by which he [the subject] hath already undertaken to be guided.'[10]

Yet in circumscribing people's actions, in denying subjects the ability to act autonomously, Hobbes does not, in his theory, dismiss the importance of salvation. Because the issues over which the sovereign has power to legislate are insignificant with respect to salvation – in other words, they do not aid or hinder salvation – subjects should not experience an inner struggle of the Puritan kind. The only things necessary to salvation, in Hobbes's estimation, were faith in God and obedience to the earthly sovereign. All other matters, from praying positions to choice of prayer book, were indifferent to salvation, and thus did not warrant disobedience or resistance. In assessing Hobbes's use of the terms public and private, it is important to understand the intellectual framework in which he was operating, and also to recognize that for him, just as the private is not natural, the civil is not free.

Unlike liberal thinkers, Hobbes assigns to his sovereign absolute power to govern subjects' actions.

All of this is not to deny that Hobbes's understanding of the public and private dichotomy in civil society is gendered. It is reasonable to assume that women do not take part in the social contract, and that they are embedded in the family and thus the private realm. However, Pateman's general statement that this private sphere is womanly is again inapplicable to Hobbes; his private sphere is no more womanly than it is natural. If anything, woman disappears altogether from Hobbes's theory – even from his discussion of the family and the private sphere – once the social covenant is formed, an issue that Pateman explores. How can the sphere be both womanly and appear on the surface not to have a woman inhabiting it?

For Hobbes, as for his contemporaries, there is no idealized, womanly private sphere in which women are described as performing their complementary functions to the male role of citizenship. The public/private dichotomy that Hobbes abandons in the state of nature and inserts in civil society is not the fully modernized, sentimental one that is manifest in the theory of Rousseau or Hegel. Mary Beth Norton points out that in early seventeenth-century English thought, no exclusive equation was made between the terms private and female, nor between private and family.[11] Indeed, Hobbes distinguishes between what he considers public and what private, and the family is used as one example of a private association; but nowhere does he draw a connection between the female and the private.[12] Even in Locke's theory, where the separation between public and private corresponds to a division between civil and natural, the private sphere is not womanly.

Among the classic contractarians whom Pateman analyses, Rousseau is the only one who depicts the private sphere as the womanly domain, controlled by her and shaped by her influences. In the thought of both Hobbes and Locke, the husband/father is the person who shapes the private as well as the formal, public realm; both realms are thoroughly masculine. Hobbes's family is ruled in the same way as the commonwealth: the ruled are embodied in every action that is taken by the ruler because they have authorized all of his actions through their (hypothetical or actual) consent.

Pateman's general theory of the public/private dichotomy has merit when applied to contemporary liberal society, but it is less useful when applied to Hobbes specifically. In Pateman's defence, it should be noted that her stated interest in *The Sexual Contract* is more contemporary than historical. She is more interested in criticizing modern liberal society than she is in clarifying the ideas of specific contract thinkers. Pateman expresses her purpose as follows: 'I am resurrecting the story in order to throw light onto the present-day structure of major social institutions in Britain, Australia and the United States – societies which, we are told, can properly be seen as if they had originated in a social contract.'[13] Her contemporary focus is evidenced by her lengthy discussion in the text of such practical, contemporary issues as prostitution, surrogate motherhood, and the marriage contract. Nevertheless, in the process of conceptualizing the workings of liberalism and the dynamics of the marriage contract, Pateman does engage in the interpretation of historical texts, interpretation that is crucial to the development of her theory of the sexual contract itself, as we will see. In short, she formulates the sexual contract in response to the idea of the social contract, and therefore the quality of her analysis of historical texts is an important criterion in determining the value of the sexual contract as a conceptual device.

While my reading of Hobbes takes much from Pateman, and is in an important sense made possible by her innovative work, it is my view that Pateman's treatment of public and private in Hobbes is indicative of a general lack of historical and textual specificity in her theory. Pateman effectively treats the three primary social contract theorists, Hobbes, Locke, and Rousseau, as if they are writing in the same period of history, and as if gender relations within their periods are roughly similar.[14] Her generalizations often obscure more than they reveal. The point here is not to critique Pateman for the book she did not write, nor is it to claim that the only approach to political theory is a historical one. But if her intent is to trace the outline of the historical development of modern patriarchy, it is essential that she differentiate, to take one example, between the early modern, Aristotelian-influenced familial structure and the sentimental family. There are traces of sentimental familial relations in the early modern period in England, but the notion that women contribute their unique feminine traits to the private realm while men contribute to the public sphere is not yet present. More important, Hobbes's theory of the family as he describes it in the state of nature represents a rare break in the transition from earlier hierarchical familial forms and the sentimental family, a point Pateman overlooks in her efforts to cast Hobbes as a patriarchal thinker.

## 2. The Conjectural History of Woman's Defeat

Women's position in the family, and their real or presumed consent to their subordinate position, leads to the overarching issue of the sexual contract itself. In Pateman's interpretation, women in Hobbes's civil society must enter into the marriage contract; there is no possibility for them to be independent contractors with men. To understand how this arrangement came to be she shifts the focus from civil society to the state of nature using the logic that women's exclusion from the social contract presupposes their prior subordination. 'There is only one way,' Pateman writes, 'in which women, who have the same status as free and equal individuals in the state of nature as men can be excluded from participation in the social contract.'[15] Women must have been conquered by men and submitted to the sexual contract in the state of nature. This is a crucial point in Pateman's hypothesis: if men alone make the civil contract we must assume that 'all the women in the natural condition have been conquered by men and are now their subjects (servants).'[16] Pateman confirms women's status as servants in civil society using Hobbes's description of the family, which 'consists of a man and his children; or of a man and his servants; or of a man, and his children, and his servants together.'[17]

Recognizing the inconsistencies between equality and subjection in Hobbes's theory, Pateman attempts to correct them in order to complete the story of woman's defeat in the state of nature. She presumes that, through her efforts of textual reconstruction and by reading between the lines, she can render Hobbes consistent on the question of gender relations; he can be made to tell the whole story of woman's subordination. The extent of what Hobbes tells us is that 'for the most part Common-wealths have been erected by the Fathers, not by the Mothers of families,'[18] a descriptive rather than an explanatory statement. From what little Hobbes does say, Pateman formulates the hypothesis that the family has its origins in conquest.[19] We need to be clear at the outset that Hobbes makes no such assertion, and that the story that follows is Pateman's alone.

Pateman's conjectural history proceeds in the following manner. Despite their original equality with men, and their mother-right, women's consent to raise their children puts them at a 'slight disadvantage against men' because they have not only themselves but their children to defend. Thus, one man is able to defeat one woman-child dyad, and to form a protective confederacy or family.[20] Mother-right is only a fleeting condition; 'for a woman to become a mother and a lord is her downfall,' because it gives her male enemy an opening 'to outwit and vanquish her in the ceaseless natural conflict.'[21] The new patriarchal protective confederacy, presented as an intermediate social formation between atomized individuals and the social contract, would not arise from consent but from conquest, because no woman would voluntarily place herself in submission. Indeed, Pateman makes much of Hobbes's fine distinction between conquest and consent[22] as she attempts to show how sexual coercion lies beneath the surface of the supposedly consensual social compact.

Her narrative continues: once one woman is conquered, so too are the others. It may be that eventually all the unconquered women, that is, women without children, die and leave behind only women who are tied to a patriarchal unit. However, Pateman concludes that it is more likely that women 'must all be conquered in the first generation.'[23] At least this is the way the story has to proceed, as she knows Hobbes's conclusions. The male heads of these households make the social covenant and presumably institute the marriage contract to ensure women's continued subservience. Women are legally 'included' in their husbands and have no independent will or political right of their own. Thus, the one-sided story of the social contract is broadened to include the origins of women's subordination in civil society.

The argument that Pateman puts forth is not a straightforward one, nor is it rooted firmly in Hobbes's texts. To understand how she formulates her story of the sexual contract, we need to focus attention on its two central elements: the protective confederacy, which Pateman views as akin to a patriarchal family; and conjugal right as the first political right. Certainly, Pateman acknowledges some problems with her conjectural history; for example, she queries why any person in Hobbes's state of nature would contract to parent a child given the risks that she assumes are involved. Furthermore, she asks, how could all men defeat all women in the state-of-nature when Hobbes tells us that there is no substantial difference in size and strength to determine rule automatically? Strong women could form protective confederacies as well.[24] Pateman is right; by Hobbes's logic, all of the strong men and women would more likely band together to defeat the weaker state-of-nature inhabitants.

Yet there are further, unacknowledged discrepancies between her story and that of Hobbes; the issue of the patriarchal protective confederacy remains a key one. Pateman reads Hobbes's statement that no man can defend himself 'without the help of Confederates' as an indication that families do come into existence in the state of nature.[25] These are not normal families, but are instead composed of a man and his servants and are formed through conquest.[26] Leaving aside the fact that Pateman extracts Hobbes's definition of the family from his discussion of civil society and applies it to the state of nature, the question remains, How firmly rooted in Hobbes's texts is this idea that men conquer women and other weaker men, making them all servants, in order to form families or protective confederacies?

Hobbes mentions the term confederates in the context of discussing the third law of nature, the keeping of covenants made. He is making his very important case, with the use of some examples, that it is always reasonable to perform one's part of a covenant. Even in a state-of-nature situation in which all are afraid for their own lives, it is unwise and against reason for a man to renege on a covenant, to 'deceive those that help him,' that is, his confederates, for he will then be an outcast and will be forced to survive on his own. The discussion of confederates is not connected to any suggestion about the formation of families. Nor is Hobbes positing the existence of confederates as an intermediate stage between the isolated individuals in the state of nature and the social contract. Rather, the confederate serves as an analogy for the leviathan. Just as it would be foolhardy to betray those who protect you, it would be unwise to break the covenant that created the leviathan. Hobbes's basic point is that nothing, not even the desire to attain 'an eternall felicity after death,' justifies the breaking of a covenant once made.[27] In this passage, Hobbes solidifies his ongoing argument for irrevocable political obligation against those who would claim the right to resist political authority on religious grounds.

The other textual evidence Pateman uses to advance her theory of patriarchal confederacies in the state of nature relates to what Hobbes alternately calls paternal or patrimonial kingdoms. In fact, these two topics, confederates and paternal kingdoms, are unrelated in the text, but Pateman nonetheless connects them in her argument. She also counterposes Hobbes's clear statements about the existence and primacy of mother-right in the state of nature to his comments about paternal kingdoms to make her argument that there must be a transformation from 'mother-right to the patriarchal family in the state of nature.'[28] Yet it is far from clear that Hobbes meant that there was a transformation from mother-right to patrimonial kingdoms or patriarchal families in the state of nature. Pateman, intent to expound the story of woman's defeat in the state of nature, extracts, decontextualizes, and then juxtaposes passages from Hobbes to establish her point. In constructing her narrative, however, she obfuscates Hobbes's original intent in these key passages.

Hobbes refers to paternal kingdoms in the course of his discussion of the varieties of sovereignty. He devotes the greatest amount of attention to sovereignty by institution, but he must also account for sovereignty by acquisition, 'wherein the Soveraign Power is acquired by Force.'[29] Paternal kingdoms are those in which a family dynasty conquers another, or in which it declares itself sovereign over a territory and people. If a family grows,

> by multiplication of children, either by generation or adoption; or of servants, either by generation, conquest, or voluntary submission, to be so great and numerous, as in probability it may protect itself, then is that family called a Patrimonial Kingdom, or monarchy by acquisition.[30]

Hobbes is not referring to families in the state of nature but to actual families that have usurped or declared power. History being filled with examples of familial dynasties, most of which were led by men, Hobbes would be remiss if he failed to account for their existence. His central point remains that, regardless of whether sovereignty comes into being through institution or conquest, the 'Rights, and Consequences of Soveraignty, are the same in both.'[31] He must show that his theory of political obligation applies not only to sovereignty that comes about through a hypothetical contract, but also to the common example of sovereignty by acquisition. Hobbes calls the product of sovereignty by acquisition a patrimonial kingdom, or a paternal kingdom, but he also suggests that sovereignty can be held by women, hence his reference to the Amazons and queens. Against patriarchalists, Hobbes asserts that sovereignty flows from consent rather than from generation. Certainly, Pateman is right to call attention to the inconsistency in naming parental and political dominion *paternal*.[32] However, there is no textual evidence to support Pateman's claim that Hobbes thought maternal right would give way to a paternal body politic in the state of nature. By extension, her central argument that a patriarchal confederate-family roams the state of nature must be cast into doubt.

The mythical story of the sexual contract becomes murkier when

Pateman puts forth her other important claim that the original political right is conjugal. Her point is that in order for a woman to exercise maternal right – which Hobbes claims is original – procreative sexual relations had first to be negotiated. About this fact, she is not wrong. But Pateman describes this negotiation as *conjugal right*, implying not consent, but *male access to the female body*, or rape.[33] At other points in the story, however, Pateman seems to suggest that sexual relations in the state of nature would be, at least initially, consensual. Is she suggesting that men actually conquer women for access to their bodies, but call conquest consent? Or do sexual relations in the state of nature begin consensually but eventually become non-consensual? If it is the latter, what causes the change? How does consensual coitus give way to conjugal right and, more peculiarly, how does conjugal right (rape) produce mother-right?

Pateman has no direct response to these questions except to say that coitus and birth are sufficiently temporally separated that the identity of the father cannot be established with certainty. Mother-right must prevail by default, but it is ultimately replaced by conjugal patriarchal right. Pateman never produces satisfactory evidence from Hobbes's text, or from her reconstructive exercise, to substantiate her claim or to show how the transformation occurs. I take as axiomatic the feminist assertion that (hetero)sexual relations themselves have a political dimension, and that Hobbes and other social contract thinkers tend to overlook the power involved in conjugal negotiation. It remains curious, however, that Pateman assumes that if heterosexual conjugal negotiation occurs in the state of nature it has to be, in the end, forced by men. In this argument, Pateman echoes a radical feminist position on heterosexual sex; this fact has implications for her theory of consent, as we will discuss.

The as-yet-unsettled problem of original rape in the state of nature stems from the fact that Pateman's argument is driven, not by Hobbes's theory itself, but by Freud's story of the primal scene. Whereas Hobbes represses the story of how woman 'could forcibly be subjugated,' Freud explains the 'true' story much more clearly in Pateman's view. Borrowing from, and reinterpreting, Freud's case history of the Wolf Man, and using contemporary evidence that many of the sexual acts currently deemed consensual are actually coercive, Pateman constructs a story about primal rape. The borrowed case history describes the trauma of a son witnessing a sexual encounter between his parents, an encounter that appears to him to be – and may in fact be – violent. This encounter, combined with the father's sexual monopoly on women, angers the son, who then conspires to commit patricide, an act that Pateman metaphorically connects with the social contract theorists' successful overthrow of paternal-patriarchalist political theory.[34] The sons/brothers (contract theorists) are subsequently led to make a fraternal pact that ensures their equality with one another, but which also establishes their equal sexual access to women.[35] The sons/brothers seize '*both* dimensions of the defeated father's political right, his sex-right as well as his paternal right.'[36] Thus the fraternal pact, or social contract, is made, and thereafter 'male sex-right extends to all men, to all members of the fraternity.'[37] Like Hobbes, then, Pateman is attentive to the violence of beginnings, but for her that violence is sexual.

The use of Freud to fill the gaps of the sublimated story of the sexual-social pact told by contract theorists is metaphorical but nonetheless enormously problematic. From a historical perspective, we must question the relevance of Freud to Hobbes's project.[38] Anachronism aside, Pateman makes no attempt to clarify the relationship between Hobbes's description of the state of nature in order and the conjectural story of primal rape and the sexual contract. Just exactly where the original rape occurs in the story of the social contract is still vague and uncertain. Does it occur at the formation of the mythical patriarchal confederacies, or is all sex in the state of nature actually rape? After the investigation of Freud, we are no closer to an answer. In either hypothesis, Pateman would have to overlook as well as supplement what Hobbes actually tells us about the state of nature in order to advance her narrative. It appears that Pateman develops the concept of the sexual contract and of original conjugal right in the abstract, drawing on a variety of sources including Freud's primal scene narrative, and subsequently applies it, unsuccessfully in my view, to the individual social contract theorists.

I rehearse this litany of apprehensions about Pateman's reading of Hobbes to expose the internal tensions in the sexual contract, as her reading bears only a tangential relationship to Hobbes's texts. Pateman's analysis of Hobbes begs too many questions precisely because Hobbes's theory is itself ambiguous. Hobbes does not explain thoroughly his transition from the state of nature to civil society, and too much is left unsaid for us to make any reasonable conjecture. We should question, of course, why Hobbes would introduce his innovations in gender relations and then exclude women from the social contract. He has told us that women are not predictably weaker in strength than men, that battle will have to be the arbiter in determining who will rule the family, if one is formed at all. Yet once civil society is established, the discussion of women's maternal dominion is abandoned, women disappear, and the remainder of *Leviathan* proceeds as though this elaborate argument has never been conceived. Is it reasonable to assume, however, that there is an argument latent in the narrative that will explain why woman vanishes from civil society? Pateman does. She writes:

> Hobbes's theory is an early version of the argument, presented in the later nineteenth and early twentieth centuries in elaborate detail and with reference to much ethnographic data, that civilization and political society resulted from the overthrow of mother-right and the triumph of patriarchy.[39]

It is not likely, in my view, that Hobbes understood his own theory in these terms, but even more important, *he does not recite such a narrative.* It is Pateman who offers this story, borrowing as we have seen from Freud and others to fill in the gaps of Hobbes's theory.

The fact that women mysteriously disappear from Hobbes's origin narrative once the state of nature is transcended in no way implies that Hobbes repressed an all-out battle between men and women that resulted in women's defeat. Indeed, when we reconsider Hobbes's purpose in discussing the family – as a way of analysing consensual political right – it seems highly *unlikely* that he envisioned such a scenario. If we want to know *why* Hobbes abandons his earlier arguments, we need only revert to his original political purpose: to counter patriarchalist, along with other, constitutional theories. He is far more concerned to defeat *paternal patriarchalist arguments* than he is to defeat patriarchy as a *conjugal relation between men and women*. Hobbes is caught between a rational but purely strategic argument for the equality of women and men, on the one hand, and a traditional reliance on custom and manners, on the other. Once his purpose is served, he reverts to the common assertions of gender inequality, such as men 'are naturally fitter than women, for actions of labour and danger.'[40] Reverting to custom – despite his criticism of others for doing so – he claims that it is necessary that either the wife or the husband govern, and 'therefore the man, to whom for the most part the woman yieldeth the government, hath for the most part also the sole right and dominion over the children.'⁴¹ As unsatisfactory as this reliance on tradition is from an otherwise rigorously rational thinker, it reveals neither a 'conjuring trick' nor a lost battle, but indicates rather that gender itself is instrumental, strategic, and symbolic for Hobbes no less that it is for his contemporaries. I am deliberately not offering an alternative narrative to Pateman's that will describe what actually happens to women in Hobbes's theory precisely because, in my view, any such narrative can be based only on speculation – speculation that is of questionable value in our attempts to understand either Hobbes or the politics of origins. Despite Pateman's attempts, a consistent story cannot be forced from Hobbes when the question of patriarchal social relations was so clearly not at the forefront of his enterprise.

### 3. Masculine Birth Story?

Up to this point, this chapter has enumerated the historical and interpretive problems with Pateman's discussion of the public/private dichotomy in Hobbes's theory and with her theoretical formulation of the sexual contract. Pateman also claims that Hobbes's social contract is a story of masculine political birth, and that its political implications are deleterious to women on procreative and political grounds. This provocative assertion remains to be considered. If Pateman is correct, Hobbes should be placed firmly in the tradition of Plato, who tells perhaps the most elaborate of these masculine stories in the *Timaeus*. When Pateman's hypothesis is unravelled, however, it becomes apparent that it rests on a faulty assumption about Hobbes.

In general, Pateman is very critical of the pervasive use of origin stories in the tradition of political thought. 'Political argument must leave behind stories of origins and original contracts,' writes Pateman, because 'to look to an original act of contract is systematically to blur the distinction between freedom and subjection.'⁴² She reasons that part of the allure of origin stories stems from 'the fact that the human beginning – or even if there was one – is a mystery.'⁴³ But the other reason for their popularity, and the one she is most interested in, has to do with their expression of a 'specifically masculine creative power, the capacity to generate, to give birth to, new forms of political life.'⁴⁴ Pateman hints at two stages of the story of masculine political birth. The first occurs when men discover their role in reproduction, which marks a 'crucial turning-point in Bachofen's conjectural history of the overthrow of matriarchy and the creation of civilization.'⁴⁵ J.J. Bachofen, the author of the influential text *Mutterrecht und Urreligion*, hypothesizes a transformation from an original matriarchy or mother-right to patriarchy.⁴⁶ At this stage of paternal patriarchy to which Pateman refers, men 'defeat' women and establish themselves as the rulers of families and polities. The arrival of modernity signifies the second stage of masculine political birth, in which the father is defeated and the civil fraternity is established, as we have already seen. At this stage, 'all men, not just fathers, can generate political life and political right,' and 'political creativity belongs not to paternity but to masculinity.'⁴⁷

Hobbes details the second stage of masculine birth, as is evident in the fact that he defeats paternal patriarchalism and establishes the fraternal social covenant. According to Pateman's logic, Hobbes empowers all men *as* men with the ability to generate political life, by which she means not just that men alone make the social contract. She believes Hobbes to be an advocate of patrogenesis, suggesting that he understands men to be the principal agents in reproduction – just as Filmer did – and that he uses that patrogenic power to enhance men's political power and autonomy. Hobbes's social contract is one more 'male replica of the ability which only women possess.'⁴⁸ It is 'an example of the appropriation by men of the awesome gift that nature has denied them,' writes Pateman.⁴⁹ In appropriating that gift, men disempower women procreatively and politically.

In other words, Pateman's assessment that Hobbes arrogates the primary reproductive power to men is central to her overall argument about the masculine quality of his origin story. Pateman is not the only feminist to posit Hobbes as a patrogenic thinker, for Mary O'Brien hints at the same in *The Politics of Reproduction*, arguing that Hobbes's sovereign is capable of self-regeneration, 'without any need for females.'⁵⁰ Pateman's argument sounds very similar to, and may well have been influenced by, O'Brien's appropriation thesis. Christine Di Stefano also sees in Hobbes's theory a tendency toward father-driven theories of reproduction as well as a denial of the '(m)other.'⁵¹ She argues that Hobbes 'never embraced' his passages on mother-right – an unsubstantiated allegation that fails to recognize the presence and significance of the theory of original maternal dominion in his political theory from the beginning.

As we know from the previous chapter, categorizing Hobbes as a patrogenic thinker is highly problematic. In contrast to Filmer and Plato before him, Hobbes acknowledges women's unique contribution to reproduction; he recognizes the limits on paternal certainty; and he even accords mothers dominion over children where there is no prior agreement to the contrary. Consider Hobbes's explicit comments on the maternal contribution in *De Corpore Politico*, in which he discusses how men become subject to one another and by 'what title one man cometh to have propriety in a child, that proceedeth *from the common generation of two, (viz.) of male and female.*' He continues:

> And considering men again dissolved from all covenants one with another, and that every man by the law of nature, hath right or propriety to his own body, the child ought rather to be the propriety of the mother (*of whose body it is part*, till the time of separation) than of the father.[52]

Of course, that he recognizes the child's emergence from the mother's body is no guarantee that Hobbes does not believe the father to be the 'principal agent' in reproduction, but if he does hold that belief, he gives no indication of it.

To suggest that Hobbes presents a story of masculine political birth is to imply, or at least to open up the possibility, that he exhibits anxiety and tension regarding the issues of women, reproduction, and birth. Theorists who are either consciously or unconsciously preoccupied with masculine birth typically give clues as to their obsession in the way of masculine fantasies about reproduction, as in the case of Plato. Or such theorists might reveal their anxiety about gender in frequent references to witches, appropriate wifely behaviour, or the proper patriarchal rule of the family, as in the case of James VI and I and Filmer. Hobbes provides no such clues, and is exceptional for his lack of masculine anxiety, for at every turn he does more to open up the space for a conception of woman as autonomous than do most other ancient or modern thinkers. If anything, Hobbes's strategic use of Amazons and queens symbolically – although unintentionally – empowers women, both politically and reproductively.

If Hobbes does not arrogate primary reproductive power to men, and if he communicates no particular fixation on the issue of reproduction, Pateman's theory that his is a masculine birth story is substantially weakened. Hobbes's social contract is a masculine birth story *only insofar as it portrays (exclusively) men consenting to the social contract and setting up civil society.* In this sense, however, Hobbes tells a story that is as masculinist – no more and no less so – than most other political theorists. The O'Brien appropriation thesis that Pateman imports has value and meaning only when applied to a story like Plato's

*Timaeus*, where the imagery of birth is clearly central. In implicitly categorizing Hobbes with Plato, Pateman risks obscuring Hobbes's actual innovations in gender hierarchies and casts him as one in a long, undifferentiated line of patriarchal thinkers.

I suggest, then, that Pateman's theory misrepresents Hobbes's origin story and its political implications. In my view, the more important implication of Hobbes's origins theorizing is the lesson he offers to those theorists who would use origins to come to terms with the present. Hobbes's significant insight on the origins discourse is his recognition that political solutions cannot be found in the narratives of mythical, historical, or customary beginnings. Pateman's attempts to locate the origins of modern patriarchy in contract theory, and Second Wave feminist attempts to locate an original matriarchy, fail to appreciate Hobbes's lesson; there is nothing about an original matriarchy, or fanciful reconstructions of patriarchy's beginnings, that can solve the problems of present-day gendered power relations. More often than not, the search for origins involves the creation of narratives that embody our present political concerns, narratives that can do more to limit our understandings of political problems and solutions than to aid them. Hobbes too is guilty of creating this kind of narrative in the state of nature. The lesson Hobbes offers, then, lies in his critique of genetic theory as opposed to his actual origin story. We should note, finally, that Hobbes's theoretical disagreement with genetic approaches actually produces insidious results on the issue of gender: despite roughly egalitarian origins, the hierarchical status quo is legitimate because it rests on contract. After having levelled all hierarchies, he re-establishes new and perhaps more profound hierarchies in civil society. That Hobbes saw no problem with this resolution is the real complication for feminists.

## 4. An Origin Story of Her Own

Pateman expressly states that her intent is not to replace 'patriarchal tales with feminist stories of origins,'[53] and yet in her extension and supplementation of Hobbes's theory this is exactly what she has accomplished. However, she is by no means the first to tell the story of woman's defeat, for *The Sexual Contract* is one of the last in a long line of similar, Second Wave feminist attempts. In this final section, attention is turned to the politics informing Pateman's own origin story.

While many feminist origin stories focus on the ancient past, trying to recover a lost Western pre-history, Pateman offers a story of modern, contractual patriarchy. She critiques other feminist origin narratives for looking too far back in the past for patriarchy's roots, for risking an ahistorical description of patriarchy when, in her view, 'there are stories available of a much closer origin.'[54] In Pateman's assessment, her own project improves on the earlier stories and escapes the ahistorical trap. It is my contention, however, that Pateman's origin narrative is of a piece with the earlier feminist stories, even if it surpasses them in rigour and theoretical complexity. Whether Pateman acknowledges it or not, her story of the sexual contract exhibits many of the same problems, and arises from the same political desire, as most other political origin stories, including that of the social contract.

Like all origin stories and all political theory, the story of the sexual contract is deeply influenced by the politics of its author. The political dimension of Pateman's work does not distinguish her from most other theorists. The problem arises, however, when her political interests overtake her project to provide a plausible and historically accurate account of the sexual contract. In her earlier work, Pateman had written extensively and critically on consent and obligation in liberal theory, and had discussed the 'women question' only in passing. As her career progressed, however, she recognized that she had 'underestimated the depth and complexity of the problem'; she criticized her earlier analysis for not going far enough.[55] As she writes in the 1985 afterword to *The Problem of Political Obligation*:

> The development of democratic theory has to take criticism of social life a good deal further than I pursue it in this book. Apart from my brief references to promising to obey and marriage, I concentrated on the private and public spheres as conventionally discussed. But my argument has to be extended to the repressed realm of personal, sexual and familial relations.[56]

As Pateman was increasingly influenced by radical feminism,[57] she began to view the radical democratic theorists with whom she had associated as being implicated in the problem. Her more recent research has led her

> to the conclusion that a distinctively feminist perspective in political theory provides as searching and as fundamental a critique of radical democratic theory as it does of liberalism, precisely because both theories are

sexually particular, predicated upon the patriarchal separation of private and public, women and men.[58]

Pateman underwent a significant transformation in her thinking as she turned her attention to the private, female realm of subordination. It is this focus on the private realm that led her to develop the theory of the sexual contract. Her origin story of the sexual contract, like other Second Wave feminist stories of origins, serves an explicitly political purpose in that it is part of an effort to assert the structural autonomy, historical longevity, and persistence of patriarchy. This assertion was a step toward achieving the recognition of gender as a central, rather than a marginal, category of analysis. An analysis of women could not be 'tacked on' to class analysis, nor could women and men be treated as if their experiences in the labour market or in politics were analogous. In particular, *The Sexual Contract* is a message to political theorists who had dismissed the private realm and feminism in their theory, and who continued to discuss politics as if the private realm either did not exist or had no political implications for society. Perhaps more importantly, Pateman delivers a message to radical thinkers and to socialists (a broad designation meant to include anarchists and left thinkers of all varieties) who, in spite of their focus on relations of power, also ignore the specificity of women's subordination. This intransigence of gender issues is part of a systemic problem – in other words, a problem that is deeply embedded in the Western political system itself – in Pateman's view. In rejecting the radical democratic line on women, and in turning to a feminist origin story, Pateman is repeating a pattern laid out by radical feminists in the late 1960s and early 1970s.

The radical feminist underpinnings of her story are manifest most clearly in her preoccupation with sexual domination, with the problems of consent and coercion in sexual relations. In fact, we could say that the central theme of *The Sexual Contract* is the sexual conquest of women's bodies by men. As we have seen, Pateman enters the discussion on the origins of women's oppression with an eye to demonstrating the coercion that lies behind the veil of consent in the arena of sexual relations. Too often, apparently consensual relations are actually coercive; too often, women feel that for economic, safety, or other personal reasons, they must 'consent' to sex, marriage, or prostitution. Pateman's point is that this consent cannot be legitimate because it occurs in an environment in which women are not truly free. Moreover, it is 'consent to' an option proposed by the other party, rather than a mutually agreed-upon decision. How valid can consent be for women if they are forever in the position of consenting to another party's agenda? She detects in the marriage contract 'echoes of the story of the primal scene.' While the original sexual contract is 'made only once ... it is replicated every day as each man makes his own "original" marriage contract.'[59] Through the marriage contract a woman becomes a 'wife,' and a man 'gains right of sexual access to her body ... and to her labour as a housewife.'[60]

To the extent that Pateman reveals the coercive underside of 'apparent' consent, her project is essential to feminist politics. She aims to separate the interwoven strands of conquest and consent, and she is rightly critical of Hobbes for positing that consent is always voluntary and thus unproblematic. In her narrative, however, she inverts Hobbes's error, manufactures the theory of conquest, and reads conquest into every act formerly declared consensual. In replacing his consensual script of citizenship with one of conquest and violence, she once again reweaves the strands of consent and conquest and obscures any kind of negotiation, any grey areas, behind the facade of conquest. In this way, she too blurs 'the distinction between freedom and subjection,' for to assume that women's position must be the result of conquest is to grossly oversimplify a complex problem. For one thing, it bears reiteration that we, in Western society at least, do not know the origins of patriarchal social relations, just as we do not know the origins of politics and power. Furthermore, it seems unnecessary and even dangerous for feminists to relinquish entirely the concept of consent on the basis that it always disguises subjection. Even in the most egalitarian society, a notion of consent would probably still be necessary to negotiate human interactions. To be fair, of course, we should note that Pateman wants to replace the flawed discourse of consent, which she sees as hopelessly one-sided, with a discourse of promising, in which the 'content of the promise is a matter for [the parties'] own judgement.'[61] Insofar as Pateman is arguing that the language of consent may not be adequate to represent egalitarian negotiation of sexual relations, I am sympathetic. I am suggesting, however, that the idea of the sexual contract glosses over the difficult interchange between consent and coercion, opting for dramatic narrative over nuanced analysis to capture the reader's imagination.

Indeed, this criticism gets to the heart of the problem with feminist origin stories themselves. Feminist origin stories are not the result of benign or impartial historical inquiry, but are imbued with the politics of the Second Wave women's liberation movement. They tend to present a dramatic and stark picture of gendered social relations in an effort to legitimate their politics. But to generate such a narrative elides the very complex evolution and development of patriarchal social relations. Diane Purkiss detects a similar elision of historical complexity in the dominant feminist approach to the European witch hunts.[62] Feminists have tended to resist historical accuracy regarding the variability within, and the multifarious causes of, the witch hunts; to Purkiss, their resistance to historical accuracy is evidence that the myth of the Burning Times has political value for feminism. The myth of a patriarchal war against women simplifies history – it refuses historicity in a sense – and favours instead 'a story with clear oppositions' between oppressed and oppressor, between the innocent and the guilty.[63] The narrative about the oppression of witches, according to Purkiss, acts as a 'Holocaust of one's own'[64] for feminism, helping radical feminists demonstrate the existence and severity of women's oppression to both men and women.

I contend that Pateman's radical feminist leanings represent the strength and the weakness of her text. Despite its shortcomings, Pateman's text does serve several political purposes – it provides an important critique of contemporary liberal and left political theory. It also revises the social-contract theorists' script of citizenship that posits consent and voluntarism as the basis for all social relationships in civil society. At the same time, however, Pateman's political purpose is undermined by a refusal of historicity, by a radical feminist desire to prove conquest. It relies on conjecture when historical and textual accuracy is impossible. A more historically oriented theory of patriarchal relations would see the disruptions as well as the continuities in social relations between pre-modern and early modern society. While it is important to investigate whether, and to what extent, early modern gender relations were transformed by the prevalent contract discourse, it is essential to recognize that the transformation was far more gradual than the metaphor of the sexual contract captures. Indeed, neither liberalism nor capitalism themselves had dramatic births, but rather evolved and took shape over the course of decades and centuries. Even if the sexual contract is taken as a metaphor rather than a statement of fact or historical truth about the origins of modern patriarchy, it remains problematic. To focus exclusively on the origins of sexual relations is really to disregard the many ways in which gender relations are reproduced and reconstituted on an ongoing – even a daily – basis. In the end, Pateman's desire to 'leave behind stories of origins and original contracts' is undermined by her creation of the sexual contract, which perpetuates contractual and origins-thinking rather than terminating it.

Throughout this chapter I have shown that Pateman favours a fabricated, metaphorical narrative of an original rape over textual specificity, that she casts aside historical precision for the political benefits of a story of woman's sexual defeat. The utility of filling the gaps of Hobbes's already conjectural story remains elusive, for it would seem that Pateman's attempt to reconstruct the origins of modern patriarchy produces more confusion than clarity. While Pateman obviously recognizes that the social contract is a hypothetical device, at times she implies that the sexual contract did occur in history, that it is manifest in the institutions and practices of contemporary liberal society. For a theorist intending to reveal the fallacies of hypothetical consent, and to expose the problems with imaginary beginnings, this slippage between myth and history is troubling.

These criticisms notwithstanding, Pateman's theory of the sexual contract does mark an improvement in feminist origins-theorizing, as many of her predecessors failed to pay even lip service to the ideal of historical objectivity. Myth and history are fused into one as radical feminists of the Second Wave turned to origin narratives in an effort to legitimate an autonomous women's movement. Exactly how this autonomy was asserted, and what kinds of stories were used to justify radical feminist politics, is the subject of consideration in the final chapter.

*Chapter Six*

# Getting to the Root of Patriarchy: Radical Feminism's Quest for Origins

*Power to all the people or to none.* All the way down, this time.
— Robin Morgan[1]

... we must invent a past adequate to our ambitions
we must create a future adequate to our needs
— *Quicksilver Times*[2]

In the beginning, woman was the superior sex, the model of the human species. She was idolized and worshipped in the form of a goddess at the same time as she ruled politically. The feminine principle, embodied in the culture, derived from woman's primal reproductive power. Peace prevailed; men were little more than helpmeets, cogs in the wheel of the great matriarchy. Aristotle was wrong; according to the rejuvenated myth of the lost matriarchy, he had inverted the truth.

This matriarchal myth was first advanced by the ancient Greeks, but was later popularized by thinkers such as J.J. Bachofen, Friedrich Engels, and Erich Fromm.[3] Early Second Wave radical feminists revived it for their own purposes. Indeed, radical feminist writing in the early stage of the Women's Liberation Movement is replete with metaphors and stories of origins; with references to goddesses, Amazons, and matriarchy; and with narratives about the cause of women's oppression. That the telling of origin narratives was a passing phase for feminism raises the question as to why origins were so central to early radical feminists. Why, at the beginning of their movement, from the late 1960s through the mid-1970s, did radical feminists turn to the question of origin? What political purpose did origins serve for radical feminism?

This chapter is an attempt to come to terms with these formerly unexamined questions in feminist historiography. To this end, it examines the development and politics of the Women's Liberation Movement, in particular the radical feminist stream.[4] While the origin narratives invoked in radical feminism exhibit a range of political and historical difficulties – not to mention biological ones – the point here is to do more than reveal their shortcomings. The origins discourse in feminism needs to be placed in the political context in which women's oppression came to be treated as an autonomous political issue worthy of attention and analysis.

## 1. The Nature of the Origins Discourse

To be sure, questions about origins and about Western prehistory have always loomed large in feminism because, from the beginning of recorded history, hierarchical gender relations have prevailed. In a certain sense, feminism cannot escape the unanswered question of origins, as being a feminist necessarily entails asking how things got to be the way they are. For this reason, feminists have long expressed an interest in origin myths, especially the Genesis myth at the core of three major religions, because they provide an account of the origins of women's oppression. Thus we find Sarah Grimké, in her 1838 *Letters on the Equality of the Sexes and the Condition of Woman*, providing a rendition of biblical creation. Properly to assess 'The Province of Woman,' she writes, demands that 'we must first view woman at the period of her creation.'[5] Archaeology and anthropology have a similar importance as they offer fragments of insight into human beginnings. It makes logical sense that the authors of *A History of Their Own*, to take one instance, began their comprehensive history of European women with an examination of these fragments in a chapter entitled 'Buried Traditions: The Question of Origins.'[6]

Ultimately, the question of origins presents an aporia to feminists. Important as the quest to understand patriarchy's beginnings might be, the answers remain elusive. There is no answer – and there might never be an answer – to the question of origins. There may not, in the end, be an identifiable and discrete historical event that explains the rise of patriarchal social relations. Nevertheless, Second Wave radical feminists have focused attention on this question. While it can be productive to interpret myth or to piece together the fragments of archaeological, anthropological, and historical evidence about origins, these kinds of scholarly enterprises have not captivated the interest of radical feminists to the extent that we might expect. Rather, radical feminists have reconstructed and revitalized myths about an ancient matriarchy and, in the process, have collapsed any distinction between myth and historical inquiry. Their origin stories pick up where history and evidence left off. Unhindered by this lack of evidence, the more recent theorists of matriarchy, and the feminists who have co-opted and refashioned their myth, have synthesized a universal story about the replacement of female rule by patriarchy. Drawing on a series of examples, this section aims to show both the prominence of, and the distinct approach to, the question of origins in this period of feminist analysis.

In this examination of Second Wave feminist narratives, I am interested not only in the full-length versions of the stories, of which there were several, but also in the proliferation of the theme of origins within the Women's Liberation Movement. Many of the activists who did not themselves generate an origin story nevertheless used, borrowed, and quoted from these stories. Segments of origin stories appeared in feminist newspapers, political speeches, and written polemics. Feminists invoked origins almost as a matter of course in discussions of strategy and theory. This emphasis on origins is most evident during the years in which radical feminism was born and peaked as a political movement, from 1968 to 1975. Following this period, the myths do not entirely disappear, but they take different forms.

Given their importance at the beginning of the women's movement, feminist newspapers and underground publications are a good starting point for assessing the proliferation of origin myths. Although radical feminists had no formal strategies for communicating with each other, they developed extensive informal networks through which ideas about feminism and political action reports were circulated. Newspapers and newsletters such as *off our backs*, *Everywoman*, *her-self*, *Voice of the Women's Liberation Movement*, and *The Other Woman* formed an important part of this network, as many activists joined newspaper collectives that in turn received the newspapers of other feminist groups located across North America. The republication of stories from other papers was common, and in some cases articles were cut and pasted wholesale from other papers. The feminist papers were thus mutually influencing with respect to content: if one group covered a particular story or controversy, it was likely that others would as well. While each newspaper had a different focus, all typically covered a standard range of topics from political rallies and protests to the latest news from the war in Vietnam; they also provided space for discussions about feminist theory and strategy; and they offered detailed advice on practical matters from plumbing and car repair to gynecology. In sum, these small feminist newspapers were key to the transmission of feminist thought and strategy.

It is not surprising, given their range of topics, that the theme of origins surfaced repeatedly in these papers. Origin stories were often included in lists of recommended reading published in the newspapers. Feminist book lists were a staple in the early Women's Liberation Movement; it was widely understood that women needed to educate themselves in their own history and in current feminist theory. The New York Radical Feminists went so far as to devise a program of study for new feminist groups under their umbrella organization: each group had to commit to six weeks of intensive reading in contemporary movement literature as well as six weeks of reading in the feminist classics and feminist history to be admitted as members.[7] Shulamith Firestone's *The Dialectic of Sex* and Kate Millet's *Sexual Politics* were most commonly cited on book lists as representing the cutting edge of feminist theory and as essential reading for any member of women's liberation.[8] Also recommended, however, was a variety of origin stories about the rise of patriarchy: Elizabeth Gould Davis's *The First Sex*, Helen Diner's *Mothers and Amazons*, Engels's *The Origin of the Family*, Robert Briffault's *The Mothers*, Bachofen's *Mother Right*, Mary Daly's *Beyond God the Father*, Elaine Morgan's *The Descent of Woman*, and Wolfgang Lederer's *The Fear of Women*.[9] Each of these texts presents an account of the 'world historic defeat of the female sex.'[10]

Long excerpts from feminist origin stories commonly appeared in the feminist newspapers, situated either in book reviews or in 'herstory' sections. Davis's *The First Sex*, for example, was reviewed in the Canadian paper *The Other Woman*. Quoting extensively from the text, the reviewer, Pat Leslie, concludes with Davis's statement that '[r]ecorded history starts with a patriarchal revolution. Let it continue with a counter-revolution that is the only hope for the survival of the human race.' Leslie suggests that 'it is not so important to quibble over whether the matriarchy was egalitarian or supremacist as it is to have free-flowing discussion on our own female past.'[11] Leaving aside for the moment the content of Davis's origin story, it is particularly noteworthy that, from the outset, feminists acknowledged that the theory of matriarchy does not rest on secure historical ground, and moreover, if matriarchy once existed, its characteristics were as yet undetermined. In short, while Davis might not have been correct about the details on matriarchy, she nevertheless remained essential reading for feminists – in Leslie's words, 'highly recommended by all of us who have read it.'

*Everywoman*, published in Venice, California, assisted women in the project of feminist self-education by running a regular 'Herstory' section along with a 'Herstory Almanac.' The 'Almanac' commemorates the acts of great women in history, matching the date of the paper with important dates in women's past.[12] The lengthier 'Herstory' section provides excerpts from authors on specific topics, like matriarchies and Amazons.[13] In her piece 'Amazons and Battle-Axes,' Barbara Miles tries to correct the 2000-year-old patriarchal tradition that has portrayed and disparaged Amazons as merely mythical beings. 'The real story,' she asserts, 'as usual, is more interesting.' First, she reports, Amazons were real, not just mythical. Second, they were beautiful, 'healthy-bodied' women who made excellent fighters. Since there were many generations of Amazons, the author claims, 'we can assume they engaged in heterosexual activity now and then; or there [was] always parthenogenesis.' Parthenogenesis, a recurring theme in the feminist origins discourse, refers to spontaneous reproduction by women without the aid of fertilization – the opposite of patrogenesis. Feminists drew upon this lost mythical history to fill in the blank spots of women's history.

The theme of origins also routinely surfaced in newspaper articles on feminist theory and politics. Because the radical feminist movement arose out of, and in opposition to, the New Left, one of the most common points of debate was the accuracy of Engels's *Origin of the Family and Private Property*. Some feminist writers used Engels to show that patriarchy has not always existed.[14] Those feminists who remained within the left organizations, that is, those who did not become radical feminists, tended to view the cause of women's oppression in the terms Engels set out, with women's oppression being incidental to the development of private property. Others claimed that feminism needed to develop its own analysis of women's oppression, but paradoxically they still used Engels to show that the family is fundamental to the economic base of capitalist societies.[15] And still others pointed to

Engels's sexist bias, recognizing his efforts to explain women's oppression, but rejecting the notion that Lenin, Marx, or Engels can 'tell us how to change it.'[16] Engels, then, frequently served as the starting point and the springboard for feminist debate about origins.

In point of fact, feminist writers during this period raised the topic of origins as if feminist strategy could not be discussed without some prior discussion of it, no matter how brief. Dawn Chalker begins her analysis of 'The Economics of Oppression' in *her-self* with a short description of the biologically based cause of women's subordination:

> This attempt to synthesize ideas into a feminist theory accepts the premise that women's position of inferiority and subservience to man developed out of her role in reporduction [sic] which incapacitated her at certain times and forced her into the position of caring for children.

Chalker must preface her feminist theory with an argument about why women are oppressed, an argument

> based on the belief that *men have always been in awe of women's reproductive powers and, although respecting this power, finally turned it against women.* In an attempt to control nature which he feared, man began to assert himself over woman whom he has also feared as a powerful and unexplainable force in nature.[17]

In a few short sentences, Chalker summarizes the popular feminist origin narrative, the one that so many writers have recited in one form or another. Chalker's narrative strays considerably from a historical analysis of the cause of oppression: in attributing male dominance to biological envy of women Chalker provides an early articulation of the envy-appropriation thesis used later by both O'Brien and Pateman.

Even a brief examination of this cross-section of feminist newspapers provides a sense of the pervasiveness of the feminist origins impulse. Indeed, the theme of origins is ubiquitous. In New York City, undoubtedly one of the most important centres for the Women's Liberation Movement, one could take classes such as 'The Origins of Women's Oppression and Male Chauvinism' in 1970.[18] At the Ontario Institute for Studies in Education (OISE) in Toronto, a group of feminists created a kit for teachers who wanted to teach women's history and feminism to their classes but who lacked the materials necessary to do so. 'The Women's Kit'[19] is a large box containing a guide book by the same title and countless clippings, articles, pamphlets, bound essays, posters, postcards, and even record albums, all on the topic of women, their status and their history. Assembled and distributed between 1972 and 1974, the kits represent a kind of time-capsule from this period of early feminist activism: the contents reveal the diversity of interests within feminism, the international focus even at this stage, and, not surprisingly, an interest in origins. Included in 'The Women's Kit' are the short, bound essays 'The Great Goddess' and 'Fear of Women.' These two short texts, both written and compiled by Pamela Harris, combine a series of quotes from other authors on these topics with some photographs and comments from Harris herself. Both texts retell the story of woman's mystical reproductive power and try to account for the rise of patriarchy by resorting to an argument about men's fear and jealousy of women. In 'Fear of Women' Harris explains that 'woman is put down and kept down, not because men really see her as inferior, but because they see her as superior.'[20] In the goddess text she surmises that these goddess-worshipping societies 'were conquered by other male-dominated, women-suppressing societies.'[21] Harris's language about origins reflects and reinforces radical feminist belief in an early matriarchy. Most of the feminists who engage with the origins discourse allude to a 'before,' a universal, primordial matriarchy, a point in history when woman controlled society and the world was a more nurturing, peaceful place. All of these authors rely heavily on male theorists like Engels and Bachofen, attempting to harness their insights for the benefit of the feminist movement.

Even major feminist writers whose intent was not specifically to develop an origin story felt the compulsion to respond to the question of origins, or to give an interpretation of existing evidence of matriarchy. Simone de Beauvoir, ever-influential to the creators of the Women's Liberation Movement, theorized the Golden Age of matriarchy to have been a myth. Radical feminist believers in the matriarchy were obviously undeterred by Beauvoir's statement that 'we must be careful to note that the presence of a woman chief or queen at the head of a tribe by no means signifies that women are sovereign therein.'[22] Later, Sarah Pomeroy entered the debate, ultimately concluding that the evidence was not sufficient to determine the historicity of matriarchy.[23] Adrienne Rich took up the issue of matriarchy in *Of Woman Born*, cautious about feminist historical sources, but at the same time aware that 'a critical exploration backward in time can be profoundly radicalizing.'[24] Rich was somewhat more sympathetic than Pomeroy to those feminists who wished to begin this exploration, those who were curious to investigate history, 'not as verifiable evidence of things done' but as 'something like the notebooks of a dreamer.'[25]

Ms. magazine also contributed to the origins hype by republishing a collection of William Moulton Marston's *Wonder Woman* comic strips. This 1972 collection was introduced by Gloria Steinem herself and contained an interpretive essay about Amazons by Phyllis Chesler. Steinem's foray into the subject of matriarchy and Amazons is particularly intriguing simply because she was not a radical feminist, and she did not participate in fanciful theorizing. Steinem's interest in Wonder Woman stems from her desire for girls to have a positive action heroine of their own with whom they can identify. While she is not convinced that Wonder Woman's mythical inspiration – the Amazons – actually existed, she claims that 'being a writer, not a scientist tied to proven fact,' gives her licence to fuse together 'the sometimes contradictory versions of Amazonia into one amalgam; into a story that sounds right to me.' And so she recounts the Amazon myth in the standard way, complete with the biological-envy thesis. She claims that if it is shown to be factual at some later point, Wonder Woman will then become 'one small outcropping of a larger human memory'; and the 'girl children who love her' will have been 'responding to one small echo of dreams and capabilities in their own forgotten past.'[26]

Chesler's piece in *Wonder Woman* is similarly provocative. She begins with a recreated conversation between herself, Helen Diner, and Johann Bachofen.[27] Here and in her groundbreaking *Women and Madness*, Chesler touches on Greek myth, the historicity of matriarchy, and the relevance of Wonder Woman herself. She gives a positive reading of the myth of the Amazons, arguing that the image of these past creatures 'produces fear and disbelief – together with an overwhelming sense of pride and excitement.'[28] Furthermore, feminist visions of the Amazons are not just about dismantling patriarchal history, but contribute to positive feminist self-understandings. Indeed, a number of radical feminists declared themselves to be modern-day Amazon women; among the most famous was Ti-Grace Atkinson in her collected writings entitled *Amazon Odyssey*.[29] A Milwaukee collective named itself after the Amazons and published a newspaper by the same name. 'We call our paper, Amazon as a tribute to [Amazon] women, and a challenge to male society,' reads their mission statement; 'we are on the road to building a new identity for women. This is the road to liberation.'[30] Chesler is ambivalent about such categorical statements, for she cautions that it may be 'unrealistic and perhaps dangerous' to take Amazon fantasies too far, but she asserts nonetheless that these visions must be respected as 'difficult truths with which to inform our lives – in some way.'[31]

Amazon warriors are also a focal point in Elizabeth Gould Davis's work; indeed, this overview of the feminist origins discourse would not be complete without a discussion of *The First Sex*. Davis wrote the most comprehensive, and the most contentious, feminist origin story of the early 1970s. Radical feminists of this period relied heavily on Davis's narrative, as her claims about the primacy of women and the historicity of a primordial matriarchy appeared in countless feminist works.[32] In fact, Davis proved to be far more influential on the subject of matriarchy than the feminists who were writing in a more historically informed manner.[33] Significantly, Davis was a generation older than the women who were active in creating the radical feminist movement, but she was aware of their struggles in the student movement and she spoke to them in a language to which they were increasingly attuned.[34]

Davis presents women not only as superior beings, but as the first beings on the earth. Parthenogenesis was the original human means of reproduction.[35] The deity was also originally 'all female,' although gradually she transforms to incorporate the male and female in one, becoming the 'creator and begetter in one body.'[36] Davis cites Plato's discussion of the original unity of male and female in the *Symposium* as evidence for this hermaphroditic deity. When the male of the human species did come into existence, it was as a mutation, an 'accident of nature.'[37] Evidence for this is adduced in women's more 'highly evolved' reproductive organs, and in the deformity of the Y chromosome. 'Geneticists and physiologists tell us,' writes Davis, 'that the small and twisted Y chromosome is a genetic error,' and thus that, 'man is an imperfect female.'[38] In Davis's rendering of creation, maleness is nothing more than a 'recessive genetic trait like colour-blindness and hemophilia with which it is linked.'[39]

Throughout the ancient world, man was enslaved by woman; he was dominated by her immense, Amazonian power. Woman 'held the secrets of nature' and was the 'originator and repository' of all culture. Women provided food and shelter for their families, 'discovered' agriculture, constructed implements; and the law and economy revolved around them. By contrast, men were the objects of scorn and derision and had to be dragged kicking and screaming into civilization.[40] This matriarchal age is represented by Davis as a universal stage in human civilization, lasting for millennia in prehistory, following which cultures dispersed across the globe. We should note, too, that matriarchy refers here to an organization of society in which women rule; it is not merely an egalitarian arrangement, but a reversal of the patriarchal hierarchy. According to Davis, a feminine-centric culture, if not a gynocracy, lasted into the period of recorded history. That this universal stage was peaceful is attributed to the worship of the Goddess, for unlike the father God who punished his worshippers, the mother Goddess 'loved all her children equally' and unconditionally.[41] Moreover, gynocratic society was marked by a 'real democracy in which the happiness and fulfillment of the individual'[42] superseded all other societal goals.

Eventually, however, female supremacy met with a counter-revolution that resulted in its collapse under patriarchy. Men had been convinced of their inferiority for so long that they developed a subconscious but 'everlasting resentment against women.'[43] As Bachofen, whom Davis quotes extensively, explains, it is the very 'strictness of the patriarchal system' that 'points to an earlier system that had to be combated and surpassed.'[44] Fear of woman, pregnancy- or womb-envy, and resentment of their past subordination: each of these is offered as a factor in explaining the creation of patriarchal society by men. With the advent of patriarchy came war, property rights, arrogance, self-interest. Woman's body and her accomplishments were disparaged and she was forced to relinquish her autonomy. The end of gynocracy did not mean, in Davis's view, the end of human connection to the Goddess, for the Celts retained their connection to the Goddess long after the rise of patriarchy; moreover, a desire to retain that connection is evident in many Goddess symbols and markers that Davis enumerates throughout the text.[45]

In sum, *The First Sex* is devoted to the detection and exposition of evidence that supports the matriarchal theory of women's history. The existence of a primordial matriarchy is demonstrated to Davis by the fact that the beginning of recorded history shows goddesses among the Greek deities. For Davis, as for Bachofen, myth is evidence enough; myth is a transparent window on the past. Myth reflects history. The Greek myths about Amazons, goddesses, and matriarchies are a repository of truth about an earlier age. Therefore, in addition to the irrefutable archaeological evidence that she argues does exist, Davis (selectively) offers the texts of Hesiod, Homer, Herodotus, Plato, and Aristotle – presenting these thinkers as accurate reporters of the past – as evidence that a matriarchal age preceded their own. Again, to quote Bachofen, '[T]he mythical tradition is to be seen as an authentic, independent record of the primordial age.'[46] If goddesses existed in myth, that alone was evidence for Davis that a gynocratic age once existed.

Putting aside for the moment the obvious shortcomings in Davis's methodological approach, we need to achieve some understanding of her purpose. It is evident from her final two chapters, which are given over to the discussion of contemporary politics, that Davis's preoccupation is with the present and the problems engendered by patriarchy. She concludes the introduction of the book by inviting a matriarchal counter-revolution: a transformation of society to end the 'rot of masculine materialism' that threatens the very core of life. Yet she is vitally aware of the socialization that has convinced women of their inferiority, a socialization that hinders the possibility of any counter-revolution. 'In order to restore women to their ancient dignity and pride,' Davis writes, 'they must be taught their own history, as the American blacks are being taught theirs.'[47] *The First Sex* is designed to fill that very mandate, though Davis herself did not witness the results of her effort, as she died in 1974. In the lengthy *Ms.* eulogy to Davis, Rhoda Lerman affirms Davis's origin story as the movement's 'own myth,' its bible.[48] It is biblical, Lerman clarifies, not because it is entirely accurate as history – for she concedes it may be 'faulty, insufficient, wrong,' and 'incomplete' – but because it 'uplifted, inspired, and brought light.' In short, it was empowering and thus politically useful.

## 2. The Emergence of Radical Feminism

To understand just how empowering and useful the myth of the lost matriarchy was to feminism at this point in its development, it is first necessary to achieve a sense of why radical feminists were drawn to origins. The answer to this question is related to the rise, and nature, of radical feminism as a movement. As we examine this history, it becomes evident that the origins focus of radical feminism is a logical outcome of women's experiences in the civil rights movement and the New Left. Indeed, radical feminism is built on the premise of getting to the root of women's oppression, a goal that overtly prioritizes the need for a theory of origins.

Most of the women who would create the radical feminist movement received their political education and experience in the civil rights movement.[49] Indeed, it would be fair to say that the entire northern student movement learned the skills of political activism and analysis from the civil rights movement. Participating en masse in the activities of the Student Nonviolent Coordinating Committee (SNCC), northern and southern students alike began 'to see the south through the eyes of the poorest blacks.'[50] The movement organized the 1964 Freedom Summer, a mass voter-registration campaign in which many whites actively participated. Student activists, while 'putting their bodies on the line,'[51] were aware that the danger and violence they encountered was a pale reflection of that facing southern blacks. Nevertheless, those involved with SNCC were inspired by its idealism in the face of racist hatred and violence, by its radically egalitarian principles of organization, and by its commitment to grass-roots politics. To all who participated, especially in contrast to the hostile political climate of the south, the movement was the 'beloved community.'[52]

By most accounts, women and men participated in the civil rights movement on a roughly equal level.[53] In particular, black women of SNCC held positions of power and were involved in the decision-making process of the committee's inner circle. White women participated in the voter-registration drives and demonstrations, and went to jail alongside the men. At the same time, however, both black and white women were aware that most of the SNCC leadership was male, and that attitudes about women's position in society were not as progressive as they could be. There was a brief moment, in fact, during which these women 'shared a feminist response to the position of women in SNCC,' but, as Sara Evans explains, they lacked the solidarity and trust to extend their shared observations into anything deeper.[54] It is significant to note that while relations between white and black women were by no means idyllic – and in fact they were strained further by the sexual relationships that sprouted between white women and black men – black women activists were role models to white women in the organization, who could find no comparable models in American society at large.

White women's participation in SNCC ended in 1965, but not by their own choice. By this point, SNCC had turned irreversibly toward Black Power and away from the idea of a 'beloved community' in which all, including whites, could participate. As black activists focused on defining the movement for themselves, white activism within SNCC was discouraged. This transformation within SNCC had a disillusioning effect on many of the white women who had devoted years to the civil rights movement.[55] Mary King, for example, remembers the disappointment she felt at the shift, claiming to be most affected by 'the way that the Black women turned against me.'[56] Carol Hanisch similarly recalls that, while she understood the incentive for Black Power, it was nonetheless difficult to face the fact that she 'really didn't belong in that struggle anymore.'[57] Nevertheless, white women departed the civil rights movement equipped with organizing skills, an appreciation for non-hierarchical decision-making, and a sense of what political solidarity could look like. Perhaps even more importantly, the civil rights movement taught women the necessity of rediscovering and reclaiming their own history, of getting to the root cause of oppression. Although they did not act upon it immediately, the significance of that lesson was not lost on them.

Upon returning to the north, many of the women activists became involved in student movements such as the Northern Student Movement, and particularly in Students for a Democratic Society (SDS). But these New Left organizations offered a very different experience for women; whereas the civil rights movement had women organizers, SDS did not. SDS, committed to achieving a total analysis of class oppression in America, was an inwardly focused, cerebral, and intellectually competitive movement. Of course, the movement was also directed toward action; 'action was the core of the movement's identity,' according to former SDS president Todd Gitlin.[58] Certainly women participated in the demonstrations, the occupation of the Columbia campus, the anti-war marches, and the national student conferences and were members of the newspaper collectives. But their participation was at a different level from that of men. When it came to policy formulation and decision-making, women were excluded for the most part. A sexual division of labour, which women in radical movements had already rejected in the larger society, prevailed within SDS and the New Left in general. Active in the National Mobilization Committee to End the War in Vietnam, Leslie Cagan was relegated to 'mimeoing,' addressing, and mailing, 'while the men would sit in one of the offices making the decisions.'[59] As the New York Radical Women later remarked, 'Even within the radical movement we are relegated to service: typing, mailing, and food preparation, with sexual service on the side.'[60]

Not only were women assigned to housekeeping and caretaking tasks and excluded from decision-making, their attempts to generate a critique of this contradiction were met with outright hostility.[61] This hostility and antagonism toward 'chicklib,' as SDS'er Mark Rudd called it, was extensive and acted as a catalyst to the development of radical feminism. Certain events in particular pushed radical women away from the left and toward their own movement. One such event occurred at the 1967 National Conference for New Politics (NCNP) in Chicago. The NCNP, a meeting of 2000 activists from all over the United States, was intended to unite the movement. As Alice Echols explains, one of the key issues for the movement at this convention was Black Power and the relationship between white and black activists; the black caucus made several demands of the delegation, including that Blacks receive 50 per cent representation on each of the committees, and a 50 per cent share of the convention vote.[62] White delegates conceded this demand as well as others, although this ultimately generated little in the way of the desired consensus.

Demands made by women who had drafted a resolution for presentation to the NCNP were treated rather differently.[63] The women, in fact, could not even get their resolution on the agenda for discussion, but were encouraged to draft a new resolution with another group of women who had already submitted one. Although they complied, the content of the second, reformed resolution did not reflect the essence of the original, a fact that enraged Ti-Grace Atkinson and Shulamith Firestone, who were involved in drafting the original. Atkinson and Firestone drafted yet another resolution, which demanded among other things that women receive 51 per cent of the votes. After threatening to tie up the entire convention, the two were successful in getting their resolution on the agenda and proceeded to make 2000 copies for circulation. In the end, however, only the second, reformed proposal was discussed while Atkinson and Firestone's resolution was ignored. Jo Freeman later reported that, following the rebuff, the chair of the conference proceeded to pat 'Shulie on the head,' saying 'Move on little girl; we have more important issues to talk about here than women's liberation.' According to Freeman, 'That was the genesis.'[64] And so it was: the first autonomous women's liberation group was founded a week later in Chicago.

For a time, radical women continued to work within the left, some within women's caucuses, which Firestone named 'Ladies' auxiliaries of the Left.'[65] Although SDS put together their 'SDS National Resolution on Women,' in which they acknowledged that women endure a 'qualitatively different kind of oppression which they experience as women in addition to the exploitation of all working people,' the situation changed very little for women in SDS and other radical groups.[66] This fact is made evident in the infamous 1969 counter-inaugural demonstration incident. SDS activist Marilyn Webb took the stage to speak about women's liberation only to be interrupted by male calls to '[t]ake her off the stage and fuck her!'[67] No reproach was made by male activists; rather, the women were told by the organizers that they were going to cause a riot if they did not cease speaking.[68] It is interesting to note that Webb had been among a group of SDS women arguing *against* a separate women's liberation movement, an argument she retracted following this experience. A short time later, Shulamith Firestone, who admonished the men at the demonstration for their behaviour, wrote a response to the incident in the *Guardian*. In her words,

> We say to the left: in this past decade you have failed to live up to your rhetoric of revolution ... Women's liberation is dynamite. And we have more important things to do than to try to get you to come around ... The message being: Fuck off, left. You can examine your navel by yourself from now on. We're starting our own movement.[69]

This tension between the New Left and radical women was an important incentive to the feminist turn to origin narratives. Put simply, *the hostility felt by radical feminists toward the left cannot be overstated.* From a feminist perspective, movement men embodied an insidious contradiction in fighting for liberation while living out a bourgeois existence vis-à-vis both their sexual and political relationships with movement women. That they refused to take action to resolve this contradiction, that they wilfully mocked and baited the women who challenged them, only added fuel to the fire. By the time the counter-inaugural incident occurred, radical women had already successfully carried out the Miss America protest,[70] and they were already developing a new confidence in their own political skills. Their experiences in the civil rights movement and the New Left had given them a new awareness of their own abilities, even as it relegated them to menial tasks. As Evans explains, the feminist movement 'was born in that contradiction – the threatened loss of new possibility.'[71]

It is in this context that the Women's Liberation Movement came into being. And it is also in this context that radical feminists turned to narratives of origins to justify and augment their separatist politics. Yet their turn to origin narratives was more than a reaction *against* the larger movement; it was also a direct consequence of their experiences in the broader movement. As much as the emergent radical feminist movement was premised on rejection of the sexism of the civil rights and New Left movements, it also took crucial lessons from both. Radical women in the civil rights movement witnessed the reclamation of black history and the search for the roots of racial oppression. They too perceived a need to get to the root of their own oppression. The analogy of racial oppression was to become a fruitful one for feminists, as we saw in Davis's call for women to learn their own history just as Blacks were learning theirs. Civil rights activists, feminists, and SDS'ers all adhered to the view that a strategy for change requires a theory about the nature and origin of the problem. For the civil rights movement, oppression had an identifiable beginning – slavery – if not an obvious solution. Similarly for the New Left, the root cause of oppression was capitalism, the rise and history of which was knowable. Not so, however, for women, who, as I have already pointed out, were unable to draw on a readily available history of their oppression. Up to the point of the formation of the radical feminist movement, radical women had been convinced that the primary source of their oppression was American capitalist, racist society. When they turned their energies to foment a feminist revolution, they also had to name the cause, hence the origin, of their subordination to men.[72] Shulamith Firestone was the first to revive the word patriarchy to connote the system that oppressed women, but it would be other radical feminists who would hypothesize its origins.

As much as radical feminists borrowed from the civil rights movement, they also appropriated from the left the distinction between reform and radical change. This new stream of feminists used the word radical deliberately. 'I call myself a radical feminist, and that means specific things to me,' writes Robin Morgan. 'The etymology of the word "radical" refers to "one who goes to the root."'[73] Radical feminists were also led to the quest for the origins of patriarchy by their rejection of the reform agenda that they associated with the National Organization for Women (NOW) and liberal feminism. In the period of the late 1960s and early 1970s all feminists, liberal and radical, were preoccupied with socialization patterns, with the reproduction of patriarchal ideas and attitudes among new generations of women and men. All feminists focused a keen eye on advertising, media, political rhetoric, literature, and anything else that portrayed women as passive, feminine, sexual objects. The formation of NOW and the Kennedy

Commission on Women both contributed to the creation of a climate in which it was again acceptable to articulate women's concerns. Yet what differentiated radical feminists, what made them a completely different breed of activist, was their emergence out of the student movement. From SDS and the broader movement they absorbed the significance of the difference between reform and revolution, and they viewed anything short of revolution as a failure. While they still focused on the question of socialization, radical feminists also theorized that the source of women's oppression must lie in a deeper, structural relation between the sexes, and that reforms that were aimed at minimizing oppression would not uncover its root cause.

### 3. 'Goodbye to All That': The Politics of Origins

In the foregoing I suggest that the origins impulse is implicit in the defining ideas of radical feminism, as theorizing the structural configuration of patriarchy led naturally to the question of its beginnings. As several feminists openly concede, however, the stories formulated about patriarchy's beginnings may not rest in a firm historical foundation. So why rely on an origin story at all? Recall Lerman's eulogy to Elizabeth Gould Davis, in which she presciently alludes to the utility of *The First Sex*. Radical feminists began to invent a story of women's past that would be useful to them politically, a story that would be 'adequate to their needs.' For the purposes of illustrating the close relationship between origin stories and politics in the women's liberation movement, I have chosen a small case study. There are few feminist works that highlight the value of the origins discourse to an emerging movement, that demonstrate the connection between the use of origin narratives and the radical feminist rejection of the left, as clearly as those of Robin Morgan and Jane Alpert.

Their life stories intertwined, Morgan and Alpert were friends and political allies. They are both notorious for their vehement rejections of the left, and they also shared the view that an ancient gynocracy had once existed. Although it was Alpert who wrote a short origin narrative in the form of an essay, 'Mother Right: A New Feminist Theory,' Morgan was her informal editor for the piece before it was submitted and published in *Ms*. Moreover, Morgan's own work, including her poetry and political tracts, is infused with the language of origins and matriarchy. Of course, the ideas put forward by Alpert and Morgan did not go uncontested in the Women's Liberation Movement: in particular, Alpert's piece served to polarize feminist debate on the question of the matriarchy.

Morgan and Alpert worked together at *Rat*, one of the many 'subterranean' newspapers of the left. They were among the group of radical women in the editorial collective who seized control of the paper in 1970. Before the takeover, *Rat*, like so many underground papers, took a less-than-enlightened view of women and feminism. In fact, *Rat*'s line seemed to be that women's liberation was a bourgeois concern only, that it was part of the problem rather than the solution. As Morgan stated in a 1969 interview with the *New York Times Magazine*, by the left's standards, 'a liberated woman was someone who was indiscriminate about whom she sleeps with'; there was little recognition that 'women don't want to be objects.'[74] Drawings, stories, and poetry in *Rat* and the other papers verged on the pornographic, representing what Tom Hayden called the 'hip version of the morality of the dirty old man.'[75] But *Rat*'s days as a pornographic paper were numbered, for Morgan and Alpert and the new editorial collective published their own feminist version following the takeover.

By far the most important article that ran in the first feminist edition of *Rat* was Morgan's landmark diatribe against the left, 'Goodbye to All That.' Drawing on countless examples of male sexism and outright misogyny, Morgan admonishes, and finally dismisses, the left for its irrelevance to the feminist struggle. A professional writer, Morgan summons powerful rhetoric to legitimate her political transformation. Throughout she repeats her wish to get to the bottom of the problem, to 'run it on down,' claiming that a revolution led by white male radicals is hardly going to solve the problem, since they too are implicated in the oppression of women. Morgan bids goodbye to her brothers in the peace movement and the New Left, who offer nothing more than women's caucuses toward the goal of liberation; she incites women members of the Weathermen[76] to 'Left Out,' or to cease rejecting 'their own radical feminism for that last desperate grab at male approval that we all know so well.'[77] The only option, Morgan asserts, is to 'seize our own power into our own hands, all women, separate and together, and make the Revolution the way it must be made – no priorities this time, no suffering group told to wait until after.'[78] Leaving behind what she terms variously the 'counterfeit Left,' the 'counterleft,' and the 'boys movement,' Morgan calls for a real revolution, 'All the way down, this time.'[79]

What makes the piece so significant, aside from her rhetorical skill, is the fact that Morgan had tried to combat women's oppression from within the confines of the left.[80] As a member of the New York Radical Women (NYRW), and a key organizer of the Miss America protest, Morgan had been critical of sexism in the left all along, but she nonetheless continued to defend the movement against the criticisms of radical feminists who argued for total separation. When NYRW divided into subgroups, Morgan founded the politico subgroup WITCH (Women's International Terrorist Conspiracy from Hell) rather than join the radical feminist subgroup, Redstockings. As a politico group, WITCH was committed to the left's analysis of the cause of the problems in American society. Whereas Redstockings turned to consciousness-raising, WITCH turned to performing 'zap actions.'[81] Morgan's history with the left made it all the more surprising when she abandoned it outright and endorsed radical feminism; and it made her rejection that much more virulent.

Morgan's repeated call to run the analysis 'all the way down' symbolizes her commitment to get to the root and origin of women's oppression. She endorses the radical feminist view that women's oppression is the original oppression, the template for all others. Sexism, until it is uprooted, 'will continue to put forth the branches of racism, class hatred, ageism, competition, ecological disaster, and economic exploitation.'[82] She recites the need to recapture the ancient gynocracy, 'the oldest culture of all,' in which equality and peace prevailed before the rise of the 'death-dealing sexual, economic and spiritual repression of the Imperialist Phallic Society.'[83] By invoking origins, Morgan demonstrates to male leftist activists, and to the women who remain active in the left, that women's oppression is older than any other, that its longevity and severity requires separate political organizing. Her intent is to foment a mass-based, feminist revolution, the consequences of which will be far greater than any revolution brought forth by the 'boy's movement.'

That origins imperative, latent in 'Goodbye to All That,' comes to the surface in Morgan's other work. In her writings as well as her many public speeches, Morgan combined her criticism of the left[84] with discussion of the lost matriarchy,[85] the Goddess religion, and the age-old persecution of women. She admits to having been profoundly influenced by both Davis and Diner[86] and recommends their work to other feminists. Like others, Morgan admits that these works are somewhat flawed but still 'indispensable.'[87] She is self-critical in *Going Too Far* of her devotion to the left and of zap actions, lamenting that WITCH 'always *meant* to do the real research' on witches, matriarchy, and the Goddess faith.[88] She developed something akin to a religious faith centred on the Goddess and, in the process, glorified the female role in reproduction. To honour the Goddess, she invented a new religious ritual of symbolically drinking menstrual blood.[89] She concluded one famous speech with the request that the participants join hands to recite an initiation chant from her WITCH coven to the Goddess, who has 'been with thee from the beginning.'[90]

In Morgan's rendering, radical feminist activism became a matter of life and death: nothing short of a gynocidal war awaits women. The mass murder of women, and especially of those whom she calls witches, is a recurring theme in Morgan's writing. Witch history is part of women's 'entombed history, a remnant of the Old Religion which pre-dated all patriarchal faiths and which was a Goddess-worshipping matriarchal faith.'[91] Identifying with witches reconnects women with their history and with the worship of the Goddess, but it also constructs a story of their brutal victimization. In a speech at the University of Maryland, Morgan called upon women to initiate a militant struggle against the 'primary contradiction' – sex – because the risks to women who identify with feminism are increasing. 'Women used to risk losing friends, maybe a job; now they are risking losing their children and losing their lives.'[92] The focus on mass victimization is made particularly clear in Morgan's famous poem 'The Network of the Imaginary Mother,'[93] in which she lists the names of women who were hanged or burned in the Burning Times. Each section of the poem concludes with some version of the same question, 'What have they done to us?'

While Morgan was spreading the radical feminist message across the country, Alpert was living underground to escape the charge of conspiracy for a Manhattan bombing. As a member of the Weather Underground, Alpert was a self-described militant leftist whose primary commitment had been to violent 'actions' against the capitalist state, but she had been introduced to feminism while at *Rat*. After living underground in isolation from the Weathermen and women, and after attending regular sessions of a radical feminist consciousness-raising group, Alpert too began to question her participation in left organizations.[94] She wrote a short origin story entitled 'Mother Right: Toward a New Feminist Theory,' which addressed the tension between radical women who wanted to retain ties to the left and those who wanted to sever those ties.[95] Alpert's strategy to convince women to follow her path comes to light in the two parts of her essay. The first part is both a virulent critique of male politics and a personal attack on her former partner, Sam Melville, who also had participated in the bombing. During Alpert's time underground, Melville was killed in the Attica prison uprising of 1971. While the Weather Underground as a whole mourned the victims of Attica and protested their murder, Alpert admonished her sisters for sending her letters and clippings on the subject. 'You fast and organize and demonstrate for Attica,' she writes. 'I will mourn the loss of 42 male supremacists no longer.'[96] Separating herself from the women in the Underground, she exclaims: 'As long as you are working politically with men, as long as you are letting men define your attitudes, behavior, and standards, then we stand on opposite sides of a line.'[97]

The second section of 'Mother Right' pieces together the skeleton of an origin story. Here she asserts her position that 'female biology is the basis of women's powers.'[98] Unlike feminists such as Firestone who see female biology as an obstacle to be overcome, Alpert argues that in biology lies the source of the feminist revolution. She insists that female biology is powerful whether or not a woman ever actually gives birth to a child. On a historical level, Alpert is persuaded by the theory that ancient gynocracies and Amazons once existed. She is influenced by a copy of *The First Sex* given to her by Morgan, and affirms the text as 'visionary' despite its being 'somewhat factually problematic.'[99] Radical feminism, in Alpert's rendering, is not narrowly 'political,' but is rather 'closely tied to theories of awakening consciousness, of creation and rebirth, and of the essential oneness of the universe – teachings which lie at the heart of all Goddess-worshipping religions.'[100] A feminist revolution must recreate the conditions of matriarchy – whether or not it ever existed historically – and put an end to all forms of oppression.

In assessing the political rhetoric of Morgan and Alpert, it is essential to recognize that they do not simply turn to spirituality from politics, as might be assumed by their interest in goddess worship. Rather, their turn to the theory of primordial matriarchy is deeply political and directed toward the achievement of specific feminist goals. In the writings of Morgan and Alpert, the connection between origin stories and politics is laid bare. The language of an originary matriarchy did political work for feminism, facilitating the development of the movement's autonomy. Alpert, like so many feminists during this period, legitimates a separatist politics for feminism. 'I urge women to leave the left and leftist causes and begin working for women, for ourselves.'[101] In other words, it is against the left that women can join together and fight the feminist cause. Other radical feminists, like Ellen Willis, sought the same end, arguing that women's struggle was not secondary, that feminism would not take a back seat to any other movement, and that one does not get radical fighting other people's battles.[102] The more feminists used the language of 'foundational oppression' and the 'primary contradiction' of sex, the more feminism was legitimated as an autonomous movement, apart from the broader movement. As in the political theory of Plato and Hobbes, the origin story in feminism was seductive, politically appealing, and highly persuasive. Whereas Plato and Hobbes desired to influence their contemporaries, to convert them to a different way of thinking about politics and power, radical feminists were building a political movement, and the origin story was seductive to those coming to feminism for the first time, or to those who were dissatisfied with the movement as a whole. The central problem with both Morgan's and Alpert's work is that, in asserting the need to discover the roots of patriarchy, they revert to an ahistorical, unsubstantiated, mythical story. That feminists commonly acknowledged the flaws in the matriarchal theory, but continued to use it nevertheless, confirms again the political utility of the origin story for feminism.

In addition, the origin story is a normative and prescriptive script of citizenship for radical feminists, offering an imagined past as a justification for a more meaningful and woman-affirming future. If matriarchy is a true stage in human history, the door is open for a feminist revolution and the recreation of matriarchy. Alpert calls for the reversion to, and resumption of, matriarchal principles, asking her readers, 'Do we dare demand less?' Recall that Davis too desired a matriarchal counter-revolution to end the masculine cycles of destruction. But what exactly did matriarchy prescribe? For one thing, a more peaceful society, one in which women held political and spiritual power. Religion was intrinsic to life, in Alpert's description, such that women could not be worshipped as deities yet simultaneously be devalued in practice. No 'sharp division' existed between life in the domestic sphere and social life, and women were integral to both.[103]

In linking past and future, feminists found models and justifications for radically egalitarian, non-hierarchical organizations and political groups. While the left paid lip service to such a model, radical feminists enacted these principles, adopting consensus as the only route to decision-making. Such an emphasis was placed on consensus that radical feminist groups were bogged down in their meetings; they were slow to take decisions; and many feminists experienced exhaustion and burn-out as a result. In keeping with the ideal of leaderless groups, radical feminists also curtailed the activities of those among them who were skilled speakers and writers, preventing them from making public appearances and speeches, lest other members of the group not be given due credit. Many feminists later viewed these strategies as significantly flawed for suppressing women's different abilities and strengths.

To the extent that radical feminism was also about creating a new self-image for women, origin stories assisted by offering a glorified image of woman on which a new identity could be based. Memorialized by Davis and others as strong, independent, nurturing, life-centred, and mothering, matriarchal and Amazon women provide a normative model of womanhood. And those who adhered to the matriarchal theory often explicitly acknowledge their search for a new identity, as Alpert did:

> [F]eminist culture is based on what is best and strongest in women, and as we begin to define ourselves as women, the qualities coming to the fore are the same ones a mother projects in the best kind of nurturing relationship to a child: empathy, intuitiveness, adaptability, awareness of growth as a process rather than as goal-ended, inventiveness, protective feelings toward others, and a capacity to respond emotionally as well as rationally.[104]

The suggestion seems to be that women have a true identity that has been corrupted by patriarchal society and needs only to be rediscovered. On the one hand, radical feminists seek to value women as women, to affirm their qualities rather than accepting the male view of them. On the other hand, however, the new identity being forged has little to do with past matriarchy, but is rather a construction, one which is then read back into the past and sanctified for the future.

Up to this point, we have assessed the prevalence of origin stories, and enumerated their political uses for radical feminism. I am suggesting that it is important to understand the reasons underlying the feminist use of origin stories, to understand their immense political value to an emerging radical feminist movement seeking to 'trump' the male left and caught up in the process of self-definition and invention.

150  Origin Stories in Political Thought

While the feminist turn to origins makes sense in this context, the origin stories themselves are rife with contradictions and problems.

## 4. The Perils of Inventing a Past

'Mother Right' proved, in the end, to be a highly divisive piece, bringing to the forefront the latent tensions within radical feminism regarding the theory of the matriarchy. Alpert elicited a polarized response: feminists either found the piece empowering and uplifting or specious and reactionary.[105] The critiques raised by Alpert's opponents underscore the larger problems in the radical feminist origins discourse. My intent here is not to dissect each origin story to reveal its logical flaws, but rather to draw out the historical, ontological, and political problems common to the stories. In historical terms, these stories combine a faulty historical methodology with inaccurate and fanciful assessments of the past. They also manipulate biology in such a way as to invert an already-problematic Aristotelian ontology. Finally, the political result of the origins discourse was not to promote mass support of feminism – as was intended – but to undermine and divide the movement.

As much as origin stories assisted in the legitimation of the Women's Liberation Movement, they also relied on a fundamental misperception about history: that myth and history are nearly synonymous. In Davis's analysis we witnessed a heavy reliance on myth as a source of historical information; but for Davis, as for Bachofen and other matriarchal theorists, that relationship is conceived in an all-too-simplistic fashion. While historians of ancient societies study myth for the historical information it can reveal, they recognize the inherent limitations of such an approach and use caution when making generalizations about their subject. Myth is a complex composite of history, politics, and fantasy; but this should not lead us to the altogether different conclusion that the ultimate truth about a bygone age is crystallized within it or that it is a straightforward repository of historical information.[106] Davis assumes that the existence of powerful queens in a particular age indicates a contemporaneous matriarchal political structure. Sarah Pomeroy undermines this logic by asking whether the reigns of Mary Stuart, Mary Tudor, and Elizabeth I will connote the existence of matriarchy to future historians.[107] Ultimately Davis grounds too many of her claims about the past gynocracy in this reductionist and simplistic view of history, and those who use Davis inevitably import her errors into their analyses.

Aside from the methodological errors implicit in this understanding of history are the substantive errors in content. The question of whether there existed matriarchies or Amazons remains unanswered, and is perhaps unanswerable. To the best of historians' current knowledge, the Amazons did not exist but were rather a fantasy of the Greek imagination.[108] Moreover, they were a fantasy that served a particular purpose for their creators; they were used as a counterpoint to ancient Greek society to show the normalcy and the logic of patriarchal arrangements. It is to this end that Hobbes's contemporaries revived the Amazon myth as a political and literary tool. Hobbes, as I have shown, inverted this use of the Amazons and lauded their independence and power, but he was drawn to them as an example for the same reasons that his opponents were: to service an immediate political goal. The examples of the Greeks and of Hobbes should remind us that the Amazons are always invoked for specific political reasons. Feminist use of Amazons is no different, despite the apologies made toward reclaiming women's past. While the value of learning women's history is unquestionable, these feminists invoke the Amazons and matriarchy to recast history in a more favourable light for women, to summon an Amazon identity for women, and, in effect, to create a feminist script of citizenship. That their interest in history is subordinate to their political interests is evident from their hostility to those who discredit their thesis.

Any attempt to question the validity of this feminist myth/history is cast as a patriarchal attack, even if the questions come from feminist scholars in the relevant fields of history, archaeology, and anthropology. One feminist mocks the 'rigorous rules of research' that guide male academics, and credits the 'Amazon dream/reality' for removing women 'from the context of having only Victim images.'[109] In her assessment of the matriarchy theory, Leah Zahler echoes this sentiment: '[T]he important question ... is not the historicity of matriarchy but our feelings about it.' She explains that the 'idea of matriarchy helps establish a sense of community among women, a shared culture,' and we ought, therefore, to turn away from the question of its veracity and toward the discovery of what it can do for feminism.[110] In an academic exchange between Merlin Stone, the author of *When God Was a Woman*, and Sally Binford, a feminist anthropologist, on the question of matriarchy and Goddess worship, Stone proclaims that 'entering into a discussion about whether or not ancient Goddess worship existed ... is much like inviting us into a discussion of whether or not World War II actually occurred.'[111] For her part, Binford is 'persuaded that logic, reason, and arguments based on knowledge of the data cut no ice at all' with believers in the matriarchy. As an anthropologist, Binford finds herself fascinated by the tenacity with which women cling to this belief, and she 'can explain it only as a religious phenomenon.'[112] This is undoubtedly true about goddess worship per se. Yet feminist myth/history is not just spiritual; it is explicitly political in its wilful defiance of evidence, in its refusal of historicity.

The underlying assumption of Morgan, like Pateman and others, is that without a dramatic story of victimization – original rape, mass slaughter of witches, or a worldwide historical conquest of women – feminism is not justified. Something akin to a holocaust of women, as Purkiss has named it, is the political prerequisite for a legitimate feminist movement, because only something that dramatic could provide the clear political oppositions that feminism needs. Only something that dramatic could create the unequivocal script of citizenship required to draw women into the movement. If women were harmed en masse in the past, then, the logic goes, knowledge of that harm could form the basis of a united opposition against their oppressor. Here we see the value of origin story as political rhetoric, and the choice to proliferate rhetoric about women's common historical bond at the expense of historical accuracy.

As well, the existence of an ancient matriarchy is posited as the historical precedent for the liberation of women in this century. Yet as Hobbes understood clearly, history cannot be the determinant of the future. Empowering as the notion of matriarchy might appear to be, it 'would weaken us if it was based on only illusion.'[113] Indeed, as one feminist argues in response to Alpert's piece, history, and the study of the past, cannot 'reveal a blueprint for the future.' In Ti-Grace Atkinson's view, by invoking a matriarchal past feminists like Alpert 'reveal a doubt' by 'searching for proof that women can fulfill their humanity. We should not need proof.'[114]

In defence of matriarchal theory, however, Judy Antonelli suggests that women are not seeking proof; rather they are gaining their 'heritage, something every oppressed group must do. We are building a future by discovering our past, a past which has been consciously suppressed by men to keep themselves in power.'[115] It would seem that Antonelli, like feminists who participate in the origins discourse, confuses the process of 'discovering' women's history – which is as she says vital to any oppressed group – with the practice of inventing a past. The distinction between the two, *discovering* and *inventing*, is lost in the feminist origins discourse.

Historical problems that surface in the origins discourse are matched by problems of flawed biological analysis. Deeply skewed and unsubstantiated genetic theories attesting to the primacy of the X chromosome underlie Davis's theory that women are the primary beings of the human species. Like Aristotle and other male theorists who search for a biological justification for what are social and political hierarchies, Davis (and thus those who build on her work) 'advance' the political goals of matriarchal feminism through the use of biological theories that verge on the absurd. Nor should we underestimate the influence that Davis and those like her held over feminists. Even feminists who did not support Alpert's 'Mother Right' assert uncritically that 'the female is most likely biologically superior to the male,'[116] or that woman's body 'is the more creative.'[117] Rosalind Miles reiterates Davis's theories in her 1981 origin story entitled *The Women's History of the World*. Miles supplements Davis's hypothesis of the originary status of women with the paleoanthropological discovery that human beings are descended from a single female living in Africa a couple of hundred thousand years ago. This female has been named Eve and is thought to carry the gene-print of the entire human species.

While it is true that Eve is an important piece of the puzzle that is our genetic past, what follows from this assertion is not entirely clear. For Miles, the ramifications of this discovery are feminist and political. Eve, who 'could have been our grandmother,' substantiates her theory that woman is the 'original, the first sex,' and man is a 'biological afterthought' deriving from a 'genetic error.' According to Miles, Eve's discovery is confirmation that *'femaleness is the norm, the fundamental form of life.'*[118] The idea here seems to be that if woman is primary, feminism is justified as a movement. I suggest, alternatively, that there is no obvious political implication stemming from Eve's discovery and, moreover, that feminists must exercise caution when attempting to read political implications from paleoanthropological discoveries. If research had not led to Eve's discovery, would feminism have no justification, no legitimacy?

Radical feminists who assert female primacy and superiority fail to recognize that they are merely inverting the language of Aristotle. How else are we to read statements that the Y chromosome, and therefore maleness, developed as a genetic mutation? Or that women alone hold the key to the destiny of the human race? The message is that women are the biological norm from which men are only a deviation.[119] Because these statements are based on incorrect biology, we can only conclude that they are overtly political. If we are to be critical, as feminists, of ancient political theorists who universalize the traits of *one sex* as *human* traits, and who find the 'opposite' sex deficient in these traits and thus in humanity, we should not make an exception for feminists who merely invert the sexes and retain the same universalizing, phallocentric language.

Indeed, one of the central problems with all of the feminist origin stories is their uncritical celebration of women's biology. Davis and Alpert both generate a new ontological argument about the sexes and reproduction. In contrast to phallocentric ontology, this feminist ontology establishes women's consciousness as a product of their reproductive capacity, regardless of whether they have children or not. In this view, there appears to be a singular experience of being a woman that is determined by biology. All women are by nature nurturing, good, life-giving beings. The key to creating a better polity is to restore women to power, and by virtue of their different ontology, peace would be achieved. Biology, then, is presented as both the source of women's superiority and the cause of their oppression.

In reverting to an ontological argument, feminists must face the unfortunate consequence of turning the oppression of women into biological destiny, for it is men's envy of women's biological power that causes them to create the structures of patriarchy in the first place. On this point, recall Mary O'Brien's theory of masculine envy and appropriation. O'Brien articulated most clearly the view to which Davis and her followers adhere, which is that the only 'safe' period for women occurred before knowledge of men's reproductive contribution. Once man learned of his importance in the process, woman's fate was sealed. This argument turns on two disputable points: the first is that there was a stage in human history in which no one understood the process of conception; the second is that women's reproductive power is superior to that of men and thus worthy of envy. With respect to the first point, the belief that men were once ignorant of their contribution to reproduction is unconfirmed. Brian Hayden has argued that 'it is naive to believe that groups intelligent enough to invent language,' were not intelligent enough to 'make the association between sex and reproduction.'[120] If they were not ignorant, then the thesis that men worshipped women for their parthenogenetic reproductive power is erroneous.

As to the second point, we have already recounted the problems associated with the envy-appropriation thesis in the discussion of Plato. In that discussion, O'Brien's theory of masculine envy and appropriation was found lacking because it rests on a political value judgment about women's biological superiority rather than an objective, biological truth. I argue that Plato's glorification of reproduction and birth should be interpreted, not as an instantiation of his envy of woman's actual power, but as a masculine fabrication. To argue differently is to imply that differences between men and women are ontological and originate in reproductive biology. Indeed, O'Brien implies that women's reproductive role is superior, and that men know it is superior. She wants to suggest that women's biology has some inherent meaning – always the same, always powerful and awe-inspiring – yet this idea works against her other claim that reproduction and birth are not merely physical processes, but are also thinking processes. If reproduction and birth are more than base biological functions, if they are mediated by woman's consciousness, how can we argue that they have a constant, unchanging meaning? Would not the meaning of reproduction and birth vary in accordance with historical and cultural context? By arguing, as O'Brien, Davis, and others do, that woman has an enviable, all-powerful role in reproduction, we would be committing ourselves to the view that hierarchical gender relations are inevitable, that their cause lies in unchangeable facts of nature rather than in power and politics. This kind of argument is untenable and it has the effect of rendering political struggle irrelevant.

Indeed, feminist origin stories occupy a difficult political space, inspiring at one and the same time a brand of feminist nationalism and a de-politicized, feminist spirituality. Because they are used normatively, origin stories are told with an eye to the restoration of female rule, the resumption of gynocracy after 5000 years of patriarchy. Ti-Grace Atkinson, following her rejection of radical feminism, criticized the matriarchy camp for a 'reactionary nationalism' in which the power structure is revised but not ultimately challenged.[121] Women are meant to view themselves and their past through the lens of the feminist origin story and to use it as the basis for action – as a script that identifies women's primacy, not only in this political struggle, but in life. While radical feminists undoubtedly had created a dramatic origin story, as a basis for action it remains troublesome. Origin stories tend to portray women as a class, the class that experiences the most pervasive and detrimental kind of oppression. The origins discourse encouraged radical feminists to adopt and then invert the left's line on foundational oppression; Morgan, in Todd Gitlin's analysis, 'offered a recycled version of the Left's hierarchy of suffering.'[122]

While radical feminists made an important advance in bringing women's oppression to the forefront of politics, the language of foundational oppression ultimately undermined the cause of radical feminism by alienating those who experienced more than one kind of oppression. Hence the current conversation in feminism about diversity and differences among women. In this sense, the feminist origins discourse, by opting for the uncomplicated story of conquest to galvanize support and thus suppressing the messiness of actual oppression, did more to derail attempts to find meaningful political solutions to the problems women faced.

As overtly political as this feminist brand of nationalism appears to be, Morgan, Alpert, Davis, and others portray the feminist revolution as beyond the political, as something more than a political shift. In Morgan's writing, the revolution would resemble a 'sea-change,' equivalent to major transformations in thinking like the Reformation or the Copernican revolution. In short, the revolution that origins theorists seek is presented as less political than a class-based revolution, and thus *more significant* because of its complete transformation of patriarchal culture. This kind of thinking has the ironic consequence of producing a depoliticized reaction; greater emphasis is placed on the peaceful, cooperative aspects of goddess-worshipping societies, on lesbian and feminist separatism, and on the creation of a woman's culture, and much less emphasis is placed on political transformation.[123] Significantly, while the drive to tell origin stories is political, their effect can be to promote a feminist *evasion* of politics. As Atkinson asserts, origins thinking can lead women to 'escapism, fantasy, [and] spiritualism.'[124] It encourages individualist solutions to social problems, and turns feminists away from concrete politics toward the otherworldliness of the Goddess and spirituality.

The evasion of politics emerges in a call for separatism. As a group, The Feminists argue that Alpert's one downfall is her suggestion that men and women can live together while women work to create a matriarchal society. 'Living with men precludes actual collectivity,' they write. Living in feminist collectives is the 'physical requirement' to 'self-preservation and the building of power.'[125] According to this view, rebuilding the matriarchy is a task that women must perform alone and in isolation from all men. This separatism is fuelled as well by theorists like Morgan who depict the feminist struggle as an all-out war of women against men, who copy 'movement machismo' but replace it with 'their own version of revolutionary apocalypse.'[126] In this view, women are each other's only allies. Again, as important as it was for radical feminism to draw attention to the specificity of women's oppression and to organize separately from other movements, the intense political separatism encouraged by the movement did not bring about the desired goal of a mass solidarity.

My characterization of this strand of radical feminism should in no way lead to the conclusion that all radical feminists accepted the matriarchal theory – for we have seen that they did not. Nor was it the case that all radical feminists had become cultural feminists by the mid-1970s, as Alice Echols has suggested in *Daring to Be Bad*. If anything, the turn to origins created a profound division in the feminist movement, a division that centred on the utility of Alpert's piece, women's identity, and the direction of feminist struggle. Within radical feminism there emerged a call for a return to 'true radicalism' in the early 1970s, and among this subgroup the matriarchy theory carried virtually no weight.[127] Indeed, the reconstituted Redstockings group cited the popularity of origin stories as a primary indicator of de-radicalization. Unfortunately this point was accompanied by some outrageous claims that undermined the import of their political message.[128] Nevertheless, the new Redstockings group made an important connection between the emphasis on origins and the decline of radicalism in the feminist movement.

After the mid-1970s the fervour about origins subsided to a large extent. The reasons for this are not entirely clear, but I will offer a few suggestions to account for the decline in their popularity. First, origin stories were not as politically necessary to feminists once the movement was under way. The turn to *origin stories* was driven by a political imperative specific to the *origins* of the Second Wave radical feminist movement; once the legitimation of an autonomous feminist movement had been achieved, feminists may have felt less inclined to use these narratives. Second, feminists who continued to think in terms of origins and matriarchy tended to focus their attention on the feminist spirituality movement and later the ecofeminist movement, both logical destinations for those interested in the Goddess. These 'cultural feminist' movements were, and continue to be, harshly criticized by the now more dominant stream of feminist thought that emphasizes differences between women and women's experiences rather than women's biological and social similarities. Finally, I suggest that, in some circles at least, the debate about origins continues. At least two popular feminist books pick up the theme: Rosalind Miles's *The Women's History of the World* and Riane Eisler's *The Chalice and the Blade*.[129]

In the final analysis, given the ambiguity and historical uncertainty surrounding the rise of patriarchal social relations, it is doubtful that feminists will ever abandon entirely the question of origins. Yet, the origins impulse has proved to be an aporia for feminism. The inquiry into the origins of patriarchy, I have argued, is a logical one insofar as feminism has a commitment to understanding women's oppression. Moreover, origin stories performed a critical political function in the radical feminist movement and in the feminist movement at large. In the end, however, origins thinking worked against the discovery of viable political solutions to practical political problems and conflicts. While it would be too simple to argue that the turn to origins *caused* a significant decline in radical feminist activism by the mid-1970s, or that it alone is responsible for radical feminism's theoretical difficulties, it is nonetheless the case that an important moment of action was lost when the creation of a woman's culture became the focus of feminism. The critical edge of radical feminism – the radical momentum that feminists gathered as they moved away from the left to create the Women's Liberation Movement – was worn away in part by the fruitless search for the golden age of matriarchy.

# Conclusion

In *Amazon: A Novel*, Barbara G. Walker uses the now familiar feminist origin narrative as the basis for a story about a Black Sea Amazon named Antiope who, as a rite of passage, is forced to travel ahead in time several millennia into late-modern America. Antiope's entry into present-day America begins with her sudden and unexpected arrival by the side of a busy highway. Completely bewildered by her surroundings, and confused about how she arrived in this foreign place, Antiope is greeted almost immediately by a hostile group of young men who identify her idle (and naked) presence by the side of the road as a sexual invitation. Although she cannot understand the language they speak, she understands very well their intentions. As a trained and experienced warrior, she handily defends herself with the aid of her sword – which has made the journey in time with her – and slices three fingers off one of her aggressors' hands. Similarly bewildered and frightened by what they have encountered, the young men retaliate by shooting and wounding Antiope in the leg before they retreat in fear.

Both science fiction and social critique, *Amazon* contrasts the conditions of late modern America with those of Antiope's pre-patriarchal, matrifocal, and matrilineal society. Although rescued by a caring older woman, Diana, who nurses her back to health and eventually writes a book about her, Antiope is shocked by the differences between this world and her own. Following her violent initiation into the present, the protagonist assesses her situation: 'My pain was increased by the shock of so much strangeness, the bad air, the ugly sky, the demonic vehicles, the mindless hostility of the only other human beings I had seen.'[1] She describes how she began to 'open [her] eyes to the alien world around [her].'² Some of the surprises are technological. Her first experience in a moving car, for example, is alarming as the car 'followed, passed, or dodged around others at a horrifying rate ... At first I covered my eyes and waited for a crashing impact, but the car kept going.'³ On a different note, Antiope is amazed at both the size of modern libraries and the extent to which the youth in the culture seem to dislike the information contained within them; the people here, she concludes, starve 'their minds in the midst of a feast of knowledge such as my world could not even have imagined.'⁴

Yet Antiope is confused even more by the social and political differences between this world and her matriarchal past. In one scene, Antiope and Diana witness an abusive situation in a parking lot in which a man is threatening and bullying his wife and child. Antiope cannot resist stepping in to scare the man and defend the woman, for which Diana chastises her afterward. In response to the information that what she did was against the law, Antiope asks, 'It is not against the law for men to hit women? It is against the law for a woman to defend another woman from a man who attacks her? What kind of laws here, Diana? All laws invented by men?'⁵ Aghast at the norms of the patriarchal world she exclaims, 'In my country, women protect each other.'⁶ Later in the novel, in a television interview following the release of Diana's book about her – also called *Amazon* – Antiope is given an opportunity to explain what it was like to live in her world:

> My people did not have your beautiful lights, your tall buildings, your miraculous stores, your wonders of communication and engineering. But no woman, no child, was ever threatened with harm anywhere, at any time, in any part of my country. It would never occur to even one of our men to attack a woman or a child. It would never occur to any woman or child to fear a man. That is civilized.⁷

As an outsider to North American patriarchal society, Antiope is uniquely positioned to take the veil off our culture, to expose us to our own reality.

Walker's purpose in writing the novel is found in an admission from Antiope, who, after having experienced life in the patriarchal world, begins to see the political value of Diana's book.

> For the first time I began to see the truth in Diana's view that just providing a detailed description of a nonpatriarchal culture would give many

women in this country a new philosophy of human behavior to consider – one that they never dreamed of before because they had no models.[8]

Just as the fictional women who read the novel *Amazon* are profoundly affected, so too are real women meant to read *Amazon: A Novel* as an exercise in awakening. True, the story does borrow the plot line from the stock Second Wave feminist origin narrative, and it is at times tedious in its equation of matriarchy with good, patriarchy with evil. Indeed, the climax of the story is a confrontation between good and evil, between Antiope and a male character who attempts unsuccessfully to destroy a new temple to the Goddess. Nevertheless, by telling the story with humour and irony, Walker generates a powerful critique of contemporary gender relations. Seeing the world from Antiope's perspective, the reader is invited to stand back and marvel at the absurdities of patriarchal social relations – to 'open [her] eyes to the alien world' around her.

The all-important difference between Walker's *Amazon* and the origin stories under consideration here is the form or genre in which they are told. *Amazon* is fiction; it does not pretend to be anything else. As such it can offer us an imaginative opportunity – it can open us up to think new thoughts about the possibilities of non-patriarchal social relationships. It uses the myth of a pre-patriarchal past, and the idea of origins, to entreat us to ask thoughtful questions such as 'How has violence against women become so normalized in our culture?' or 'What if patriarchal social relations are not inevitable?' Effective social critique ought to move us in exactly this way; it ought to inspire us to think new thoughts and to ask new questions. To the extent that literature and art have the potential to fulfil this role, we cannot deny their significance in politics. As Martha Nussbaum has pointed out, the narrative imagination is essential to arriving at mutual citizen understanding. Literature can awaken us; it can generate awareness and empathy; and it can provoke.

At the end of the day we have to be able to assess what sorts of stories contribute to a mutual citizen understanding and what kinds of stories impede us. I have argued that origin stories, while they are often motivated by the desire to think outside the prevailing political framework, take us to a different and less opportune place. Again, this is not to say that these are not compelling stories. Plato, Hobbes, and the feminist thinkers all developed very compelling stories indeed, stories that undoubtedly served both a heuristic and a political purpose.

At the same time, however, these stories have a way of limiting our thinking, of narrowing our perspectives, precisely because they presuppose a belief in essences, original orders, and primordial truths. They deny the complexity and the messiness of politics as a strategy to galvanize support. While Walker's *Amazon* also presents a one-dimensional picture of the patriarchal world, it is not being offered as the cornerstone to a political program. It can take liberties and opt for simplicity without ultimately undermining itself *because* it is a work of fiction.

What I see in the origins discourse is a kind of political holding pattern, or the aporia of origins. While we cannot know our political origins, we are nonetheless attracted to origin stories and the vision that they offer us as a way of making sense of ourselves and our politics. We may be particularly in need of these kinds of stories in times of instability or when we perceive that dramatic change is imminent. For instance, a fear and anticipation of the millennium contributed to a revival of interest in Genesis, a revival evident at not only a religious, but also a scholarly level. The mid- to late-1990s witnessed a flurry of Genesis translations, interpretations, and commentaries.[9] When people fear change, or when they are trying to make sense of profound societal shifts, they turn to myths such as that of Genesis to help them understand their place amidst that change. Almost intuitively, people look to origin stories out of a sense that these stories can help orient them in times of uncertainty. Moreover, in late-modern North America, we are grasping to recover or revive a sense of the meaning and purpose of human life. In a world in which all that is solid melts into air, to borrow a phrase from Marx, the neat answers provided by an origin story such as Genesis can be enormously comforting. People drawn to Genesis are convinced that within its lines lies a clue about life's real significance.

This relationship between societal change and origin stories is certainly evident in the stories examined here. Each represents an attempt to grapple with and make sense of profound change. The tentative status of the Athenian polis as a form of political organization, along with what Plato perceived to be the instability of the new democratic regime, can be seen as motivating factors for Plato's entry into the origins discourse. Similarly with Hobbes, the climate of the mid-seventeenth century was deeply unstable for a theorist intent on establishing order. The Civil War, the competing political interpretations of the regime's proper configuration, the religious enthusiasts: together these sources of instability drove Hobbes to try to make better sense of politics through the use of origins. At the rise of their new movement, feminists too were pushing for, and on the cusp of, dramatic change in the makeup of human relationships and of political and social structures. Change and (perceived or real) instability inspire the turn to origins, because origin stories are unique in offering theorists an opportunity to make sense of chaos and posit political meaning and solutions. They provide a foundation.

In spite of the problems associated with them, origin stories are not likely to disappear, largely because human beings are inescapably involved in assigning meaning to their experience. In other words, what distinguishes human beings – our consciousness, our ability to think rationally as well as mythically – is also what creates this 'aboriginal human need' to speculate about our beginnings and the nature of existence. As much as human beings strive for scientific, anthropological, archaeological, and historical accounts of beginnings, it is also quite likely that even the most comprehensive scientific explanation will fail to satisfy the desire to render meaningful human origins and existence.

To take this a step further, human beings will always be involved in this process of meaning-production, of myth-making, precisely because we are afraid of the consequences of not producing meaning. Myths of origin serve as a means of evading the uncomfortable recognition that life is devoid of inherent meaning. It is on this basis that, throughout this study, I have indicated the danger in arguing the deep meaning and significance of reproduction. This is not to say that interpreting such human events is not a worthy exercise, or that we could stop doing so if we tried, but rather that we should not assume that a true and final meaning can be posited once and for all. The point is that, in creating myth, and assigning value and significance to human events and processes, we may also be avoiding the abyss of our meaninglessness.

The question we are left with is, if we make a conscious effort to turn away from origin stories, what will then serve as the foundation for politics? And more specifically, if we turn away from the drama and violence that make up the feminist origin story, can feminism proceed as a movement and a politics? Can feminism do without an origin story as its beacon? Perhaps what we can take away from this inquiry into origin stories is the recognition that there is a better, and more productive question to ask: could feminism have survived if it continued to use a simplistic origin story as a script for action? The divisions that resulted from the radical feminist turn to origins and matriarchy are evidence enough that it could not have. Indeed, what emerges from this study is the recognition that there is no one script that effectively and completely captures the complexity of women's oppression or their agency, just as there is not one script on which we can rely to meet the challenges of late capitalist liberal democracy. Nonetheless, in literature, art, and music, and most importantly in critical historical inquiry, we can nevertheless piece together the basis for an enlarged human understanding and a vibrant social critique. Thus we can find value in Walker's *Amazon* as fiction, for it uses the idea of origins to stimulate our imaginations and invite conversation without offering itself as a political origin story or a script of citizenship.

We can carve out a political vision, or multiple visions, without relying on origin stories as a foundation. We can forge new scripts of citizenship using our narrative imagination without grounding them in specious claims about our original nature. While we may not be able, nor perhaps should we try, to put an end to our curiousity about beginnings, being more critically aware and reflective about the function of origin stories and their more pernicious falsehoods and uses can only advance our search for an equitable politics.

# Notes

**1: The Origins Imperative in Political Theory**

1 Edward Said, *Beginnings: Intention and Method* (New York: Basic Books, 1975), 5.
2 Plato, *Republic* in *The Collected Dialogues of Plato Including the Letters*, ed. Edith Hamilton and Huntington Cairns (New York: Pantheon Books, 1961).
3 Arlene W. Saxonhouse, 'Myths and the Origins of Cities: Reflections on the Autochthony Theme in Euripides' Ion,' in J. Peter Euben, ed., *Greek Tragedy and Political Theory* (Berkeley: University of California Press, 1986).
4 Nicole Loraux, *The Children of Athena: Athenian Ideas about Citizenship and the Division between the Sexes*, trans. Caroline Levine (Princeton, NJ: Princeton University Press, 1993), 17.
5 Ibid.
6 David Adams Leeming with Margaret Adams Leeming, *Encyclopedia of Creation Myths* (Oxford: ABC-CLIO, 1994), vii.
7 Marie-Louise von Franz, *Creation Myths*, rev. ed. (Boston and London: Shambhala, 1995), 11.
8 See Bill Moyers, *Genesis: A Living Conversation*, ed. Betty Sue Flowers (New York: Doubleday, 1996).
9 See Barbara G. Walker, *The Woman's Dictionary of Myths and Secrets* (San Francisco: Harper & Row, 1983); Judith Plaskow, 'The Coming of Lilith,' in C.P. Christ and J. Plaskow, eds, *Womanspirit Rising: A Feminist Reader in Religion* (San Francisco: Harper & Row, 1979); Aviva Cantor Zuckoff, 'The Lilith Question,' *Lilith* 1:1 (Fall 1976). Most recently, Lilith became a pop-culture icon as a result of the women's music tour named in her honour.
10 There are other ways of reading the story of Eve in Genesis. For example, she is also interpreted by feminists to be 'the brave one in the biblical story'

(Cheris Kramarae and Paula A. Treichler, *A Feminist Dictionary* [London: Pandora, 1985], 145); and 'the most important woman character in the drama enacted in the Garden of Eden' (John A. Phillips, *Eve: The History of an Idea* [New York: Harper & Row, 1984]). Elizabeth Cady Stanton gave voice to what has become a common theme in defences of Eve when she described her as 'fearless of death if she can gain wisdom.' In other words, Eve's actions are taken as a sign not of weakness, sin, or temptation, but of inquisitiveness, curiosity, and independence. See Elizabeth Cady Stanton, *The Woman's Bible* (Boston: Northeastern University Press, 1993). For additional interpretations that do not place the missing figure of Lilith at the centre, see Elaine Pagels, *Adam, Eve, and the Serpent* (New York: Vintage, 1988); and Karen Armstrong, *In the Beginning: A New Interpretation of Genesis* (New York: Ballantine, 1996).
11 Deborah F. Sawyer, 'Wisdom, Lilith and Mothers,' chap. 8 in *Women and Religion in the First Christian Centuries* (New York: Routledge, 1996), 139.
12 Michel Foucault, 'Nietzsche, Genealogy, History,' in Paul Rabinow, ed., *The Foucault Reader* (New York: Pantheon, 1984), 78.
13 Ibid., 79.
14 Ibid., 78.
15 Roland Barthes, *Mythologies*, trans. Annette Lavers (Toronto: Paladin, 1973), 143.
16 Foucault, 'Nietzsche,' 79.
17 I explore this point further in chapter 2.
18 Hannah Arendt, *On Revolution* (New York: Viking Press, 1963), 10.
19 Bonnie Honig, 'Declarations of Independence: Arendt and Derrida on the Problem of Founding a Republic,' in Frederick M. Dolan and Thomas L. Dumm, eds, *Rhetorical Republic: Governing Representations in American Politics* (Amherst: University of Massachusetts Press, 1993), 216.
20 On money-making, see David Bedford, 'The Politics of Appetite: Plato on Money-making,' paper presented at Canadian Political Science Association meetings, Quebec City, 2001; and David Bedford and Thom Workman, 'Recalling Plato from Exile: The Pursuit of Reasoned Moderation in International Relations,' paper presented at New England Political Science Association meetings, Portland, ME, 2002.
21 Arendt, *On Revolution*, 10–11.
22 Bernard Bailyn, *On the Teaching and Writing of History: Responses to a Series of Questions*, ed. Edward Connery Lathem (Hanover, NH: Montgomery Endowment, Dartmouth College, 1994), 12.
23 Ibid.
24 Foucault, 'Nietzsche,' 81.

25 Quentin Skinner, *Reason and Rhetoric in the Philosophy of Hobbes* (New York: Cambridge University Press, 1996), p. 8.
26 Quentin Skinner, 'Meaning and Understanding in the History of Ideas,' in James Tully, ed., *Meaning and Context: Quentin Skinner and His Critics* (Princeton, NJ: Princeton University Press, 1988), 65.
27 Ibid.
28 These exceptions include Gordon Schochet, whose works in historical political thought include consideration of gender dynamics, and James Tully, whose historical analysis includes consideration of various power dynamics, most particularly those between Aboriginal nations and European immigrants to North America. See, for example, Gordon Schochet, 'The Significant Sounds of Silence: The Absence of Women from the Political Thought of Sir Robert Filmer and John Locke (or, "Why can't a woman be more like a man?"),' in Hilda L. Smith, ed., *Women Writers and the Early Modern British Political Tradition* (New York: Cambridge University Press, 1998); Schochet, 'Thomas Hobbes on the Family and the State of Nature,' *Political Science Quarterly* 82:3 (September 1967); Schochet, *Patriarchalism in Political Thought: The Authoritarian Family and Political Speculation and Attitudes Especially in Seventeenth-century England* (Oxford: Basil Blackwell, 1975); and James Tully, *Strange Multiplicity: Constitutionalism in an Age of Diversity* (New York: Cambridge University Press, 1995).
29 Vere Chappell, ed., *The Cambridge Companion to Locke* (New York: Cambridge University Press, 1994); and Tom Sorell, ed., *The Cambridge Companion to Hobbes* (New York: Cambridge University Press, 1996).
30 The defence of her exclusion from discussions in historical political thought might be that she does not make history her primary focus. Her aim is not to place Hobbes and Locke in their historical context. However, she makes claims that are substantive – and indeed radical – enough that they ought to be considered, even if to be disagreed with.
31 Examples include Susan Moller Okin, *Women in Western Political Thought* (Princeton, NJ: Princeton University Press, 1979); and the articles in Mary Lyndon Shanley and Carole Pateman, eds, *Feminist Interpretations and Political Theory* (University Park: Pennsylvania State University Press, 1991).
32 See, e.g., Wendy Brown, *States of Injury: Power and Freedom in Late Modernity* (Princeton, NJ: Princeton University Press, 1995). See also such popular 'feminist' books as Elizabeth Fox-Genovese, *'Feminism is not the story of my life': How Today's Feminist Elite Has Lost Touch with the Real Concerns of Women* (New York: Nan A. Talese, 1996); Christina Hoff Sommers, *Who Stole Feminism? How Women Have Betrayed Women* (New York: Simon &

Schuster, 1994); and Katie Roiphe, *The Morning After: Sex, Fear, and Feminism on Campus* (Boston: Little, Brown & Co., 1993).
33 Mary O'Brien, *The Politics of Reproduction* (Boston: Routledge & Kegan Paul, 1981), 8; italics in original.
34 Ibid., 131.
35 See Mary O'Brien, *Reproducing the World: Essays in Feminist Theory* (Boulder, CO: Westview Press, 1989).
36 Laura M. Purdy, *Reproducing Persons: Issues in Feminist Bioethics* (Ithaca, NY: Cornell University Press, 1996), 94.
37 Robbie E. Davis-Floyd and Carolyn F. Sargent, eds, *Childbirth and Authoritative Knowledge: Cross-cultural Perspectives* (Los Angeles: University of California Press, 1997).
38 O'Brien's writings exhibit a tension in this respect. She tends to present reproduction in a biologically determinist light, as I have argued, but the core of her project is emancipatory. These two things stand in obvious tension, for if human beings are biologically determined, it is difficult to theorize that social relations might be altered or women emancipated. In my view, this is a problem that is never fully resolved in O'Brien's work.
39 Anthony D. Smith, *National Identity* (Reno: University of Nevada Press, 1991), 22.
40 See Bruce James Smith, *Politics and Remembrance: Republican Themes in Machiavelli, Burke, and Tocqueville* (Princeton, NJ: Princeton University Press, 1985), 11.
41 E.J. Hobsbawm, *Nations and Nationalism since 1780: Programme, Myth, Reality* (New York: Cambridge University Press, 1990), 12.
42 The origins impulse takes different forms in political theory. For example, Machiavelli is a thinker driven by beginnings, but his interest is confined primarily to the foundations of cities and republics and to the lessons of history – he is not a theorist who tells his own origin story per se. For discussion of Machiavelli's interest in foundations, see Smith, *Politics and Remembrance*.
43 Martha C. Nussbaum, *Cultivating Humanity: A Classical Defense of Reform in Liberal Education* (Cambridge, MA: Harvard University Press, 1997), 86.
44 Ibid., 85.

### 2: Plato's Creation Politics

1 For an excellent discussion of Plato's ambiguity, see Dorothea Wender, 'Plato: Misogynist, Paedophile, and Feminist,' in John Peradotto and J.P. Sullivan, eds, *Women in the Ancient World: The Arethusa Papers* (Albany:

State University of New York Press, 1984). For a Straussian reading, see Allan Bloom, 'Interpretive Essay,' in *The Republic of Plato*, trans. Allan Bloom (New York: HarperCollins, 1991).
2 I am deliberately sidestepping the debate about whether or not Plato ought to be considered a feminist. Such a debate applies an anachronistic usage of 'feminist' to ancient Greece; it also relies upon a narrow understanding of feminism in the sense that, whatever Plato's intentions in theory, he did not behave as a feminist might toward historical women. Finally, this debate fails to appreciate the competing strain that runs through Plato's theory: a sometimes overt, at other times subtle, phallocentrism. For a critical commentary on Plato's feminism, see Julia Annas, 'Plato's Republic and Feminism,' *Philosophy* 51 (1976). For competing interpretations, see Arlene W. Saxonhouse, *Women in the History of Political Thought: Ancient Greece to Machiavelli* (New York: Praeger, 1985) and 'Eros and the Female in Greek Political Thought: An Interpretation of Plato's *Symposium*,' *Political Theory* 12 (1984); Giulia Sissa, 'The Sexual Philosophies of Plato and Aristotle,' in Pauline Schmitt Pantel, ed., *A History of Women*, vol. 1, *From Ancient Goddesses to Christian Saints* (Cambridge, MA: Belknap Press of Harvard University Press, 1992); Susan Hawthorne, 'Diotima Speaks through the Body,' in Bat-Ami Bar On, ed., *Engendering Origins: Critical Feminist Readings in Plato and Aristotle* (Albany: State University of New York Press, 1994); and Gregory Vlastos, 'Was Plato a Feminist?' *Times Literary Supplement*, 17–23 March 1989.
3 Plato, *Timaeus* in *The Collected Dialogues of Plato Including the Letters*, ed. with intro. and prefatory notes Edith Hamilton and Huntington Cairns (New York: Pantheon Books, 1961).
4 R.B. Rutherford, *The Art of Plato: Ten Essays in Platonic Interpretation* (Cambridge, MA: Harvard University Press, 1995), 288.
5 See note 18 below.
6 There is a debate about how seriously Plato's assertion of a god should be taken. Warrington, for one, faults interpreters who overlook 'the purely mythical character of the Demiurge, crediting him with attributes proper to the God of Jewish-Christian theology and representing Plato as a monotheist on the threshold of Christianity!' Guthrie, conversely, insists that Plato's idea of the Demiurge should be read as 'philosophy, not myth.' In a similar vein, Norbert Samuelson suggests that Timaeus's arguments are an 'attempt to synthesize the explanations of Greek philosophers with the stories of Greek religion.' It is likely that Plato was attempting to come to terms with Hesiodic and Homeric gods, but just how he intended his Demiurge to be interpreted is difficult to ascertain. The most important point for my purposes is that, in using a creator god, Plato escapes having

to account for why the world transformed the way it did when it did. It permits Plato to attribute to this Being a vast plan or scheme for order. For discussion, see John Warrington, 'Introduction' to Plato, *Timaeus*, ed. and trans. John Warrington (Dutton, NY: Everyman's Library, 1965), viii; W.K.C. Guthrie, *A History of Greek Philosophy*, vol. V, *The Later Plato and the Academy* (New York: Cambridge University Press, 1978), 255; Norbert M. Samuelson, *Judaism and the Doctrine of Creation* (New York: Cambridge University Press, 1994), 175.

7 W.K.C. Guthrie, *The Greek Philosophers from Thales to Aristotle* (New York: Harper & Row, 1960), 24.
8 G.S. Kirk and J.E. Raven, *The Presocratic Philosophers: A Critical History with a Selection of Texts* (New York: Cambridge University Press, 1957), 197. See also the English translation of Heraclitus, *On the Universe*, in *Hippocrates*, vol. 4, trans. W.H.S. Jones (London: Heinemann 1931).
9 Guthrie, *The Greek Philosophers*, 88.
10 Ibid., 277.
11 Judith Genova provides a useful discussion of Platonic dualism at the ontological and metaphysical level, but mistakenly equates his dualism with that of Pythagoras. To see Plato as merely a Pythagorean dualist obscures the innovation he forges that takes him distinctly beyond Presocratic thought. See Judith Genova, 'Feminist Dialectics: Plato and Dualism,' in Bat-Ami Bar On, ed., *Engendering Origins: Critical Feminist Readings in Plato and Aristotle* (Albany: State University of New York Press, 1994).
12 Ibid., 237.
13 Francis MacDonald Cornford, *Plato's Cosmology: The Timaeus of Plato Translated with a Running Commentary* (London: Routledge & Kegan Paul, 1966), 6.
14 Because this is the point in the dialogue at which Plato begins to discuss the creation of human beings, it will be my focus. It should be noted, of course, that this is but one part of the creation story he offers.
15 Guthrie, *History of Greek Philosophy*, vol. 5, 307.
16 David Farrell Krell, 'Female Parts in *Timaeus*,' *Arion: A Journal of Humanities and the Classics*, new series, 2:3 (1975): 400.
17 Ibid., 404.
18 It is likely that Krell derives his argument in turn from A.E. Taylor, *A Commentary on Plato's Timaeus* (Toronto: Oxford University Press, 1928), 10–11. Taylor also posits Timaeus as a real Pythagorean figure, and maintains accordingly that we will not find 'any revelation of distinctively Platonic doctrines' in the dialogue. More convincing is Cornford's assessment on this front: 'There is no evidence for the historic existence of Timaeus of

Locri. If he did exist, we know nothing whatever about him beyond Socrates' description.' Therefore, 'we may regard his [Timaeus's] doctrine simply as Plato's own.' This does not mean, of course, that Plato was not influenced by any number of Presocratics, including the Pythagoreans. See Cornford, *Plato's Cosmology*, 2–3.
19 Guthrie, *History of Greek Philosophy*, vol. 5, 307.
20 For a discussion of how Plato ties women to the body, see Elizabeth Spelman, 'Woman As Body: Ancient and Contemporary Views,' *Feminist Studies* 8 (1982).
21 Francis Cornford argues that 'we are not to suppose that there ever existed a generation of men before there were any women or lower animals' (*Plato's Cosmology*, 291–2). Plato, he says, postpones discussion of the differences between male and female until the end of the dialogue because these details are 'irrelevant to the whole account of our human nature which fills most of the remaining discourse' (142).
22 See *A Commentary on Timaeus*, 635.
23 Nancy Tuana, *The Less Noble Sex: Scientific, Religious, and Philosophical Conceptions of Woman's Nature* (Indianapolis: Indiana University Press, 1993). In a 1975 article, Anne Geddes provides an insightful if brief analysis of Plato's usage of patriarchal theories in embryology. See 'The Philosophic Notion of Women in Antiquity,' *Antichthon: Journal of the Australian Society for Classical Studies* 9 (1975). Even more brief is Susan Moller Okin's mention of *Timaeus*, and it too is restricted to the secondary birth of women on the earth; see *Women in Western Political Thought* (Princeton, NJ: Princeton University Press, 1979), 26.
24 Luce Irigaray, *Speculum of the Other Woman*, trans. Gillian C. Gill (Ithaca, NY: Cornell University Press, 1985), 307.
25 Ibid.
26 Sue Blundell, *Women in Ancient Greece* (Cambridge, MA: Harvard University Press, 1995), 128.
27 Pericles' speech is known to us through Thucydides, *History of the Peloponnesian War*, vol. 1, trans. Charles Forster Smith (Cambridge, MA: Harvard University Press, 1935), 2: XLV, 341.
28 Aristotle's paraphrase of Sophocles. Aristotle, *The Politics*, trans. Ernest Barker, rev. with intro. and notes R.F. Stalley (New York: Oxford University Press, 1995), 1260a24, p. 36.
29 Mogens Herman Hansen, *The Athenian Democracy in the Age of Demosthenes*, trans. J.A. Crook (Cambridge: Blackwell, 1991), 81.
30 Thuc. 2: XL, 329.
31 It is important to note that not all women were located primarily in the pri-

vate realm. Courtesans and prostitutes are an exception, as they did enter the public sphere to some extent. And some of Socrates' monologues come from courtesan philosophers, Diotima and Aspasia in particular. Whatever their public roles, these female philosophers never actually appear in Platonic dialogues themselves, nor was philosophic participation similar to men's even a possibility for them. Women could be active in the private realm, but their action in the public realm was 'firmly rejected.' On this latter point see Nancy Demand, *Birth, Death, and Motherhood in Classical Greece* (Baltimore: Johns Hopkins University Press, 1994), 127.

32 David M. Halperin, 'Why Is Diotima a Woman? Platonic Erós and the Figuration of Gender,' in David M. Halperin, John J. Winkler, and Froma I. Zeitlin, eds, *Before Sexuality: The Construction of Erotic Experience in the Ancient Greek World* (Princeton, NJ: Princeton University Press, 1990), 291.

33 Ibid., 289.

34 Simon Goldhill, *Foucault's Virginity: Ancient Erotic Fiction and the History of Sexuality* (New York: Cambridge University Press, 1995), 142.

35 Blundell, *Women in Ancient Greece*, 157.

36 The marriage contract also was necessary to ensure the legitimacy of children. This contract was not between man and woman, but was a oral agreement between father and son-in-law, whereby the son-in-law received the hand of his wife as well as her dowry. Marriage contracts did not establish women as property of their husbands in fourth-century Athens, but did establish a husband's guardianship over his wife, and assigned to her the status of a minor. See Claudine Leduc, 'Marriage in Ancient Greece,' in Pauline Schmitt Pantel, ed., *A History of Women* (Cambridge, MA: Harvard University Press, 1992), 1: 272–5.

37 Halperin, 'Why Is Diotima a Woman?' 278.

38 Aeschylus, *Eumenides*, in *Greek Drama*, ed. with intro. Moses Hadas (Toronto: Bantam, 1982), 70.

39 Ibid., 71.

40 Ibid., 69.

41 This might mean she nourished him with their shared blood while he was in the womb. Or Aeschylus might believe what the Hippocratic writers did: that menstrual blood nourished the fetus. This they based on the observation that menstruation ceased during pregnancy.

42 Aristotle, 'On the Generation of Animals,' excerpted in Mary Briody Mahowald, ed., *Philosophy of Woman: An Anthology of Classic and Current Concepts* (Indianapolis: Hackett, 1983), 268.

43 Ibid., 267.

44 Ibid., 268.
45 Aristotle has his defenders, however, who attempt to rescue his views on reproduction from the charge of misogyny. Among them is D.M. Balme, who argues that Aristotle understood the mother to contribute to 'the formation and development of the fetus in a way that bears some analogy to the male' (21). Leaving aside the phallocentric manner in which Balme formulates his thesis, the argument remains problematic. He suggests that Aristotle considers matter to be in some sense preformed, or at least highly diversified. Menstrual blood, according to this theory, has all of the potential body parts of both sexes, and the male seed brings to the matter (or menstrual blood) activity and motion; it 'brings the fetus form and defining character' (23). This is precisely the point: the female contains the raw materials and the male contributes the vital 'soul movements.' Even the most extreme patrogenic belief will not deny the mother as contributing *something*, be it gestative nourishment or matter. Aristotle's is but another variation on patrogenesis, and it is a mistake to equate his theory of reproduction with a benign scientific one. See D.M. Balme, 'Anthropos Anthropon Genna: Human Is Generated by Human,' in G.R. Dunstan, ed., *The Human Embryo: Aristotle and the Arabic and European Traditions* (Devon: University of Exeter Press, 1990).
46 *Regimen I:* XXVII, in *Hippocrates*, vol. IV, trans. by W.H.S. Jones (London: Heinemann Ltd., 1931), 265.
47 Hippocrates, 'On the Nature of the Child,' quoted in Helen King, 'Making a Man: Becoming Human in Early Greek Medicine,' in Dunstan, ed., *The Human Embryo*, 16.
48 King, 'Making a Man,' 17.
49 Hippocrates, 'On the Generating Seed and the Nature of the Child,' in Mary R. Lefkowitz and Maureen B. Fant, eds, *Women's Life in Greece and Rome: A Source Book in Translation* (Baltimore: Johns Hopkins University Press, 1982), 86.
50 Hippocrates, 'Diseases of Women 1,' in Lefkowitz and Fant, eds, *Women's Life in Greece and Rome*, 90.
51 Thomas Laqueur, *Making Sex: Body and Gender from the Greeks to Freud* (Cambridge, MA: Harvard University Press, 1990), 26.
52 Ibid., 62.
53 Mary O'Brien, *The Politics of Reproduction* (Boston: Routledge & Kegan Paul, 1981).
54 Robbie Pfeufer Kahn, *Bearing Meaning: The Language of Birth* (Urbana and Chicago: University of Illinois Press, 1995), 4. For further elaboration of the

appropriation thesis see Page duBois, *Sowing the Body: Psychoanalysis and Ancient Representations of Women* (Chicago: University of Chicago Press, 1988), esp. chap. 8.

55 Feminist theorists have made this point forcefully. Mary O'Brien is foremost among them in *The Politics of Reproduction*. Virginia Held as well makes the case that to locate birth in the solely physical realm severs it from a truly human experience, and confines it to the status of animalistic processes. See Virginia Held, 'Preconceptions of Birth and Death,' in *Feminist Morality: Transforming Culture, Society, and Politics* (Chicago: University of Chicago Press, 1993).

56 The critique of appropriation has its origins in Halperin (1990), who argues that Plato is unable to recognize the contribution of woman to reproduction in the *Symposium*. It is in response to Halperin's point that I began to conceptualize Plato's reproductive metaphor as fantasy and fabrication rather than straightforward appropriation.

57 Laqueur, *Making Sex*, 58.

58 As Mary Seller points out, even after women's contribution was scientifically proven, there was a reluctance to abandon patrogenesis. See Mary J. Seller, 'Short Communication: Some Fallacies in Embryology through the Ages,' in Dunstan, ed., *The Human Embryo*, 224.

59 For elaboration of this point see Sheldon S. Wolin, *Politics and Vision: Continuity and Innovation in Western Political Thought* (Toronto: Little, Brown 1960), 32–44; and Gregory Vlastos, ed., *Plato: A Collection of Critical Essays, Vol. II* (Notre Dame, IN: University of Notre Dame Press, 1971).

60 Bedford and Workman, 'Recalling Plato from Exile,' 10 (see chap. 2, n. 20).

61 Ibid., 8.

62 One of the best discussions of Platonic ideals of masculinity is found in Halperin's 'Why Is Diotima a Woman?'

63 Wendy Brown, '"Supposing Truth Were a Woman ...": Plato's Subversion of Masculine Discourse,' in Nancy Tuana, ed., *Feminist Interpretations of Plato* (University Park: Pennsylvania State University Press, 1994), 162.

64 Ibid., 162.

65 Ibid., 163.

66 For a discussion of Plato's architectonic vision, see Wolin, *Politics and Vision*, chap. 2.

### 3: Hobbes and the Discourse on Origins

1 For an analysis of Hobbes on the subject of origins see Matthew H. Kramer, *Hobbes and the Paradoxes of Political Origins* (New York: St Martin's Press, 1997).

2 Thomas Hobbes, *Leviathan*, ed. Richard Tuck (New York: Cambridge University Press, 1991), part II: chap. 17, p. 117 (abbreviated hereafter as *Lev*).
3 *Lev* I: 13, 87.
4 Ibid.
5 *Lev* I: 13, 88. Hobbes makes a nostalgic example of ancient Greece, the 'golden age' of great 'simplicity' in which subjects obeyed authority and did not entertain the 'folly' of 'measuring what was just by the sayings and judgments of private men.' By contrast there is nothing nostalgic about the state of nature. Thomas Hobbes, *Man and Citizen (De Homine and De Cive)*, ed. Bernard Gert (Indianapolis: Hackett, 1991), 97 (abbreviated hereafter as *De Cive*).
6 *Lev* I: 13, 89.
7 *Lev* I: 14, 92.
8 *Lev* II: 18, 121.
9 Kahn suggests that Hobbes is able to present an argument for the compatibility of consent and coercion, or the 'paradox of consent to fear.' Certainly it is true that between Hobbes's understanding of consent and coercion lies a blurry line, and that Hobbes is not concerned with the power relations that underlie consent, but I do not agree with Kahn's interpretation that Hobbes's subjects 'consent to be coerced' or that they 'consent to fear.' These terms unnecessarily confuse matters in my view. Subjects do feel fear, and rather than risk their personal security, they submit to the prevailing sovereign power. Hobbes calls this consent where most of us would probably call it coercion or at least consent under duress. See Victoria Kahn, '"The Duty to Love": Passion and Obligation in Early Modern Political Theory,' *Representations* 68 (Fall 1999).
10 G.J. Schochet, *Patriarchalism in Political Thought: The Authoritarian Family and Political Speculation and Attitudes Especially in Seventeenth-century England* (Oxford: Basil Blackwell, 1975), 21, 229.
11 Sir Robert Filmer, 'Observations *Concerning* the Originall of Government, Upon Mr Hobs *Leviathan*, Mr Milton against *Salmasius*, H. Grotius *De Jure Belli*,' in Sir Robert Filmer, *Patriarcha and Other Writings*, ed. Johann P. Sommerville (New York: Cambridge University Press, 1991), 184–5.
12 Quentin Skinner brings out this point in his discussion of Hobbes's theory of political liberty. See 'Thomas Hobbes's Antiliberal Theory of Liberty,' in Bernard Yack, ed., *Liberalism without Illusions: Essays on Liberal Theory and the Political Vision of Judith Shklar* (Chicago: University of Chicago Press, 1996), 160–4.
13 *Lev* II: 18, 127.

14 Michael Zuckert, *Natural Rights and the New Republicanism* (Princeton, NJ: Princeton University Press, 1994), 51–5.
15 Glenn Burgess, *The Politics of the Ancient Constitution: An Introduction to English Political Thought, 1603–1642* (University Park: Pennsylvania State University Press, 1992), 4–5.
16 Ibid., 11.
17 *Lev* I: 11, 73.
18 *Lev* I: 11, 74.
19 *Lev* II: 20, 145.
20 Ibid.
21 Alan Craig Houston, '"A Way of Settlement": The Levellers, Monopolies and the Public Interest,' *History of Political Thought* 14:3 (Autumn 1993): 413.
22 A.S.P. Woodhouse, ed., *Puritanism and Liberty: Being the Army Debates (1647–49) from the Clarke Manuscripts* (Rutland, VT: Charles E. Tuttle Co., 1992), 53. The use of 'man' here does not imply gender inclusivity, as the Levellers did not make an argument for the extension of the franchise to women, despite the presence of women activists in their ranks. Moreover, the extent of the Levellers' democratic initiative is the source of twentieth-century dispute. See C.B. Macpherson, *The Political Theory of Possessive Individualism: Hobbes to Locke* (New York: Oxford University Press, 1962). For a response to Macpherson's thesis, see Keith Thomas, 'The Levellers and the Franchise,' in G.E. Aylmer, ed., *The Interregnum: The Quest for Settlement, 1646–1660* (Toronto: Macmillan, 1972).
23 Woodhouse, ed., *Puritanism and Liberty*, 66.
24 It is noteworthy that the Levellers inspired fear in the ruling elites more than they actually influenced events during the late 1640s. See John Morrill, *The Nature of the English Revolution: Essays* (New York: Longman, 1993), 19.
25 See Johann Sommerville, 'Lofty Science and Local Politics,' in Tom Sorell, ed., *The Cambridge Companion to Hobbes* (New York: Cambridge University Press, 1996), 258–66.
26 Thomas Hobbes, *De Corpore*, part I, 186, in J.C.A. Gaskin, ed., *The Elements of Law Natural and Politic* (New York: Oxford Univeristy Press, 1994).
27 Ibid., pt. I, 191.
28 *De Cive*, 'Author's Preface,' 98–9.
29 Christine Di Stefano, *Configurations of Masculinity: A Feminist Perspective on Modern Political Theory* (Ithaca, NY: Cornell University Press, 1991), 78.
30 *De Cive*, 'Author's Preface,' 98.
31 See *Leviathan*, esp. book I.
32 For all the benefits of speech, Hobbes lists corresponding abuses of speech,

including the use of metaphor and the 'inconstancy of the signification of their words.' *Lev* I: 4, 25.
33 *Lev* I: 4, 28.
34 Sheldon S. Wolin, *Politics and Vision: Continuity and Innovation in Western Political Thought* (Toronto: Little, Brown 1960), 253–4.
35 Thomas A. Spragens, Jr, *The Politics of Motion: The World of Thomas Hobbes* (Lexington: University Press of Kentucky, 1973), 58.
36 *De Corpore*, VI, 197; italics in original.
37 Richard S. Westfall, *The Construction of Modern Science: Mechanisms and Mechanics* (New York: Cambridge University Press, 1977), 33.
38 Hobbes, in Gaskin, ed., *The Elements of Law*, 26.
39 Westfall, *The Construction of Modern Science*, chap. 1.
40 Ibid., 19.
41 *Lev* I: 2, 15.
42 Yves Charles Zarka, 'First Philosophy and the Foundation of Knowledge,' in Sorell, ed., *Cambridge Companion to Hobbes*, 73.
43 See J.W.N. Watkins, *Hobbes's System of Ideas: A Study in the Political Significance of Philosophical Theories* (London: Hutchinson, 1965).
44 Quentin Skinner, *Reason and Rhetoric in the Philosophy of Hobbes* (New York: Cambridge University Press, 1996); David Johnston, *The Rhetoric of Leviathan: Thomas Hobbes and the Politics of Cultural Transformation* (Princeton, NJ: Princeton University Press, 1986); and Victoria Silver, 'Hobbes on Rhetoric,' in Sorell, ed., *Cambridge Companion to Hobbes*. Note the difference between a contract theorist such as John Rawls and Hobbes: Rawls uses origins hypothetically, but does not spin a narrative to enhance the device. Hobbes's hypothetical device of origins, by contrast, is situated in the context of a narrative that has the power to increase its plausibility.
45 On this point, see Johnston, *The Rhetoric of Leviathan*, chap. 3.
46 Thomas Hobbes, *Behemoth or The Long Parliament*, ed. Ferdinand Tönnies, intro. Stephen Holmes (Chicago: University of Chicago Press, 1990), 16.
47 See Johnston, *The Rhetoric of Leviathan*, 131–3.
48 Sheldon S. Wolin, *Hobbes and the Epic Tradition of Political Theory* (Los Angeles: William Andrews Clark Memorial Library, 1970), 24.
49 Ibid., 38.
50 Although Hobbes does not limit his ideas on the natural state to one chapter in *De Cive* or *Leviathan*, I will take the chapter specified in each as indicative of his ideas on the subject for the purpose of comparison.
51 *De Cive*, chap. I, 118.
52 *Lev* I: 13, 89.

53 Ibid. This story appears briefly in the 'Author's Preface to the Reader' in *De Cive*.
54 James Tully, *Strange Multiplicity: Constitutionalism in an Age of Diversity* (New York: Cambridge University Press, 1995), 73.
55 Charles W. Mills, *The Racial Contract* (Ithaca, NY, and London: Cornell University Press, 1997), 65–6.
56 Tully, *Strange Multiplicity*, 64.
57 Christopher Hill, *The English Bible and the Seventeenth-century Revolution* (Toronto: Penguin, 1993), 7.
58 Ibid., 201–3.
59 Ibid., 20.
60 There are two different creation stories in Genesis: Genesis 1 describes the creation of the earth, and of man and woman made in the image of God; and Genesis 2 portrays the creation of Adam as from the dust, and Eve as from Adam's rib. These two together form the Judeo-Christian, or the Hebraic, creation story. Christians also take the Book of John, in the New Testament, as their creation story, because it describes beginnings ('In the beginning was the Word ...'). For the purposes of this chapter, I will take the Christian creation myth to be synonymous with the Hebraic.
61 David Adams Leeming with Margaret Adams Leeming, *Encyclopedia of Creation Myths* (Oxford: ABC-CLIO, 1994), 113.
62 Genesis 2 is thought to have been written five hundred years earlier, around 950 BCE.
63 Elaine Pagels, *Adam, Eve, and the Serpent* (New York: Vintage, 1988), 9.
64 J.R. Porter, 'Creation,' in Bruce M. Metzger and Michael D. Coogan, eds, *The Oxford Companion to the Bible* (New York: Oxford, 1993), 140.
65 Karen Armstrong, *In the Beginning: A New Interpretation of Genesis* (New York: Ballantine, 1996), 21–4.
66 Hill, *The English Bible*, 5.
67 Roger Trigg claims that Hobbes does not have a theory of human nature per se; rather, that his nominalism and anti-essentialism preclude his designating one. Roger Trigg, *Ideas of Human Nature: An Historical Introduction* (Cambridge: Blackwell, 1988).
68 *De Cive*, chap. VIII, 205. This forms the basis of Di Stefano's critique of Hobbesian ontology, an ontology that she describes as inherently masculinist because of its denial of the mother–child relationship. See *Configurations of Masculinity: A Feminist Perspective on Modern Political Theory* (Ithaca, NY: Cornell University Press, 1991). Carole Pateman critiques this view in her essay '"God Hath Ordained to Man a Helper": Hobbes, Patriarchy and Conjugal Right,' in Mary Lyndon Shanley and Carole Pateman, eds, *Feminist*

*Interpretations and Political Theory* (University Park: Pennsylvania State University Press, 1991).
69 *De Cive*, 'Author's Preface,' 100.
70 *Lev* I: 14, 93.
71 As Bernard Gert explains, 'Nothing in Hobbes's political theory requires that men not have friends for whom they are willing to make some sacrifice.' See Gert, 'Introduction' to *De Cive*, 8.
72 Ibid., 6
73 Ibid., 12.
74 *Lev* III: 35, 280.

### 4: Gender in Hobbes's Origin Story

1 Nancy J. Hirschmann, *Rethinking Obligation: A Feminist Method for Political Theory* (Ithaca, NY: Cornell University Press, 1992); Diana Coole, 'Women, Gender and Contract: Feminist Interpretations,' in David Boucher and Paul Kelly, eds, *The Social Contract from Hobbes to Rawls* (New York: Routledge, 1994); Di Stefano, *Configurations of Masculinity*. Karen Green compares Hobbes to Christine de Pisan in *The Woman of Reason: Feminism, Humanism and Political Thought* (New York: Continuum, 1995). Ingrid Makus's analysis of Hobbes raises some important criticisms of other feminist treatments. Her focus is familial relationships, but she does not read Hobbes historically. See *Women, Politics, and Reproduction: The Liberal Legacy* (Toronto: University of Toronto Press, 1996).
2 Carole Pateman, *The Sexual Contract* (Stanford, CA: Stanford University Press, 1988). See also her '"God Hath Ordained to Man a Helper": Hobbes, Patriarchy and Conjugal Right,' in Mary Lyndon Shanley and Carole Pateman, eds, *Feminist Interpretations and Political Theory* (University Park: Pennsylvania State University Press, 1991).
3 Jane Jaquette also offers a critique of Pateman. She suggests that, contrary to what Pateman argues about contract theory, Hobbes's notion of contract ought to be of interest to feminists. Moreover, she argues that 'women are not foundationally excluded from the social contract in Hobbes' (212), and sketches an alternative conjectural story about what happens to women (and men) in the state of nature. See Jane Jaquette, 'Contract and Coercion: Power and Gender in *Leviathan*,' in Hilda Smith, ed., *Women Writers and the Early Modern British Political Tradition* (New York: Cambridge University Press, 1998). See also Joanne Boucher, 'Male Power and Contract Theory: Hobbes and Locke in Carole Pateman's *The Sexual Contract*,' *Canadian Journal of Political Science* 36:1 (March 2003): 23–38.

4 This literature is vast, but among the most important recent treatments of Hobbes are Richard Tuck, *Philosophy and Government, 1572–1651* (Cambridge: Cambridge University Press, 1993); Tom Sorell, ed., *The Cambridge Companion to Hobbes* (New York: Cambridge University Press, 1996); and Quentin Skinner, *Reason and Rhetoric in the Philosophy of Hobbes* (New York: Cambridge University Press, 1996). A notable exception is the work of Gordon Schochet; see chapter 1, n. 28 above.

5 There is a sizable literature on gender relations in early modern England. Among the most recent works are Sara Mendelson and Patricia Crawford, *Women in Early Modern England, 1550–1720* (Oxford and New York: Clarendon Press, 1998); Anne Laurence, *Women in England, 1500–1740: A Social History* (London: Phoenix, 1994); Anthony Fletcher, *Gender, Sex and Subordination in England, 1500–1800* (New Haven, CT, and London: Yale University Press, 1995); and David Cressy, *Birth, Marriage, and Death: Ritual, Religion, and the Life-cycle in Tudor and Stuart England* (Toronto: Oxford University Press, 1997).

6 For an extensive discussion on this topic, see Margaret R. Sommerville, *Sex and Subjection: Attitudes to Women in Early-modern Society* (New York: St Martin's Press, 1995), chap. 2, 'The Basis of Subjection.'

7 As the emerging literature on women's political and religious activism reveals, the ideological imperative for women to confine their activity to the private realm did not prevent their actual participation in public affairs. Women had many public roles and were by no means located exclusively in the private realm; moreover, in early modern England the private realm was not considered a feminine sphere, as has sometimes been implied. Pateman, for example, implies as much in her general discussion of public and private in social contract theory in *The Sexual Contract*: 'The antinomy private/public is another expression of natural/civil and women/men' (11); and 'The private, womanly sphere (natural) and the public, masculine sphere (civil) are opposed but gain their meaning from each other' (11). That the terms public and private cannot be used to *describe* women's location has led some historians to argue against the use of the very concept of a gendered public and private division. Amanda Vickery argues that the 'rough division between private and public could be applied to almost any century or any culture – a fact which robs the distinction of its analytical purpose' (7). See Amanda Vickery, *The Gentleman's Daughter: Women's Lives in Georgian England* (New Haven, CT, and London: Yale University Press, 1998). For further critiques of the terms see Amanda Vickery, 'Golden Age to Separate Spheres? A Review of the Categories and Chronology of English Women's History,' *Historical Journal* 36:2 (1993): 383–414; and

Rachel Weil, *Political Passions: Gender, the Family and Political Argument in England, 1680–1714* (Manchester and New York: Manchester University Press and St Martin's Press, 1999).

Certainly, scholars want to avoid ahistorical simplifications about the relegation of women to the private sphere, as well as trans-historical generalizations about the pervasive existence of a public/private dichotomy. Nevertheless, I am concerned here with the political discourse of early modern England, and in the writings of Hobbes, Filmer, James, Locke, and others the public/private division features prominently. It remains, therefore, a useful term of analysis precisely because what is defined as public and what private is central to a theorist's vision of politics. I am making an important distinction, then, between the use of public and private to *describe* women's location in society, which is clearly not warranted, and the use of the terms public and private at the level of political discourse and ideology. What is of interest from a historical perspective is the changing meaning of the terms public and private and their influence on, and relationship to, gender.

8 See Fletcher, *Gender, Sex and Subordination*, 101; and D.E. Underdown, 'The Taming of the Scold: The Enforcement of Patriarchal Authority in Early Modern England,' in Anthony Fletcher and John Stevenson, eds, *Order and Disorder in Early Modern England* (New York: Cambridge University Press, 1985), 116.

9 One extensive marriage guide is William Gouge's *Of domestical duties*. Portions of Gouge's 1622 text are reprinted in Kate Aughterson, ed., *Renaissance Woman: A Sourcebook. Constructions of Femininity in England* (New York: Routledge, 1995).

10 Mary Beth Norton, *Founding Mothers and Fathers: Gendered Power and the Forming of American Society* (New York: Alfred A. Knopf, 1996), 6.

11 Although Filmer and James differ in their interpretation of how the family models the commonwealth, they both rely on the family *as a model* for understanding political relationships. For the purposes of this chapter, then, I will refer to both of them as analogical thinkers. Hobbes too participates in analogical thinking, but with a difference, as we will see.

12 Elizabeth Poole, *A Vision: wherein is manifested the disease and cure of the Kingdom being the summe of what was lately delivered to the Councel of War* (London, 1648), 1; italics in original. Other than the substitution of 's' for 'f,' no changes will be made to quotations from primary material.

13 Ibid., 3.

14 Elizabeth Poole, *An Alarum of War, Given to the Army, and to their High Court of Justice (so called) by the wille of God* (1649), 8–9.

15 Given the existing patriarchal social order, the very fact and congruence of Elizabeth's gender and her sovereignty were in tension; but Elizabeth manipulated this tension successfully with carefully chosen metaphors. On the one hand, she asserted the weakness of her female body, while on the other she declared that her heart and will were male. While casting aside demands that she marry, Elizabeth generated contradictory images of herself as Virgin Queen as well as the mother and sometimes wife to the English nation so as to command authority and respect, and to show her loyalty to the nation. Despite Elizabeth's popularity and success as a ruler, the general concept of female rule, and the specific reality of Elizabeth's rule, remained the subject of intense debate and speculation in political theory and public discourse alike. (See Lena Cowen Corlin, 'The Fictional Families of Elizabeth I,' in Carole Levin and Patricia A. Sullivan, eds, *Political Rhetoric, Power, and Renaissance Women* [Albany: State University of New York Press, 1995].) Although Elizabeth was very successful at manipulating gendered metaphors, there remained a widespread insecurity about female rule that lay 'right under the surface throughout her reign.' See Ilona Bell, 'Elizabeth I – Always Her Own Free Woman,' in Levin and Sullivan, eds, *Political Rhetoric*, 74.

16 Mark Breitenberg, *Anxious Masculinity in Early Modern England* (New York: Cambridge University Press, 1996), 3.

17 Ibid., 2. Both Fletcher and Underdown treat the subject of masculine or patriarchal anxiety. See Fletcher, *Gender, Sex and Subordination*, chap. 1; and Underdown, 'The Taming of the Scold.'

18 As Breitenberg explains, the meaning of anxiety as a 'condition of preparation for an anticipated threat whose origin "may be an unknown one"' has been relatively constant since the early modern period. See Breitenberg, *Anxious Masculinity*, 'Introduction,' 4–5.

19 I discuss the question of whether the early modern period witnessed a 'crisis in gender relations' in section 3. For now, suffice it to say that I am interested, not in actual changes to gender relations, but in the *perceived threat* to the gender order.

20 An important example of a popular early-modern tract that exhibits an overt misogyny is Joseph Swetnam's *The arraignement of lewd, idle, froward, and inconstant women*. Published in 1615, Swetnam's attack on women had ten printings before 1634. See Rosemary Masek, 'Women in an Age of Transition: 1485–1714,' in Barbara Kanner, ed., *The Women of England: From Anglo-Saxon Times to the Present* (Hamden, CT: Archon, 1979), 147–8.

21 King James VI and I, *Basilicon Doron*, in King James VI and I, *Political Writ-*

*ings*, ed. J.P. Sommerville (New York: Cambridge University Press, 1994), 38.
22 *Basilicon Doron*, 42.
23 Ibid.
24 Reprinted in G.B. Harrison, ed., *Elizabethan and Jacobean Quartos* (New York: Barnes and Noble, 1966). It is important to point out that witchcraft accusations were made predominantly but not exclusively against women; but witchcraft should not be understood as something that women practised consciously. As often as not it was a charge levelled against those who were thought to be subverting the local social order. See also Diana Purkiss, *The Witch in History: Early Modern and Twentieth-century Representations* (New York: Routledge, 1996).
25 Laurence, *Women in England*, 218. See also Deborah Willis, *Malevolent Nurture: Witch-hunting and Maternal Power in Early Modern England* (Ithaca, NY: Cornell University Press, 1995).
26 Quoted in Valerie Wayne, 'The Dearth of the Author: Anonymity's Allies and *Swetnam the Woman-hater*,' in Susan Frye and Karen Robertson, eds, *Maids and Mistresses, Cousins and Queens: Women's Alliances in Early Modern England* (New York: Oxford University Press, 1999), 235.
27 *Lev* I: 12, 81. From Margaret Cavendish's writing it is known that Hobbes devoted at least some time to the consideration of witchcraft, as he is reported by her to have spent time discussing the subject with her husband, William Cavendish, Duke of Newcastle, in Paris. Thomas Hobbes, *The Correspondence*, Vol. 2, *1660–1679*, ed. Noel Malcolm (Oxford: Clarendon, 1994), 811.
28 *Lev* I: 2, 18.
29 Sir Robert Filmer, 'Observations Concerning the Originall of Government, Upon Mr Hobs *Lev*,' in Sir Robert Filmer, *Patriarcha and Other Writings*, ed. J.P. Sommerville (New York: Cambridge University Press, 1991), 184–95.
30 Sommerville, *Sex and Subjection*, 29.
31 Sir Robert Filmer, 'The Anarchy of a Limited or Mixed Monarchy,' in Filmer, *Patriarcha*, 142.
32 Cressy, *Birth, Marriage, and Death*, 256.
33 Filmer, *Patriarcha*, 192.
34 Ibid., 187–8.
35 *Lev* II: 17, 118.
36 *Lev* II: 20, 139.
37 *Lev* II: 20, 140.
38 Ibid.
39 *De Cive*, chap. IX, 213.

40 Gordon Schochet suggests that Hobbes relies on the law of gratitude, without naming it as such, to show the obligation that is owed to those who spare us our lives. He contends that Hobbes's argument about mothers 'reveals a kind of conceptual embarrassment. Mothers did give birth in the state of nature, but Hobbes insisted upon rooting the consequences of this undeniably natural phenomenon in convention.' It seems to me that Hobbes is being strategic and, in fact, makes a convincing argument: while birth may be a *natural* event, motherhood is a *social* relationship. See Gordon J. Schochet, 'Intending (Political) Obligation: Hobbes and the Voluntary Basis of Society,' in Mary Deitz, ed., *Thomas Hobbes and Political Theory* (Lawrence: University Press of Kansas, 1990), 64.
41 *Lev* II: 20, 140.
42 *De Cive*, chap. IX, 213.
43 *Lev* II: 20, 140.
44 For an overview, see Celeste Turner Wright, 'The Amazons in Elizabethan Literature,' *Studies in Philology* 37:3 (July 1940).
45 Kathryn Schwarz, *Tough Love: Amazon Encounters in the English Renaissance* (Durham, NC, and London: Duke University Press, 2000), 14.
46 Quote from Breitenberg, *Anxious Masculinity*, 75. Spinoza also has a suggestive passage devoted to the Amazons. His desire is to determine, in a total of one page, whether or not women are naturally inferior to men. His conclusion is that, because women never do rule with or over men, they should be understood as inferior. Moreover, he writes, men's passions and lusts for women would destroy the potential for peace if they were to rule jointly. Convention appears to be normative for Spinoza. 'The Amazons, who are said by legend to have ruled in days gone by, are no exception' to the rule that men and women cannot share power harmoniously, 'for they would not allow men to stay in their native land, but used to rear females only and to kill the males they had borne.' See Benedict De Spinoza, *The Political Works*, ed. A.G. Wernham (Toronto: Oxford University Press, 1958), 443–5.
47 'The chiefe Heads of the Ladies Lawes,' in *Parliament of Ladies; With their Lawes newly enacted* (1647).
48 *Hic Mulier; or, The Man-Woman*, in Katherine Usher Henderson and Barbara F. McManus, eds, *Half Humankind: Contexts and Texts of the Controversy about Women in England, 1540–1640* (Urbana and Chicago: University of Illinois Press, 1985), 266.
49 The author scorns Lady Frances Howard, who in 1613 began an affair with one of the members of the King's court. She sought and received an annulment to her marriage and afterwards married the Earl of Somerset, with whom she had been having the affair. It came to light sometime later that

the man who had tried to intervene and stop the affair, Sir Thomas Overbury, was in fact murdered in the Tower of London by Lady Frances. Her accomplice in the murder, a woman also, was sent to the gallows, but James commuted Lady Frances's death sentence. See editor's annotations, n. 12, in *Hic Mulier*, 267.

50 Ibid., 269–70
51 The author invokes the Amazons in his quotation from Edmund Spenser's *The Faerie Queene*.
52 *Haec Vir: Or, The Womanish-Man*, also reprinted in Henderson and McManus, eds, *Half Humankind*, 289.
53 *Swetnam the Woman-hater Arraigned by Women* depicts Amazons and mannish women in a more positive light in response to Swetnam's original misogynist tract. The anonymous authors of this play create an Amazon character who shows her superiority by defeating the weak and impotent Swetnam in a duel. See Wayne, 'The Dearth of the Author,' 229.
54 Mendelson and Crawford, *Women in Early Modern England*, 19.
55 Some feminists have explained Hobbes's use of the Amazons differently. In *The Woman of Reason*, Karen Green, following an argument she attributes to Pateman, suggests that Hobbes's reference to the Amazons reveals his awareness, and retelling of, the myth of the overthrow of mother-right (p. 50). This is, I think, quite far off the mark. Hobbes's purpose in raising the spectre of the Amazons is the opposite of what Green theorizes. His words in *De Cive* state the argument best; after referring to the Amazons, he asserts, 'And at this day, in divers places women are invested with the principal authority' (chap. IX, 213). The point is to affirm the continued *possibility* that women can hold maternal dominion, not that they have forever lost it in a mythical battle.

Ingrid Makus, in *Women, Politics and Reproduction*, recognizes that Hobbes took seriously 'the Amazons as a historical example of women having dominion over children and acting as heads of households' (29). Still, she reads Hobbes's message to be that the Amazons are mere exceptions to the general rule that men are the founders of commonwealths, not women. This is how Hobbes's contemporaries use the Amazons. While Hobbes does fall back on the latter assertion about the founders of the commonwealth, his use of the Amazons, in my view, is meant to show not that maternal dominion is rare, but that it is possible. The distinction is important.
56 See Mendelson and Crawford, *Women in Early Modern England*, 349–65.
57 This justification did nothing to return him to the favour of Elizabeth. See Sommerville, *Sex and Subjection*, 74–5, n. 41. Sections of Knox's tract have been reprinted in Aughterson, ed., *Renaissance Woman*.

58 Sommerville, *Sex and Subjection*, 55.
59 Fletcher, *Gender, Sex and Subordination*, 79.
60 Sommerville, *Sex and Subjection*, 57–9.
61 It is not that Hobbes disagrees with the practice of male primogeniture, for despite the consent theory that he elaborates, he acknowledges that nations are commonly ruled by hereditary monarchs. Children of the current monarch are preferred in the order of succession, and men are preferred over women, for the former 'are naturally fitter than women, for actions of labour and danger.' *Lev* II: 19, 137.
62 *Lev* II: 20, 140.
63 Laura Gowing, *Domestic Dangers: Women, Words, and Sex in Early Modern London* (New York: Oxford University Press, 1998), 28. Gowing points out that 'the gulf between prescriptions for the ideal household and everyday life for men, women, children, and servants was manifestly wide, yet ideals of the ordered patriarchal household remained powerful' (269).
64 Lois G. Schwoerer elaborates on this point in 'Women's Public Political Voice in England: 1640–1740,' in Smith, ed., *Women Writers*.
65 Mendelson and Crawford, *Women in Early Modern England*, 432. The concept of a 'crisis in gender relations' comes from Underdown's 'The Taming of the Scold,' and has been called into question by Martin Ingram in his '"Scolding women cucked or washed": A Crisis in Gender Relations in Early Modern England?' in Jennifer Kermode and Garthine Walker, eds, *Women, Crime and the Courts in Early Modern England* (Chapel Hill, NC, and London: University of North Carolina Press, 1994). See also Lyndal Roper, *Oedipus and the Devil: Witchcraft, Sexuality and Religion in Early Modern Europe* (New York: Routledge, 1994); and Gowing, *Domestic Dangers*.
66 Mendelson and Crawford, *Women in Early Modern England*, 432.
67 Patricia Crawford, 'The Challenges to Patriarchalism: How Did the Revolution Affect Women?' in John Morrill, ed., *Revolution and Restoration: England in the 1650s* (London: Collins and Brown, 1992), 124.
68 Phyllis Mack, *Visionary Women: Ecstatic Prophesy in Seventeenth-century England* (Berkeley: University of California Press, 1992), 5.
69 Although the concept in the abstract was ungendered, the discourse about conscience, and the ability to use conscience as a justification for one's actions, was indeed gendered. See Patricia Crawford, 'Public Duty, Conscience, and Women in Early Modern England,' in John Morrill, Paul Slack, and Daniel Woolf, eds, *Public Duty and Private Conscience in Seventeenth-century England: Essays Presented to G.E. Aylmer* (Toronto: Clarendon Press, 1993).
70 Lady Eleanor Davies was among the most provocative and radical of the

female prophesiers; she had predicted the execution of Charles I, an act that earned her imprisonment at the Gatehouse. Nor did her imprisonment put an end to her religious zeal; upon her release she reportedly seated herself on the episcopal throne and sprinkled the famous mixture on the cathedral hangings. For this she was sent to Bedlam (where she predicted a fire and one occurred), and then to the Tower. See Antonia Fraser, *The Weaker Vessel* (New York: Vintage Books, 1985), 157–60; and Mack, *Visionary Women*, 98.

71 Mack, *Visionary Women*, 90–1.
72 According to Patricia Crawford's research, women may have outnumbered men in the sects by two to one. Their status as members remained ambiguous, however. Women's consent to the church covenant was required, but their names in some cases were listed separately on the church register, and Crawford notes that many of the congregations had debates about whether women should swear the covenant in the first place. See *Women and Religion in England, 1500–1720* (New York: Routledge, 1996), chap. 7, 'Separatist Churches and Sexual Politics.'
73 Which is not to say that the churches themselves necessarily saw women as ministers. See Mack, *Visionary Women*, 91. Indeed, there was resistance to women preaching; Katherine Chidley engaged in an extended debate with Thomas Edwards on, among other issues, this subject. See Thomas Edwards, *Gangraena*, repr. in Aughterson, ed., *Renaissance Woman*. See also *A Discoverie of Six women preachers, in Middlesex, Kent, Cambridgshire, and Salisbury* (1641).
74 Mary (Rande) Cary, 'To the Reader' (1651) in *Little Horns Doom and Downfall*.
75 Poole, 'The Postscript,' in *An Alarum of War*.
76 Poole, *A Vision*, 3.
77 The Army council discussed her vision at length and called her back to appear before them again; Henry Ireton questioned Poole extensively about the nature of her revelations. See Fraser, *The Weaker Vessel*, 253; Rachel Trubowitz, 'Female Preachers and Male Wives: Gender and Authority in Civil War England,' *Prose Studies* 14 (1991): 92–111.
78 Crawford, *Women and Religion*, 137.
79 Ann Hughes, 'Gender and Politics in Leveller Literature,' in Susan D. Amussen and Mark A. Kishlansky, eds, *Political Culture and Cultural Politics in Early Modern England* (Manchester and New York: Manchester University Press, 1995), 170. Hughes cautions us that Leveller women's political activity is best interpreted in the context of the Leveller movement itself, rather than as an 'episode in women's activism' (164). Indeed, Hughes's analysis of the integration of gender into Leveller writings, and the presen-

tation of the Leveller men as honest masculine defenders of their households, aids our understanding of the tone of the women's petitions.
80 Laurence, *Women in England*, 243–4.
81 *To the Supream authority of this Nation, the commons assembled in Parliament: The humble Petition of divers wel-affected Women* (London, 1649).
82 *To the Supreme Authority of England. The Commons Assembled in Parliament*, 5 May 1649.
83 Ibid. It may be the strength of the language that has led some historians to assume that women's petitions were, in fact, written by men and only delivered by women. However, desperate times require desperate measures; given the careful negotiation of submission and authority found in the petitions it is likely that women themselves were their authors.
84 Ibid.
85 John Lilburne, *Unto every individual Member of Parliament: The humble Representation of divers afflicted women-Petitioners to the Parliament, on behalf of Mr. John Lilburn*, 29 July 1653.
86 Chidley's activism was met with mockery from her male counterparts, who wrote a rhyme denouncing her religious politics as displaced lustfulness: 'Oh Kate, O Kate, thou art unclean I heare, A man doth lye betweene thy sheetes, I feare.' For a discussion, see Crawford, *Women and Religion*, 129.
87 Mack, *Visionary Women*, 87; Crawford, *Women and Religion*, 132.
88 Fletcher, *Gender, Sex and Subordination*, 12–14.
89 Nor was the disorder of the Civil War period generally as great as had been imagined. See John Morrill and John Walter, 'Order and Disorder in the English Revolution,' in John Morrill, *The Nature of the English Revolution* (New York: Longman, 1993). On the moderateness of women's claims see Mack, *Visionary Women*, 105.
90 *A True Copie of the Petition of the Gentlewomen, and the Tradesmens-wives in and about the City of London* (London, 1641); italics added.
91 This is a matter of debate among feminist historians. Ann Marie McEntee reads greater radicalism into the women's petitions in '"The [Un]Civill-Sisterhood of Oranges and Lemons": Female Petitioners and Demonstrators, 1642–53,' *Prose Studies* 14 (1991): 92–111. Diane Purkiss cautions about the real interpretive challenge involved in reading the early moderns for signs and indications of feminist sentiment. *Women, Texts, and Histories, 1575–1760* (New York: Routledge, 1992).
92 Crawford, *Women and Religion*, 142.
93 See Mack, *Visionary Women*, 106.
94 'Hobbes to Margaret Cavendish, Marchioness of Newcastle,' 9 February 1662, in Hobbes, *The Correspondence, Vol. II*: 524.

95 The Lady Marchioness of Newcastle, *Philosophical Letters: Or, Modest Reflections Upon some Opinions in Natural Philosophy, Maintained By Several Famous and Learned Authors of this Age, Expressed by way of Letters* (London, 1664), 47.
96 As Victoria Kahn points out, however, Cavendish uses the marriage contract in her drama *The Contract* to present an argument for political obligation based not on fear or Hobbesian self-interest, but on love. See 'Margaret Cavendish and the Romance of Contract,' *Renaissance Quarterly* 50:2 (1997): 526–66.
97 Victoria Kahn offers a somewhat different reading, as she sees Cavendish advocating a romanticized version of contract popular in the royalist camp. It is likely that the two disagreed on the Engagement controversy, for the *Leviathan* provides a justification for pledging allegiance to the new sovereign on the basis that he can offer protection, whereas Cavendish personally refused to take the oath and suggests in *The Contract* that fear cannot be the basis for legitimate political obligation. Here we see how Hobbes's views alienated even those with whom he was in basic political agreement. Still, how do we resolve Kahn's reading of Cavendish as a defender of love and romance with Cavendish's own desentimentalized critique of marriage and the family in her *Philosophical Letters*? It may be that Cavendish is equivocal, committed on the one hand to her own marriage and able to use it as a similitude, but aware on the other that marriage as an institution was flawed. This is a question that merits further study.
98 Quoted in Hilda L. Smith, '"Though it be the part of every good wife": Margaret Cavendish, Duchess of Newcastle,' in Valerie Frith, ed., *Women and History: Voices of Early Modern England* (Concord, ON: Irwin Press, 1995), 126.
99 She claims not to have exchanged more that a few passing words with Hobbes. See biographical notes in Hobbes, *The Correspondence, Vol. II*: 811.
100 Cavendish was so concerned, according to Anna Battigelli, that she was unable to offer a 'conclusive reforming vision' (53), because she worried that her public words might spark further controversy. Hobbes, of course, worried about controversy over public words and interpretations, but this did not prevent him from offering his own vision of how the commonwealth should be organized. In this respect, Battigelli argues, Cavendish 'was more of a Hobbesian that Hobbes' (55). See her 'Political Thought/Political Action: Margaret Cavendish's Hobbesian Dilemma,' in Smith, ed., *Women Writers*, 40–55.

101 *Lev* II: 20, 142.
102 *Lev* II: 19, 137.

### 5: Pateman's Sexual Contract

1 Carole Pateman, *The Sexual Contract* (Stanford: Stanford University Press, 1988), 36 (abbreviated hereafter as *SC*).
2 See Nancy Fraser in *Justice Interruptus: Critical Reflections on the 'Postsocialist' Condition* (New York: Routledge, 1997); Shannon Bell, *Reading, Writing, and Rewriting the Prostitute Body* (Bloomington: Indiana University Press, 1994); and Carol Johnson, 'Does Capitalism Really Need Patriarchy? Some Old Issues Reconsidered,' *Women's Studies International Forum* 19:3 (1996).
3 *SC*, 1.
4 *SC*, 11.
5 Ibid.
6 Ibid.
7 Pateman's critique of the public/private dichotomy can be found in two other important articles: 'Feminist Critiques of the Public/Private Dichotomy' and 'The Patriarchal Welfare State,' both in Carol Pateman, *The Disorder of Women: Democracy, Feminism and Political Theory* (Stanford, CA: Stanford University Press, 1989).
8 Kevin Sharpe, 'Private Conscience and Public Duty in the Writings of James VI and I,' in John Morrill, Paul Slack, and Daniel Woolf, eds., *Public Duty and Private Conscience in Seventeenth-century England: Essays Presented to G.E. Aylmer* (Toronto: Clarendon Press, 1993), 84.
9 Freedom of conscience was itself a gendered issue, as discussed in chapter 4.
10 *Lev* II: 29, 223.
11 Mary Beth Norton, *Founding Mothers and Fathers: Gendered Power and the Forming of American Society* (New York: Alfred A. Knopf, 1996), 22.
12 See *Lev* chap. 22.
13 *SC*, 4.
14 Linda Zerilli makes a similar critique in her review of *The Sexual Contract*. See 'In the Beginning, Rape,' *Women's Review of Books* 6:6 (March 1989).
15 *SC*, 48.
16 *SC*, 49.
17 *Lev* II: 20, 142.
18 *Lev* II: 20, 140.
19 Carole Pateman, '"God Hath Ordained to Man a Helper": Hobbes, Patriar-

chy and Conjugal Right,' in Mary Lyndon Shanley and Carole Pateman, eds, *Feminist Interpretations and Political Theory* (University Park: Pennsylvania State University Press, 1991), 56 (hereafter *FI* ).
20 *SC*, 49
21 *FI*, 65.
22 Hobbes writes: 'It is not therefore the Victory, that giveth the right of Dominion over the Vanquished, but his own Covenant. Nor is he obliged because he is Conquered ... but because he commeth in, and Submitteth to the Victor.' *Lev* II: 20, 141. In other words, consent is understood as the basis for dominion, even in circumstances of conquest. Moreover, that consent is given under conditions of duress does not undermine its legitimacy in Hobbes's view.
23 *FI*, 66.
24 *FI*, 65.
25 Gordon Schochet also detects the existence of patriarchal families in the state of nature, but he does so on different grounds. See 'Thomas Hobbes on the Family and the State of Nature,' *Political Science Quarterly* 82:3 (September 1967).
26 Mary Beth Norton notes that such descriptions were the norm at the time in which Hobbes was writing. It was typical for a family to include servants and all those working and living in a household and subsumed under the family head. (See *Founding Mothers and Fathers*, 17–18). Whereas Pateman makes the case that women disappear from Hobbes's descriptions of the family because they are now servants, it is more likely that they are considered subjects, or that Hobbes 'forgets' women once his purpose in discussing them has been served.
27 *Lev* I: 15, 103.
28 *FI*, 63.
29 *Lev* II: 20, 138.
30 Hobbes, *The Elements of Law Natural and Politic*, ed. J.C.A. Gaskin (New York: Oxford University Press, 1994), chap. XXIII, 133.
31 *Lev* II: 20, 139.
32 Ibid.
33 See Zerilli, 'In the Beginning, Rape.'
34 *SC*, 32.
35 *SC*, 108–9.
36 *SC*, 33.
37 *SC*, 110.
38 This critique is also raised by Susan Moller Okin in her review of *The Sexual*

*Contract*. See 'Feminism, the Individual, and Contract Theory,' *Ethics* 100 (April 1990): 661.
39 *FI*, 70.
40 *Lev* II: 19, 137.
41 *The Elements of Law*, chap. XXIII, 132.
42 *SC*, 232.
43 *SC*, 220.
44 *SC*, 220.
45 *SC*, 36.
46 Johann Jakob Bachofen, *Myth, Religion and Mother Right: Selected Writings of J.J. Bachofen*, trans. Ralph Manheim (Princeton, NJ: Princeton University Press, 1967).
47 *SC*, 36.
48 Carole Pateman, 'The Fraternal Social Contract,' in Pateman, *The Disorder of Women*, 45.
49 *SC*, 102.
50 Mary O'Brien, *The Politics of Reproduction* (Boston: Routledge & Kegan Paul, 1981), 158–9.
51 Christine Di Stefano, *Configurations of Masculinity: A Feminist Perspective on Modern Political Theory* (Ithaca, NY: Cornell University Press, 1991), chap. 2.
52 Hobbes, *Human Nature and De Corpore Politico*, chap. XXIII, 130; emphasis added.
53 *SC*, 18.
54 *SC*, 29.
55 Carole Pateman, *The Problem of Political Obligation: A Critique of Liberal Theory* (Berkeley: University of California Press, 1985), 188.
56 Ibid., 192.
57 Pateman acknowledges this point in the preface to *The Sexual Contract*.
58 Pateman, *The Problem of Political Obligation*, 193.
59 *SC*, 115.
60 Ibid.
61 Pateman, *The Problem of Political Obligation*, 21.
62 The predominant feminist approach to the witch hunts is epitomized in the writings of Robin Morgan (see chapter 6 for discussion), as well as in Mary Daly, *Gyn/Ecology* (London: Women's Press, 1979) and Barbara Ehrenreich and Deirdre English, *Witches, Midwives and Nurses* (London: Writers and Readers Publishing Cooperative, 1973).
63 Diane Purkiss, *The Witch in History: Early Modern and Twentieth-century Representations* (New York: Routledge, 1996), 8–11.
64 Ibid., chap. 1.

## 6: Radical Feminism's Quest for Origins

1 Robin Morgan, 'Goodbye to All That,' *Rat*, 9–23 Feb. 1970. Reprinted in Robin Morgan, *Going Too Far: The Personal Chronicle of a Feminist* (New York: Vintage Books, 1978); italics in original.
2 From the centerpiece of *Quicksilver Times*, special supplement: Women's Liberation, 1969. Credit/The Old Mole. New York University, Tamiment Library, Women's Liberation Newspaper Box.
3 J.J. Bachofen, *Myth, Religion, and Mother Right: Selected Writings of J.J. Bachofen*, trans. Ralph Manheim (Princeton, NJ: Princeton University Press, 1967); Friedrich Engels, *The Origin of the Family, Private Property, and the State* (New York: International Publishers, 1942). Erich Fromm popularized the writings of Bachofen in such articles as 'The Significance of the Theory of Mother Right for Today,' written in 1970. See the most recent collection of Fromm's essays: *Love, Sexuality and Matriarchy: About Gender*, ed. Rainer Funk (New York: Fromm International Publishing, 1997). These thinkers share the basic idea that prior to patriarchal social relations existed some form of maternal or matriarchal culture. However, as Joseph Campbell explains in his introduction to Bachofen's writings in *Myth, Religion and Mother Right*, 'In Bachofen's usage the term mother right ... does not require that the woman should hold political sway' (xxxi). The liberties that the early Second Wave feminists took with Bachofen's conclusions is a subject worthy of further study.
4 It should be noted at the outset that many of the authors cited here use the terms feminism and radical feminism interchangeably. To a large extent, radical feminism was the dominant stream of the Women's Liberation Movement of the late 1960s and early 1970s, and certainly radical feminism supplied much of the momentum of the movement. For the purposes of this chapter, however, I will attempt to specify whether the claims being made refer to radical feminism or to feminism in general.
5 Sarah M. Grimke to Mary S. Parker, president of the Boston Female Anti-Slavery Society, Letter 1, *Letters on the Equality of the Sexes and the Condition of Woman* (New York: Burt Franklin, 1970: originally published 1838), 3–4.
6 Bonnie S. Anderson and Judith P. Zinsser, *A History of Their Own: Women in Europe from Prehistory to the Present*, Vol. I (Toronto: Harper & Row, 1988), chap. 1.
7 In addition, each group had to undergo three months of consciousness-raising. See 'Organizing Principles of the New York Radical Feminists,' in Shulamith Firestone and Anne Koedt, eds, *Notes from the Second Year* (New York: Radical Feminism, 1970), 120.

8 Shulamith Firestone, *The Dialectic of Sex: The Case for Feminist Revolution* (London: Women's Press, 1979); Kate Millet, *Sexual Politics* (Garden City, NY: Doubleday, 1970).
9 Elizabeth Gould Davis, *The First Sex* (New York: G.P. Putnam's Sons, 1971); Helen Diner, *Mothers and Amazons: The First Feminine History of Culture* (New York: Julian Press, 1965); Mary Daly, *Beyond God the Father: Toward a Philosophy of Women's Liberation* (Boston: Beacon Press, 1973); Elaine Morgan, *The Descent of Woman* (New York: Bantam, 1972); Wolfgang Lederer, *The Fear of Women* (New York: Harcourt, Brace, Jovanovich, 1968).
10 Engels's expression from *The Origin of the Family.*
11 Pat Leslie, book review, 'The First Sex,' in *The Other Woman* (Toronto) 1:2 (September 1972): 15.
12 Mary Lyon, for example, is commemorated for founding Mt Holyoke College, the first women's college in the United States. 'Herstory Almanac,' *Everywoman* 1:2 (5 Feb. 1971): 7.
13 Ann Forfreedom quotes Helen Diner's *Mothers and Amazons* in 'Herstory: Matriarchies,' *Everywoman* 1:2 (5 Feb 1971): 7; Barbara Miles quotes from *Pandora's Box* in 'Herstory: Amazons and Battle-Axes,' *Everywoman* 1:4 (5 March 1971): 5.
14 Linda Carcione, 'True Story: The Women's Movement, Part One,' *Quicksilver Times*, special supplement on Women's Liberation, 1969: 21. New York University, Tamiment Library, Women's Liberation Newspaper Box. One of the feminists who popularized the use of Engels during this period was Evelyn Reed. Although Reed did not become a radical feminist, but rather remained within the Marxist camp, she was no less preoccupied with describing an origin theory, and she adhered to Engels's belief in an original matriarchy.
15 Barbara Mehrhof, Linda Feldman, Sheila Cronan, and Ellen Willis, 'New York Women Reply,' *Voice of the Women's Liberation Movement* 7 (11 August 1969).
16 Dawn Chalker, 'The Economics of Oppression: Women in Capitalist Society,' *her-self* 3:8 (March 1975): 13.
17 Ibid., 12; emphasis mine.
18 Advertisement for classes in 'Women's Liberation and Socialism,' New York University, Tamiment Library, Women's Liberation File, 1970.
19 'The Women's Kit,' developed by Pamela Harris and Becky Kane, with Donna James, Margot Smith, and Claire Watson (Toronto: OISE, 1974). Under 100 kits were made and distributed. They are not identical; there is some variation in feminist periodicals, depending on availability, but each contains essentially the same kinds of items. An example of 'The Women's

Kit' can be found at University of Ottawa, Canadian Women's Movement Archives.
20 Pamela Harris, 'Fear of Women,' 8, in 'The Women's Kit.'
21 Pamela Harris, 'The Great Goddess,' 24, in 'The Women's Kit.'
22 Simone de Beauvoir, *The Second Sex* (New York: Knopf, 1953), 71.
23 Sarah B. Pomeroy, 'A Classical Scholar's Perspective on Matriarchy,' in Bernice A. Carroll, ed., *Liberating Women's History: Theoretical and Critical Essays* (Chicago: University of Illinois Press, 1976).
24 Adrienne Rich, *Of Woman Born: Motherhood as Experience and Institution* (New York: W.W. Norton, 1976), 86.
25 Ibid.
26 Gloria Steinem, 'Introduction' to William Moulton Marston, *Wonder Woman* (New York: Bonanza Books, 1972), pages unnumbered.
27 Phyllis Chesler, 'The Amazon Legacy,' in Marston, *Wonder Woman*.
28 Phyllis Chesler, *Women and Madness* (New York: Four Walls Eight Windows, 1997; originally published 1972), 311.
29 Ti-Grace Atkinson, *Amazon Odyssey* (New York: Links Books, 1974).
30 Amazon Collective (Milwaukee, WI), 'Amazon? Claiming Our Culture,' *Amazon* 1:3 (July 1972).
31 Chesler, *Women and Madness*, 311.
32 The references to Davis are too numerous to list. However, it is important to mention Jill Johnston, a regular contributor to *The Village Voice*, who had an active role in popularizing Davis's work. See *Lesbian Nation: The Feminist Solution* (New York: Simon and Schuster, 1973).
33 Esther Newton and Paula Webster discuss this point in 'Matriarchy: As Women See It,' *Aphra* 4:3 (Summer 1973): 12. *The First Sex* was eventually published as an inexpensive paperback, at which point its sales and thus its influence rose dramatically.
34 See her comments in the final chapter on the subordinate role of women in the student movement (*The First Sex*, 328–9). Although a generation older, Davis did not entirely escape controversy and politics within the feminist movement. Just as many feminists disparaged her work as liked it. Furthermore, Davis was posthumously accused by the re-formed Redstockings group of being a Naval Intelligence officer. See below, n. 128.
35 Davis, *The First Sex*, 34.
36 Ibid., 33.
37 Ibid., 34.
38 Ibid. The theory of the deformity of the Y chromosome is among many assertions Davis makes that are unsubstantiated. My purpose at this stage is merely to recount her narrative, however, and so I will not dwell on her

repeated errors of fact and interpretation. See, however, the critiques offered by Amy Hackett and Sarah Pomeroy in 'Making History: *The First Sex,*' *Feminist Studies* 1:2 (Fall 1972).

39 Davis, *The First Sex*, 35.
40 Ibid., 40–1.
41 Ibid., 64.
42 The use of the term 'individual' is noteworthy. To speak of individuals even in ancient Greece is anachronistic.
43 Davis, *The First Sex*, 148.
44 Quoted ibid.
45 For one example, the fact that priests still wear robes is said to be a symbol of the ancient worship of the Goddess. See Davis, *The First Sex*, 99.
46 Ibid., 78.
47 Ibid., 18.
48 Davis, suffering from cancer, committed suicide when she was 64 years old. Rhoda Lerman, 'In Memoriam: Elizabeth Gould Davis,' *Ms.* 3:6 (December 1974): 74.
49 My focus here is the American example both because of the surplus of sources and because it is in this context that some of the most important radical feminists developed a theoretical system. We should note that the same patterns were emerging in Canada, where a number of feminists worked in the civil rights movement, joined student movements on the left, and followed the same trajectory as their American counterparts in becoming dissatisfied with left caucuses. See Myrna Kostash, *Long Way from Home: The Story of the Sixties Generation in Canada* (Toronto: James Lorimer, 1980).
50 Sara Evans, *Personal Politics: The Roots of Women's Liberation in the Civil Rights Movement and the New Left* (New York: Knopf, 1979), 43.
51 This expression is taken from Todd Gitlin, but surfaces throughout movement literature. 'Putting your body on the line' was the only way to become a member of the student and civil rights movements, which otherwise had no formal membership system. See Todd Gitlin, *The Sixties: Years of Hope, Days of Rage*, rev. ed. (New York: Bantam, 1993), 84–5.
52 Evans and Gitlin both write of the incredible idealism, but also the solidarity of the 'beloved community.' See Evans, *Personal Politics*, 36–41.
53 See Flora Davis, *Moving the Mountain: The Women's Movement in America since 1960* (New York: Simon and Schuster, 1991); and Evans, *Personal Politics*.
54 Evans, *Personal Politics*, 88. White women activists did raise the issue of women's position in SNCC, only to be met with scepticism and Stokely

Carmichael's famous utterance: 'The only position of women in SNCC is prone.'
55 Ibid., 97–8.
56 Quote ibid., 98. King and Casey Hayden wrote a memo to raise the issue of women's marginalization within SNCC, entitled 'A Kind of Memo from Casey Hayden and Mary King to a number of other women in the Peace and Freedom Movements,' reprinted in Mary King, *Freedom Song: A Personal Story of the 1960s Civil Rights Movement* (New York: William Morrow, 1987).
57 Carol Hanisch, 'Hard Knocks: Working for Women's Liberation in a Mixed (Male-Female) Movement Group,' in Firestone and Koedt, eds, *Notes from the Second Year*, 60.
58 Gitlin criticizes the lack of coherent ideology underlying the movement's actions at the same time as he praises the movement's break with what he calls 1950s complacency. See Gitlin, *The Sixties*, 84–5.
59 Leslie Cagan, 'Something New Emerges: The Growth of a Socialist Feminist,' in Dick Cluster, ed., *They Should Have Served That Cup of Coffee* (Boston: South End Press, 1979), 238. As Judith Brown put it, 'Most women are not long suffering in the movement; they never really get in, and their brief passing is hardly noted. The radical female is cooled out, very simply, because she is not wanted politically, and she cannot proffer her secretarial skills as payment for inclusion in traditionally male activity – political decision-making.' See part 2 of Beverly Jones and Judith Brown, 'Toward a Female Liberation Movement,' in Leslie B. Tanner, ed., *Voices from Women's Liberation* (New York: Signet, 1970), 393–8.
60 [Rosalyn Baxandall], 'Roz's Page,' New York Radical Women, *Notes from the First Year* (New York), June 1968, 28. There are too many feminist pieces on left sexism to count, as almost all radical feminist writing in this period excoriates the left. Among the most influential are Marge Piercy, 'The Grand Coolie Damn,' in Robin Morgan, ed., *Sisterhood Is Powerful: An Anthology of Writings from the Women's Liberation Movement* (New York: Vintage, 1970); Firestone, *The Dialectic of Sex*; and Morgan, 'Goodbye to All That,' in *Going*.
61 This was also true in the Canadian case. The Knitting Circle was formed by radical women of the New Left Caucus at the University of Toronto upon their discovery of an internal discussion paper that ridiculed its women members. The paper presents women as clucking, gossiping hens in a knitting circle, thus the women's choice of name. See their response to the men's mockery: The Knitting Circle of the New Left Caucus, 'Destruction Is the Highest Form of Creation, or The *Real* Contradictions in the Social Rela-

tionships in the New Left Caucus (Back to the Materialist *Knitty*-Gritty)' [ca. 1969], University of Ottawa, Canadian Women's Movement Archives, File: New Left Caucus, The Knitting Circle of.
62 Alice Echols, *Daring to Be Bad: Radical Feminism in America, 1967–1975* (Minneapolis: University of Minnesota Press, 1989), 46–7.
63 As Echols states, '[W]hereas radical men seemed eager to do penance for their racism, they actively resisted women's attempts to raise the issue of sexual inequality.' See *Daring*, 48.
64 Reported ibid., 49; and Marlene LeGates, *Making Waves: A History of Feminism in Western Society* (Toronto: Copp Clark, 1996), 335. See also Ellen Willis's account of this event in 'Up from Radicalism: A Feminist Journal,' New York University, Tamiment Library, Women's Liberation File (undated). Reprinted from *US* magazine (Bantam Books), no. 2, October 1969.
65 Firestone, *The Dialectic of Sex*, 39.
66 'SDS National Resolution on Women' (Boston: New England Free Press, 1968), New York University, Tamiment Library, Women's Liberation File 1968.
67 This is perhaps the most reported incident relating to sexism in the movement literature. See Echols, *Daring*; LeGates, *Making Waves*; Cagan, 'Something New Emerges'; and Gitlin, *The Sixties*, 363.
68 Gitlin, *The Sixties*, 363.
69 Quoted in LeGates, *Making Waves*, 337.
70 More than one hundred women from across the United States gathered to protest outside the 1969 Miss America contest in Atlantic City; they marched, chanted, performed street theatre, handcuffed themselves to a giant mannequin of Miss America, and crowned a live sheep as Miss America. This protest is one of the earliest acts of the Women's Liberation Movement, and incited thousands of women to join the movement. See the reports of the event in *Liberation News Service* (New York), no. 104, 17 Sept. 1969; and Robin Morgan, 'Women Disrupt the Miss America Pageant,' in *Going*.
71 Evans, *Personal Politics*, 221.
72 'Unfortunately, there has been a real lack of discussion among women's groups and individual women about what we see as the root of women's problems and how we see change coming about ... For only when women have a grasp on these questions can we build a strong and effective movement.' Kathy Kozachenko, 'The Women's Movement: Political Definitions,' *her-self* 1:5 (October 1972): 4.
73 Robin Morgan, 'Introduction: Rights of Passage,' in *Going*, 9. See also Ti-Grace Atkinson's assertion that she was 'probing deeper and deeper into the roots of the oppression of women.' *Amazon Odyssey*, xxi.

74 Quote in Peter Babcox, 'Meet the Women of the Revolution, 1969,' *New York Times Magazine*, 9 Feb. 1969: 88.
75 Tom Hayden was a leader of SDS; this statement was made in reference to the *Berkeley Barb*. Quote in Babcox, 'Meet the Women,' 92.
76 The Weather Underground, or the Weather Bureau, a leftist group that carried out several bombings, and of which Jane Alpert was a member.
77 Morgan, 'Goodbye to All That,' 123.
78 Ibid., 128
79 Ibid., 130.
80 She discusses her efforts to get the left to change its view of women's liberation in the introduction to 'Take a Memo, Mr. Smith,' in Morgan, *Going*.
81 A zap action is a creative, impromptu protest against a specific issue or event; they often took the form of street theatre in which feminists dressed in costume to attract attention and raise awareness.
82 Morgan, 'Introduction: Rights of Passage,' 9.
83 'WITCH Documents,' in Morgan, ed., *Sisterhood Is Powerful*, 605.
84 'I am not here to revive the Left, but to bury it,' Morgan stated in a speech to a Stony Brook women's centre. See 'A Woman's Perspective of Robin Morgan,' in the undated, untitled newsletter, New York University, Tamiment Library, Women's Liberation File (undated).
85 Morgan, 'Introduction: Rights of Passage,' 11.
86 Diner's book *Mothers and Amazons* was discussed at a 1969 Thanksgiving conference in Chicago. In response to that discussion Pat Hansen wrote: 'This book has been for me a starting point into a completely new understanding of female cultural history.' Women need, in Hansen's view, to reject patriarchal definitions of women and to choose instead 'the matriarchal culture that preceded the patriarchal when woman was recognized for her inherent creative potentials.' See Pat Hansen, letter to the editor, *Voice of the Women's Liberation Movement* 1:5 (January 1969): 11.
87 Robin Morgan, 'Letter to the Editors,' *oob* 2:8 (March 1972): 30.
88 Robin Morgan, 'Three Articles on WITCH,' in *Going*, 72.
89 See Claudia Morrow, 'Robin Morgan: Credit Union Benefit,' *her-self* 4:2, June 1975: 3.
90 Robin Morgan, 'Lesbianism and Feminism: Synonyms or Contradictions,' in *Going*, 188.
91 Morgan, 'Three Articles on WITCH,' 72.
92 Quoted in Fran Pollner, 'Robin: Harbinger of a New Season,' *oob* 2:7 (March 1972).
93 Robin Morgan, 'The Network of the Imaginary Mother,' in *Upstairs in the Garden: Poems Selected and New, 1968–1988* (New York: W.W. Norton, 1990).

94 At precisely this point, she became reacquainted with Robin Morgan. My interest here is less in their tumultuous friendship – which has been well described by Alpert in her memoirs – and more in their shared politics: their rejection of the left and concomitant adoption of a matriarchal feminist theory.
95 Alpert originally intended the piece to be addressed to the Weathermen, but it was Morgan who recommended that she address it 'Dear Sisters in the Weather Underground.' See Jane Alpert, *Growing Up Underground* (New York: William Morrow & Co., 1981), 343.
96 Jane Alpert, 'Mother Right: A New Feminist Theory,' *Ms.* 2:2 (August 1973): 88.
97 Ibid., 55.
98 Ibid., 91.
99 Ibid. In her memoir, Alpert concedes that 'Davis had most of her facts wrong and had grossly misinterpreted modern scholarship.' She drew this conclusion after having reread several of the ancient texts that Davis cited.
100 Alpert, 'Mother Right,' 94.
101 Alpert, 'Letter from the Underground,' *oob* 3:9 (July/Aug. 1973). *oob* published Alpert's letter as a preface to 'Mother Right,' but *Ms.* published only the piece itself with a foreword by Gloria Steinem.
102 Ellen Willis, 'Liberation Forum,' *Guardian*, 15 Feb. 1969: 11. New York University, Tamiment Library, Redstockings of the Women's Liberation Movement File.
103 Alpert, 'Mother Right,' 91
104 Ibid., 92.
105 See the controversy in *her-self* in several 1975 issues, and in *oob* from 1973, when the original Alpert piece was published, to 1975, when an interview with Alpert followed.
106 The question of how to interpret the goddesses of Greek mythology remains a contested one. See, for example, Sue Blundell and Margaret Williamson, eds, *The Sacred and the Feminine in Ancient Greece* (New York: Routledge, 1998).
107 Pomeroy, 'A Classical Scholar's Perspective,' 219.
108 See Sue Blundell, *Women in Ancient Greece* (Cambridge, MA: Harvard University Press, 1995).
109 Emily Erwin Culpepper, 'Female History Myth Making,' *The Second Wave* 4:1 (Spring 1975).
110 Leah Zahler, 'Matriarchy and Myth,' *Aphra* 4:3 (Summer 1973): 30.
111 Merlin Stone, 'Response,' in Charlene Spretnak, ed., *The Politics of Women's*

*Spirituality: Essays on the Rise of Spiritual Power within the Feminist Movement* (Garden City, NY: Anchor Press, 1982), 550.

112 Sally R. Binford, 'Are Goddesses and Matriarchies Merely Figments of a Feminist Imagination? Myths and Matriarchies,' in Spretnak, *Politics*, 542–3.

113 Betsy Warrior, 'Conviction and Faith,' letter to the editors of *oob* 3:9 (July/August 1973): 25.

114 Paraphrase of Ti-Grace Atkinson by Judy Antonelli in 'Atkinson Re-evaluates Feminism,' *oob* 5:5 (May/June 1975): 19.

115 Ibid.

116 Roxanne Dunbar in 'Dear Jane Alpert,' letters to *Ms.* 2:8 (February 1974): 61.

117 The Feminists, 'Building the Matriarchy,' letter to the editors of *oob* 3:9 (July/August 1973): 26.

118 Rosalind Miles, *The Women's History of the World* (London: Paladin, 1988), 19–20.

119 Ibid., 20.

120 Brian Hayden, 'Old Europe: Sacred Matriarchy or Complementary Opposition?' in Anthony Bonanno, ed., *Archaeology and Fertility Cult in the Ancient Mediterranean* (Amsterdam: B.R. Gruner, 1986), 22.

121 Paraphrase of Atkinson by Antonelli, 'Atkinson Re-evaluates Feminism,' 19.

122 Gitlin, *The Sixties*, 374.

123 'We must look to our matriarchal past for guidance in defining a culture that is a logical extension of nature,' writes Kathleen Barry, for 'female culture ... will reverse the subordinated link to nature [that] patriarchy forces on women.' Barry is making the case that women's studies programmes should be run by those whose first priority is to create a female culture. See Kathleen Barry, 'West Coast Conference: Not Purely Academic,' *oob* 3:10 (September 1973): 25. Another famous call for a female culture is found in the *Fourth World Manifesto* (New Haven, CT: Advocate Press, 1971) by Barbara Burris (in agreement with Kathleen Barry, Terry Moon, Joann DeLor, Joann Parent, and Cate Stadelman). In this lengthy and controversial document the 'long-suppressed and ridiculed female principle' is affirmed, and women all over the world are identified as the 'female culture' and the 'Fourth World.'

124 Paraphrase of Atkinson by Antonelli, 'Atkinson Re-evaluates Feminism,' 19.

125 The Feminists, 'Building the Matriarchy,' 26.

126 Gitlin, *The Sixties*, 373.
127 Like Alice Echols, Brooke Williams sees a shift in feminism in the mid-1970s from radical to cultural feminism. Brooke, as she calls herself, argues for the need to return, not to an original matriarchy, but to the original principles of radical feminist politics. Cultural feminism and the matriarchal emphasis that accompanies it, in Brooke's view, 'is an attempt to transform feminism from a political movement to a lifestyle movement.' See Brooke, 'The Retreat to Cultural Feminism,' in Redstockings, *Feminist Revolution* (New York: Random House, 1978), 83. See also Brooke, 'When Going Back Is Going Forward,' *Meeting Ground* 1 (January 1977); and Brooke Williams, 'The Chador of Women's Liberation: Cultural Feminism and the Movement Press,' *Heresies* 3:1 (1980).
128 A few years after the original Redstockings for Women's Liberation collective dissolved, some of its original members along with some additional feminists re-formed the group to protest the de-radicalization of the Women's Liberation Movement. The group issued a lengthy press release entitled 'Feminist Revolution,' in which they accused various feminists of being too liberal or of conspiring with the state. They claimed that Elizabeth Gould Davis was a suspicious character because she had been in the Navy, and because of her occupation as a librarian. The group was especially critical of Gloria Steinem for her liberal sympathies in *Ms.* and for being a conspirator with the CIA. Steinem (reluctantly) defended herself against the charges, and several other feminists came to her defence, including Robin Morgan. See the reprint of the press release in Redstockings, *Feminist Revolution*, ed. Kathie Sarachild (New Paltz, NY: Redstockings, 1975), Columbia University, Barnard Center for Research on Women, restricted file. For legal reasons having to do with contentious charges against Steinem, the unabridged version is not widely accessible. See also Steinem's essay and Morgan's letter, both in *her-self* 4:4 (September 1975); and Mary Thom's account of the incident in *Inside Ms.: 25 Years of the Magazine and the Feminist Movement* (New York: Henry Holt, 1997), 74–9.
129 Miles, *The Women's History of the World*; Riane Eisler, *The Chalice and the Blade: Our History, Our Future* (San Francisco: HarperCollins, 1987). As well, see Peggy Reeves Sanday's academic treatise *Female Power and Male Dominance: On the Origins of Sexual Inequality* (New York: Cambridge University Press, 1981).

## Conclusion

1 Barbara G. Walker, *Amazon: A Novel* (New York: HarperCollins, 1992), 20.
2 Ibid., 24.

3 Ibid., 24.
4 Ibid., 59.
5 Ibid., 50.
6 Ibid., 50.
7 Ibid., 83.
8 Ibid., 74.
9 Some examples include Karen Armstrong, *In the Beginning: A New Interpretation of Genesis* (New York: Ballantine, 1996); Bill Moyers, *Genesis: A Living Conversation*, ed. Betty Sue Flowers (New York: Doubleday, 1996) and the PBS Television series by the same name. An early contribution to the revived debate is Elaine Pagels's *Adam, Eve, and the Serpent* (New York: Vintage, 1988).

# Bibliography

### General Works

Abrams, M.H. *A Glossary of Literary Terms*. 5th ed. Montreal: Holt, Rinehart and Winston, 1988.

Arendt, Hannah. *On Revolution*. New York: Viking Press, 1963.

Armstrong, Karen. *In the Beginning: A New Interpretation of Genesis*. Toronto: Ballantine, 1996.

Bailyn, Bernard. *On the Teaching and Writing of History: Responses to a Series of Questions*. Ed. Edward Connery Lathem. Hanover, NH: Montgomery Endowment, Dartmouth College, 1994.

Barthes, Roland. *Mythologies*. Trans. Annette Lavers. Toronto: Paladin, 1973.

Davis-Floyd, Robbie E., and Carolyn F. Sargent, eds. *Childbirth and Authoritative Knowledge: Cross-Cultural Perspectives*. Los Angeles: University of California Press, 1997.

Foucault, Michel. 'Nietzsche, Genealogy, History.' In Paul Rabinow, ed., *The Foucault Reader*. New York: Pantheon, 1984.

Hobsbawm, E.J. *Nations and Nationalism since 1780: Programme, Myth, Reality*. New York: Cambridge University Press, 1990.

Honig, Bonnie. 'Declarations of Independence: Arendt and Derrida on the Problem of Founding a Republic.' In Frederick M. Dolan and Thomas L. Dumm, eds, *Rhetorical Republic: Governing Representations in American Politics*. Amherst: University of Massachusetts Press, 1993.

Moyers, Bill. *Genesis: A Living Conversation*. Ed. Betty Sue Flowers. New York: Doubleday, 1996.

Nussbaum, Martha C. *Cultivating Humanity: A Classical Defense of Reform in Liberal Education*. Cambridge, MA: Harvard University Press, 1997.

Pagels, Elaine. *Adam, Eve, and the Serpent*. New York: Vintage, 1988.

Porter, J.R. 'Creation.' In Bruce M. Metzger and Michael D. Coogan, eds, *The Oxford Companion to the Bible.* New York: Oxford, 1993.
Russell, Bertrand. *Religion and Science.* New York: Oxford University Press, 1997.
Said, Edward. *Beginnings: Intention and Method.* New York: Basic Books, 1975.
Sawyer, Deborah F. *Women and Religion in the First Christian Centuries.* New York: Routledge, 1996.
Skinner, Quentin. 'Meaning and Understanding in the History of Ideas.' In James Tully, ed., *Meaning and Context: Quentin Skinner and His Critics.* Princeton, NJ: Princeton University Press, 1988.
Smith, Anthony D. *National Identity.* Reno: University of Nevada Press, 1991.
Smith, Bruce James. *Politics and Remembrance: Republican Themes in Machiavelli, Burke, and Tocqueville.* Princeton, NJ: Princeton University Press, 1985.
Tully, James. *Strange Multiplicity: Constitutionalism in an Age of Diversity.* New York: Cambridge University Press, 1995.
von Franz, Marie-Louise. *Creation Myths.* Rev. ed. Boston and London: Shambhala, 1995.
Wolin, Sheldon S. *Politics and Vision: Continuity and Innovation in Western Political Thought.* Toronto: Little, Brown and Co., 1960.
Wright, Ronald. *Stolen Continents: The 'New World' through Indian Eyes.* Toronto: Penguin, 1992.

## Plato (Primary)

Aeschylus. *Eumenides.* In *Greek Drama.* Ed., with intro., Moses Hadas. Toronto: Bantam, 1982.
Aristotle. 'On the Generation of Animals.' In Mary Briody Mahowald, ed., *Philosophy of Woman: An Anthology of Classic and Current Concepts.* Indianapolis: Hackett, 1983.
– *The Politics.* Trans. Ernest Barker. Rev., with intro. and notes, R.F. Stalley. New York: Oxford University Press, 1995.
Heraclitus. *On the Universe.* In *Hippocrates*, volume IV. Trans. W.H.S. Jones. London: Heinemann Ltd., 1931.
Hippocrates. 'Diseases of Women 1.' In Mary R. Lefkowitz and Maureen B. Fant, eds, *Women's Life in Greece and Rome: A Source Book in Translation.* Baltimore: Johns Hopkins University Press, 1982.
– 'On the Generating Seed and the Nature of the Child.' In Lefkowitz and Fant, eds, *Women's Life in Greece and Rome.*
– *Hippocrates*, volume IV. Trans. W.H.S. Jones. London: Heinemann Ltd., 1931.

Kirk, G.S., and J.E. Raven, eds. *The Presocratic Philosophers: A Critical History with a Selection of Texts*. New York: Cambridge University Press, 1957.

Plato. *The Collected Dialogues of Plato Including the Letters*. Ed., with intro. and prefatory notes, Edith Hamilton and Huntington Cairns. New York: Pantheon Books, 1961.

Thucydides. *History of the Peloponnesian War*. Volume 1. Trans. Charles Forster Smith. Cambridge, MA: Harvard University Press, 1935.

**Plato (Secondary)**

Annas, Julia. 'Plato's Republic and Feminism.' *Philosophy* 51 (1976).

Balme, D.M. 'Anthropos Anthropon Genna: Human Is Generated by Human.' In G.R. Dunstan, ed., *The Human Embryo: Aristotle and the Arabic and European Traditions*. Devon: University of Exeter Press, 1990.

Bedford, David. 'The Politics of Appetite: Plato on Money-Making.' Paper presented at the Canadian Political Science Association meetings, Quebec City, 2001.

Bedford, David, and Thom Workman. 'Recalling Plato from Exile: The Pursuit of Reasoned Moderation in International Relations.' Paper presented at the New England Political Science Association meetings, Portland, ME, 2002.

Bloom, Allan. 'Interpretive Essay.' In *The Republic of Plato*. Trans., with notes, Allan Bloom. New York: HarperCollins, 1991.

Blundell, Sue. *Women in Ancient Greece*. Cambridge, MA: Harvard University Press, 1995.

Brown, Wendy. '"Supposing Truth Were a Woman ...": Plato's Subversion of Masculine Discourse.' In Nancy Tuana, ed., *Feminist Interpretations of Plato*. University Park: Pennsylvania State University Press, 1994.

Cornford, Francis MacDonald. *Plato's Cosmology: The Timaeus of Plato Translated with a Running Commentary*. London: Routledge & Kegan Paul, 1966.

*Principium Sapientiae: The Origins of Greek Philosophical Thought*. Ed. W.K.C. Guthrie. New York: Harper Torchbooks, 1965.

Demand, Nancy. *Birth, Death, and Motherhood in Classical Greece*. Baltimore: Johns Hopkins University Press, 1994.

duBois, Page. *Sowing the Body: Psychoanalysis and Ancient Representations of Women*. Chicago: University of Chicago Press, 1988.

Geddes, Anne. 'The Philosophic Notion of Women in Antiquity.' *Antichthon: Journal of the Australian Society for Classical Studies* 9 (1975).

Genova, Judith. 'Feminist Dialectics: Plato and Dualism.' In Bat-Ami Bar On, ed., *Engendering Origins: Critical Feminist Readings in Plato and Aristotle*. Albany: State University of New York Press, 1994.

Goldhill, Simon. *Foucault's Virginity: Ancient Erotic Fiction and the History of Sexuality.* New York: Cambridge University Press, 1995.

Guthrie, W.K.C. *The Greek Philosophers from Thales to Aristotle.* New York: Harper & Row, 1960.

– *A History of Greek Philosophy.* Volume I, *The Earlier Presocratics and the Pythagoreans.* Cambridge: Cambridge University Press, 1962.

– *A History of Greek Philosophy.* Volume 5, *The Later Plato and the Academy.* New York: Cambridge University Press, 1978.

Halperin, David M. 'Why Is Diotima a Woman? Platonic Erós and the Figuration of Gender.' In David M. Halperin, John J. Winkler, and Froma I. Zeitlin, eds, *Before Sexuality: The Construction of Erotic Experience in the Ancient Greek World.* Princeton, NJ: Princeton University Press, 1990.

Hampton, Cynthia. 'Overcoming Dualism: The Importance of the Intermediate in Plato's *Philebus*.' In Bat-Ami Bar On, ed., *Engendering Origins: Critical Feminist Readings in Plato and Aristotle.* Albany: State University of New York Press, 1994.

Hansen, Mogens Herman. *The Athenian Democracy in the Age of Demosthenes.* Trans. J.A. Crook. Cambridge: Blackwell, 1991.

Hawthorne, Susan. 'Diotima Speaks through the Body.' In Bat-Ami Bar On, ed., *Engendering Origins: Critical Feminist Readings in Plato and Aristotle.* Albany: State University of New York Press, 1994.

Held, Virginia. 'Preconceptions of Birth and Death.' In *Feminist Morality: Transforming Culture, Society and Politics.* Chicago: University of Chicago Press, 1993.

Irwin, T.H. 'Plato: The Intellectual Background.' In Richard Kraut, ed., *The Cambridge Companion to Plato.* New York: Cambridge University Press, 1992.

Kahn, Robbie Pfeufer. *Bearing Meaning: The Language of Birth.* Urbana and Chicago: University of Illinois Press, 1995.

King, Helen. 'Making a Man: Becoming Human in Early Greek Medicine.' In G.R. Dunstan, ed., *The Human Embryo: Aristotle and the Arabic and European Traditions.* Devon: University of Exeter Press, 1990.

Kraut, Richard. 'Introduction to the Study of Plato.' In Richard Kraut, ed., *The Cambridge Companion to Plato.* New York: Cambridge University Press, 1992.

Krell, David Farrell. 'Female Parts in *Timaeus*.' *Arion: A Journal of Humanities and the Classics,* new series, 2:3 (1975).

Laqueur, Thomas. *Making Sex: Body and Gender from the Greeks to Freud.* Cambridge, MA: Harvard University Press, 1990.

Leduc, Claudine. 'Marriage in Ancient Greece.' In Pauline Schmitt Pantel, ed., *A History of Women. I: From Ancient Goddesses to Christian Saints.* Cambridge, MA: Belknap Press of Harvard University Press, 1992.

Lloyd, Genevieve. *The Man of Reason: 'Male' and 'Female' in Western Philosophy.* 2nd ed. London: Routledge, 1993.
Loraux, Nicole. *The Children of Athena: Athenian Ideas about Citizenship and the Division between the Sexes.* Trans. Caroline Levine. Princeton, NJ: Princeton University Press, 1993.
Lovibond, Sabina. 'An Ancient Theory of Gender: Plato and the Pythagorean Table.' In Léonie J. Archer, Susan Fischler, and Maria Wyke, eds, *Women in Ancient Societies: An Illusion in the Night.* New York: Routledge, 1994.
Rutherford, R.B. *The Art of Plato: Ten Essays in Platonic Interpretation.* Cambridge, MA: Harvard University Press, 1995.
Samuelson, Norbert M. *Judaism and the Doctrine of Creation.* New York: Cambridge University Press, 1994.
Saxonhouse, Arlene W. 'Eros and the Female in Greek Political Thought: An Interpretation of Plato's *Symposium.*' *Political Theory* 12 (1984).
– 'Myths and the Origins of Cities: Reflections on the Autochthony Theme in Euripides' Ion.' In J. Peter Euben, ed., *Greek Tragedy and Political Theory.* Berkeley: University of California Press, 1986.
– *Women in the History of Political Thought: Ancient Greece to Machiavelli.* New York: Praeger, 1985.
Seller, Mary J. 'Short Communication: Some Fallacies in Embryology through the Ages.' In G.R. Dunstan, ed., *The Human Embryo: Aristotle and the Arabic and European Traditions.* Devon: University of Exeter Press, 1990.
Sissa, Giulia. 'The Sexual Philosophies of Plato and Aristotle.' In Pauline Schmitt Pantel, ed., *A History of Women.* Volume 1, *From Ancient Goddesses to Christian Saints.* Cambridge, MA: Belknap Press of Harvard University Press, 1992.
Taylor, A.E. *A Commentary on Plato's Timaeus.* Toronto: Oxford University Press, 1928.
Tuana, Nancy. *The Less Noble Sex: Scientific, Religious, and Philosophical Conceptions of Woman's Nature.* Indianapolis: Indiana University Press, 1993.
Vlastos, Gregory, ed. *Plato: A Collection of Critical Essays*, volume 2. Notre Dame, IN: University of Notre Dame Press, 1971.
– 'Was Plato a Feminist?' *Times Literary Supplement* 4:485, 17–23 March 1989.
Warrington, John. 'Introduction' to *Timaeus.* Ed. and trans. John Warrington. Dutton, NY: Everyman's Library, 1965.

### Hobbes (Primary)

Aughterson, Kate, ed. *Renaissance Woman: A Sourcebook. Constructions of Femininity in England.* New York: Routledge, 1995.

Cary, Mary (Rande). *Little Horns Doom and Downfall.* 1651.
Filmer, Sir Robert. *Patriarcha and Other Writings.* Ed. Johann P. Sommerville. New York: Cambridge University Press, 1991.
Fleming, Chief Baron. 'Bate's Case' (1606). In *The Stuart Constitution, 1603–1688: Documents and Commentary.* 2nd ed., ed. J.P. Kenyon. New York: Cambridge, 1986.
Henderson, Katherine Usher, and Barbara F. McManus, eds. *Half Humankind: Contexts and Texts of the Controversy about Women in England, 1540–1640.* Urbana and Chicago: University of Illinois Press, 1985.
Hobbes, Thomas. *Behemoth or The Long Parliament.* Ed. Ferdinand Tönnies. Intro. Stephen Holmes. Chicago: University of Chicago Press, 1990.
– *The Correspondence.* Volume 2, *1660–1679.* Ed. Noel Malcolm. Oxford: Clarendon, 1994.
– *The Elements of Law Natural and Politic.* Ed., with intro., J.C.A. Gaskin. New York: Oxford University Press, 1994.
– *Leviathan.* Ed. Richard Tuck. New York: Cambridge University Press, 1991.
– *Man and Citizen (De Homme and De Cive).* Ed. Bernard Gert. Indianapolis: Hackett, 1991.
King James VI and I. *Political Writings.* Ed. Johann P. Sommerville. New York: Cambridge University Press, 1994.
Lady Marchioness of Newcastle. *Philosophical Letters: Or, Modest Reflections Upon some Opinions in Natural Philosophy, Maintained By Several Famous and Learned Authors of this Age, Expressed by way of Letters.* London, 1664.
Lilburne, John. *Unto every individual Member of Parliament: The humble Representation of divers afflicted women-Petitioners to the Parliament, on behalf of Mr. John Lilburne.* 29 July 1653.
[Neville, Henry]. *Parliament of Ladies; With their Lawes newly enacted.* 1647.
Poole, Elizabeth. *An Alarum of War, Given to the Army, and to their High Court of Justice (so called) by the wille of God.* 1649.
– *A Vision: wherein is manifested the disease and cure of the Kingdom being the summe of what was lately delivered to the Councel of War.* London, 1648.
*To the Supream authority of this Nation, the commons assembled in Parliament: The humble Petition of divers wel-affected Women.* London, 1649.
*To the Supreme Authority of England. The Commons Assembled in Parliament.* 5 May 1649.
Swetnam, Joseph, *The arraignment of lewd, idle, froward, and inconstant women.* 1615.
*A True Copie of the Petition of the Gentlewomen, and the Tradesmens-wives in and about the City of London.* London, 1641.
Woodhouse, A.S.P., ed. *Puritanism and Liberty: Being the Army Debates (1647–49) from the Clarke Manuscripts.* Rutland, VT: Charles E. Tuttle Co., 1992.

## Hobbes (Secondary)

Bell, Ilona, 'Elizabeth I – Always Her Own Free Woman.' In Carole Levin and Patricia A. Sullivan, eds, *Political Rhetoric, Power, and Renaissance Women.* Albany: State University of New York Press, 1995.

Breitenberg, Mark. *Anxious Masculinity in Early Modern England.* New York: Cambridge University Press, 1996.

Burgess, Glenn. *The Politics of the Ancient Constitution: An Introduction to English Political Thought, 1603–1642.* University Park: Pennsylvania State University Press, 1992.

Coole, Diana. 'Women, Gender and Contract: Feminist Interpretations.' In David Boucher and Paul Kelly, eds, *The Social Contract from Hobbes to Rawls.* New York: Routledge, 1994.

Crawford, Patricia. 'The Challenges to Patriarchalism: How Did the Revolution Affect Women?' In John Morrill, ed., *Revolution and Restoration: England in the 1650s.* London: Collins and Brown, 1992.

– 'Public Duty, Conscience, and Women in Early Modern England.' In John Morrill, Paul Slack, and Daniel Woolf, eds, *Public Duty and Private Conscience in Seventeenth-century England: Essays Presented to G.E. Aylmer.* Toronto: Clarendon Press, 1993.

– *Women and Religion in England, 1500–1720.* New York: Routledge, 1996.

Cressy, David. *Birth, Marriage, and Death: Ritual, Religion, and the Life-cycle in Tudor and Stuart England.* Toronto: Oxford University Press, 1997.

Di Stefano, Christine. *Configurations of Masculinity: A Feminist Perspective on Modern Political Theory.* Ithaca, NY: Cornell University Press, 1991.

Fletcher, Anthony. *Gender, Sex and Subordination in England, 1500–1800.* New Haven, CT: Yale University Press, 1995.

Fraser, Antonia. *The Weaker Vessel.* New York: Vintage Books, 1985.

Gowing, Laura. *Domestic Dangers: Women, Words, and Sex in Early Modern London.* New York: Oxford University Press, 1998.

Green, Karen. *The Woman of Reason: Feminism, Humanism and Political Thought.* New York: Continuum, 1995.

Hill, Christopher. *The English Bible and the Seventeenth-century Revolution.* Toronto: Penguin, 1993.

Hirschmann, Nancy J. *Rethinking Obligation: A Feminist Method for Political Theory.* Ithaca, NY: Cornell University Press, 1992.

Houston, Alan Craig. '"A Way of Settlement": The Levellers, Monopolies and the Public Interest.' *History of Political Thought* 14:3 (Autumn 1993).

Hughes, Ann. *The Causes of the English Civil War.* London: Macmillan, 1991.

– 'Gender and Politics in Leveller Literature.' In Susan D. Amussen and

Mark A. Kishlansky, eds, *Political Culture and Cultural Politics in Early Modern England.* Manchester and New York: Manchester University Press, 1995.

Ingram, Martin. '"Scolding women cucked or washed": A Crisis in Gender Relations in Early Modern England?' In Jennifer Kermode and Garthine Walker, eds, *Women, Crime and the Courts in Early Modern England.* Chapel Hill, NC, and London: University of North Carolina Press, 1994.

Jaquette, Jane S. 'Contract and Coercion: Power and Gender in *Leviathan*.' In Hilda L. Smith, ed., *Women Writers and the Early Modern British Political Tradition.* New York: Cambridge University Press, 1998.

Johnston, David. *The Rhetoric of Leviathan: Thomas Hobbes and the Politics of Cultural Transformation.* Princeton, NJ: Princeton University Press, 1986.

Kahn, Victoria. '"The Duty to Love": Passion and Obligation in Early Modern Political Theory.' *Representations* 68 (Fall 1999).

– 'Margaret Cavendish and the Romance of Contract.' *Renaissance Quarterly* 50:2 (1997).

Kramer, Matthew H. *Hobbes and the Paradoxes of Political Origins.* New York: St Martin's Press, 1997.

Laurence, Anne. *Women in England, 1500–1740: A Social History.* London: Phoenix, 1994.

Mack, Phyllis. *Visionary Women: Ecstatic Prophesy in Seventeenth-century England.* Berkeley: University of California Press, 1992.

Macpherson, C.B. *The Political Theory of Possessive Individualism: Hobbes to Locke.* New York: Oxford University Press, 1962.

Makus, Ingrid. *Women, Politics, and Reproduction: The Liberal Legacy.* Toronto: University of Toronto Press, 1996.

Masek, Rosemary. 'Women in an Age of Transition: 1485–1714.' In Barbara Kanner, ed., *The Women of England: From Anglo-Saxon Times to the Present. Interpretive Bibliographic Essays.* Hamden, CT: Archon, 1979.

McEntee, Ann Marie. '"The [Un]Civill-Sisterhood of Oranges and Lemons": Female Petitioners and Demonstrators, 1642–53.' *Prose Studies* 14 (1991).

Mendelson, Sara, and Patricia Crawford. *Women in Early Modern England, 1550–1720.* Oxford and New York: Clarendon Press, 1998.

Mills, Charles W. *The Racial Contract.* Ithaca, NY, and London: Cornell University Press, 1997.

Morrill, John. *The Nature of the English Revolution: Essays.* New York: Longman, 1993.

Morrill, John, Paul Slack, and Daniel Woolf, eds. *Public Duty and Private Conscience in Seventeenth-century England: Essays Presented to G.E. Aylmer.* Toronto: Clarendon Press, 1993.

Norton, Mary Beth. *Founding Mothers and Fathers: Gendered Power and the Forming of American Society.* New York: Alfred A. Knopf, 1996.
Orlin, Lena Cowen. 'The Fictional Families of Elizabeth I.' In Carole Levin and Patricia A. Sullivan, eds, *Political Rhetoric, Power, and Renaissance Women.* Albany: State University of New York Press, 1995.
Purkiss, Diane. *Women, Texts, and Histories, 1575–1760.* New York: Routledge, 1992.
Schochet, G.J. 'Intending (Political) Obligation: Hobbes and the Voluntary Basis of Society.' In Mary Dietz, ed., *Thomas Hobbes and Political Theory.* Lawrence: University Press of Kansas, 1990.
– *Patriarchalism in Political Thought: The Authoritarian Family and Political Speculation and Attitudes Especially in Seventeenth-century England.* Oxford: Basil Blackwell, 1975.
– 'The Significant Sounds of Silence: The Absence of Women from the Political Thought of Sir Robert Filmer and John Locke (or, "Why Can't a Woman Be More Like a Man?").' In Hilda L. Smith, ed., *Women Writers and the Early Modern British Political Tradition.* New York: Cambridge University Press, 1998.
– 'Thomas Hobbes on the Family and the State of Nature.' *Political Science Quarterly* 82:3 (September 1967).
Schwarz, Kathryn. *Tough Love: Amazon Encounters in the English Rennaissance.* Durham, NC, and London: Duke University Press, 2000.
Skinner, Quentin. *Reason and Rhetoric in the Philosophy of Hobbes.* New York: Cambridge University Press, 1996.
– 'Thomas Hobbes's Antiliberal Theory of Liberty.' In Bernard Yack, ed., *Liberalism without Illusions: Essays on Liberal Theory and the Political Vision of Judith Shklar.* Chicago: University of Chicago Press, 1996.
Smith, Hilda L. '"Though it be the part of every good wife": Margaret Cavendish, Duchess of Newcastle.' In Valerie Frith, ed., *Women and History: Voices of Early Modern England.* Concord, ON: Irwin Press, 1995.
Smith, Hilda L., ed. *Women Writers and the Early Modern British Political Tradition.* New York: Cambridge University Press, 1998.
Sommerville, J.P. *Politics and Ideology in England, 1603–1640.* New York: Longman, 1986.
Sommerville, Margaret R. *Sex and Subjection: Attitudes to Women in Early-modern Society.* New York: St Martin's Press, 1995.
Sorell, Tom, ed. *The Cambridge Companion to Hobbes.* New York: Cambridge University Press, 1996.
Spragens, Thomas A., Jr. *The Politics of Motion: The World of Thomas Hobbes.* Foreword Anthony Flew. Lexington: University Press of Kentucky, 1973.

Trigg, Roger. *Ideas of Human Nature: An Historical Introduction.* Cambridge: Blackwell, 1988.

Trubowitz, Rachel. 'Female Preachers and Male Wives: Gender and Authority in Civil War England.' *Prose Studies* 14 (1991).

Tully, James. *Strange Multiplicity: Constitutionalism in an Age of Diversity.* New York: Cambridge University Press, 1995.

Underdown, D.E. *A Freeborn People: Politics and the Nation in Seventeenth-century England.* Oxford: Clarendon, 1996.

– 'The Taming of the Scold: The Enforcement of Patriarchal Authority in Early Modern England.' In Anthony Fletcher and John Stevenson, eds, *Order and Disorder in Early Modern England.* New York: Cambridge University Press, 1985

Vickery, Amanda. 'Golden Age to Separate Spheres? A Review of the Categories and Chronology of English Women's History.' *Historical Journal* 36:2 (1993).

Watkins, J.W.N. *Hobbes's System of Ideas: A Study in the Political Significance of Philosophical Theories.* London: Hutchinson, 1965.

Weil, Rachel. *Political Passions: Gender, the Family and Political Argument in England, 1680–1714.* Manchester and New York: Manchester University Press and St Martin's Press, 1999.

Westfall, Richard S. *The Construction of Modern Science: Mechanisms and Mechanics.* New York: Cambridge University Press, 1977.

Willis, Deborah. *Malevolent Nurture: Witch-hunting and Maternal Power in Early Modern England.* Ithaca, NY: Cornell University Press, 1995.

Wolin, Sheldon S. *Hobbes and the Epic Tradition of Political Theory.* Los Angeles: William Andrews Clark Memorial Library, 1970.

Wootton, David. 'Leveller Democracy and the Puritan Revolution.' In J.H. Burns and Mark Goldie, eds, *The Cambridge History of Political Thought, 1450–1700.* New York: Cambridge University Press, 1991.

Wright, Celeste Turner. 'The Amazons in Elizabethan Literature.' *Studies in Philology* 37:3 (July 1940).

Zuckert, Michael. *Natural Rights and the New Republicanism.* Princeton, NJ: Princeton University Press, 1994.

**Feminist Origin Stories (Primary)**

*Newspapers*

*Amazon*
*Everywoman*

*The Guardian*
*her-self*
*Liberation News Service*
*off our backs (oob)*
*The Other Woman (Toronto)*
*Quicksilver Times*
*The Second Wave*
*Voice of the Women's Liberation Movement*

*Books, Articles, and Ephemera*

Alpert, Jane. *Growing Up Underground*. New York: William Morrow & Co., 1981.
– 'Mother Right: A New Feminist Theory.' *Ms.* 2:2 (August 1973).
Brooke [Williams]. 'The Retreat to Cultural Feminism.' In Redstockings, *Feminist Revolution*. Abridged edition with additional writings. New York: Random House, 1978.
– 'When Going Back Is Going Forward.' *Meeting Ground* 1 (January 1977).
Burris, Barbara. *Fourth World Manifesto*. New Haven, CT: Advocate Press, 1971.
Chesler, Phyllis. *Women and Madness*. New York: Four Walls Eight Windows, 1997; first published 1972.
Davis, Elizabeth Gould. *The First Sex*. New York: G.P. Putnam's Sons, 1971.
Dunbar, Roxanne. 'Dear Jane Alpert.' Letters to *Ms.* 2:8 (February 1974).
Harris, Pamela, et al. 'The Women's Kit.' Toronto: OISE, 1974. University of Ottawa, Canadian Women's Movement Archives.
Johnston, Jill. *Lesbian Nation: The Feminist Solution*. New York: Simon and Schuster, 1973.
Jones, Beverly, and Judith Brown. 'Toward a Female Liberation Movement.' In Leslie B. Tanner, ed., *Voices from Women's Liberation*. New York: Signet, 1970.
Knitting Circle of the New Left Caucus, The. 'Destruction Is the Highest Form of Creation, or The *Real* Contradictions in the Social Relationships in the New Left Caucus (Back to the Materialist *Knitty*-Gritty)' [ca. 1969]. University of Ottawa, Canadian Women's Movement Archives, File: New Left Caucus, The Knitting Circle of.
Marston, William Moulton. *Wonder Woman*. Intro. Gloria Steinem. New York: Bonanza Books, 1972.
Morgan, Robin. *Going Too Far: The Personal Chronicle of a Feminist*. New York: Vintage Books, 1978.
– 'Letter to the Editors.' *oob* 2:8 (March 1972).

'The Network of the Imaginary Mother.' In *Upstairs in the Garden: Poems Selected and New, 1968–1988*. New York: W.W. Norton, 1990.

Morgan, Robin, ed. *Sisterhood Is Powerful: An Anthology of Writings from the Women's Liberation Movement*. New York: Vintage, 1970.

Newton, Esther, and Paula Webster. 'Matriarchy: As Women See It.' *Aphra* 4:3 (Summer 1973).

Pateman, Carole. '"God Hath Ordained to Man a Helper": Hobbes, Patriarchy and Conjugal Right.' In Mary Lyndon Shanley and Carole Pateman, eds, *Feminist Interpretations and Political Theory*. University Park: Pennsylvania State University Press, 1991.

– *The Sexual Contract*. Stanford, CA: Stanford University Press, 1988.

Redstockings. *Feminist Revolution*. Ed. Kathie Sarachild. New Paltz, NY: Redstockings, 1975. Columbia University, Barnard Center for Research on Women, restricted file.

Williams, Brooke. 'The Chador of Women's Liberation: Cultural Feminism and the Movement Press.' *Heresies* 3:1 [1980].

Willis, Ellen. 'Up from Radicalism: A Feminist Journal.' New York University, Tamiment Library, Women's Liberation File (undated). Reprinted from *US* magazine (Bantam Books), no. 2 (October 1969).

Zahler, Leah. 'Matriarchy and Myth.' *Aphra* 4:3 (Summer 1973).

## Feminist Origin Stories (Secondary)

Anderson, Bonnie S., and Zinsser, Judith P. *A History of Their Own: Women in Europe from Prehistory to the Present*. Volume 1. Toronto: Harper & Row, 1988.

Atkinson, Ti-Grace. *Amazon Odyssey*. New York: Links Books, 1974.

Babcox, Peter. 'Meet the Women of the Revolution, 1969.' *New York Times Magazine*, 9 February 1969.

Bachofen, J.J. *Myth, Religion, and Mother Right: Selected Writings of J.J. Bachofen*. Trans. Ralph Manheim. Princeton, NJ: Princeton University Press, 1967.

Bell, Shannon. *Reading, Writing, and Rewriting the Prostitute Body*. Bloomington: Indiana University Press, 1994.

Brown, Wendy. *States of Injury: Power and Freedom in Late Modernity*. Princeton, NJ: Princeton University Press, 1995.

Cagan, Leslie. 'Something New Emerges: The Growth of a Socialist Feminist.' In Dick Cluster, ed., *They Should Have Served That Cup of Coffee*. Boston: South End Press, 1979.

Daly, Mary. *Beyond God the Father: Toward a Philosophy of Women's Liberation*. Boston: Beacon Press, 1973.

Davis, Flora. *Moving the Mountain: The Women's Movement in America since 1960.* New York: Simon and Schuster, 1991.

de Beauvoir, Simone. *The Second Sex.* New York: Knopf, 1953.

Diner, Helen. *Mothers and Amazons: The First Feminine History of Culture.* New York: Julian Press, 1965.

Echols, Alice. *Daring to Be Bad: Radical Feminism in America 1967-1975.* Minneapolis: University of Minnesota Press, 1989.

Eisler, Riane. *The Chalice and the Blade: Our History, Our Future.* San Francisco: HarperCollins, 1987.

Engels, Friedrich. *The Origin of the Family, Private Property, and the State.* New York: International Publishers, 1942.

Evans, Sara. *Personal Politics: The Roots of Women's Liberation in the Civil Rights Movement and the New Left.* New York: Knopf, 1979.

Firestone, Shulamith. *The Dialectic of Sex: The Case for Feminist Revolution.* London: Women's Press, 1979.

Firestone, Shulamith, and Anne Koedt, eds. *Notes from the Second Year.* New York: Radical Feminism, 1970.

Fraser, Nancy. *Justice Interruptus: Critical Reflections on the 'Postsocialist' Condition.* New York: Routledge, 1997.

Gitlin, Todd. *The Sixties: Years of Hope, Days of Rage.* Rev. ed. New York: Bantam, 1993.

Grimké, Sarah M. *Letters on the Equality of the Sexes and the Condition of Woman.* New York: Burt Franklin, 1970.

Hackett, Amy, and Sarah Pomeroy. 'Making History: *The First Sex.*' *Feminist Studies* 1:2 (Fall 1972).

Hayden, Brian. 'Old Europe: Sacred Matriarchy or Complementary Opposition?' In Anthony Bonanno, ed., *Archaeology and Fertility Cult in the Ancient Mediterranean.* Amsterdam: B.R. Gruner, 1986.

Johnson, Carol. 'Does Capitalism Really Need Patriarchy? Some Old Issues Reconsidered.' *Women's Studies International Forum* 19:3 1996.

King, Mary. *Freedom Song: A Personal Story of the 1960s Civil Rights Movement.* New York: William Morrow, 1987.

Kostash, Myrna. *Long Way from Home: The Story of the Sixties Generation in Canada.* Toronto: James Lorimer, 1980.

Lederer, Wolfgang. *The Fear of Women.* New York: Harcourt, Brace, Janovich, 1968.

LeGates, Marlene. *Making Waves: A History of Feminism in Western Society.* Toronto: Copp Clark, 1996.

Lerman, Rhoda. 'In Memoriam: Elizabeth Gould Davis.' *Ms.* 3:6 (December 1974).

Miles, Rosalind. *The Women's History of the World*. London: Paladin, 1988.
Millet, Kate. *Sexual Politics*. Garden City, NY: Doubleday, 1970.
Morgan, Elaine. *The Descent of Woman*. New York: Bantam, 1972.
New York Radical Women. *Notes from the First Year*. New York, June 1968.
O'Brien, Mary. *The Politics of Reproduction*. Boston: Routledge & Kegan Paul, 1981.
– *Reproducing the World: Essays in Feminist Theory*. Boulder, CO: Westview Press, 1989.
Okin, Susan Moller. 'Feminism, the Individual, and Contract Theory.' *Ethics* 100 (April 1990).
– *Women in Western Political Thought*. Princeton, NJ: Princeton University Press, 1979.
Pateman, Carole. 'Conclusion. Women's Writing, Women's Standing: Theory and Politics in the Early Modern Period.' In Hilda L. Smith, ed., *Women Writers and the Early Modern British Political Tradition*. New York: Cambridge University Press, 1998.
– *The Disorder of Women: Democracy, Feminism and Political Theory*. Stanford, CA: Stanford University Press, 1989.
– *The Problem of Political Obligation: A Critique of Liberal Theory*. Berkeley: University of California Press, 1985.
Plaskow, Judith. 'The Coming of Lilith.' In C.P. Christ and J. Plaskow, eds, *Womanspirit Rising: A Feminist Reader in Religion*. San Francisco: Harper & Row, 1979.
Pomeroy, Sarah B. 'A Classical Scholar's Perspective on Matriarchy.' In Bernice A. Carroll, ed., *Liberating Women's History: Theoretical and Critical Essays*. Chicago: University of Illinois Press, 1976.
Purdy, Laura M. *Reproducing Persons: Issues in Feminist Bioethics*. Ithaca, NY: Cornell University Press, 1996.
Purkiss, Dianne. *The Witch in History: Early Modern and Twentieth-century Representations*. New York: Routledge, 1996.
Rich, Adrienne. *Of Woman Born: Motherhood as Experience and Institution*. New York: W.W. Norton, 1976.
Sanday, Peggy Reeves. *Female Power and Male Dominance: On the Origins of Sexual Inequality*. New York: Cambridge University Press, 1981.
Shanley, Mary Lyndon, and Carole Pateman, eds. *Feminist Interpretations and Political Theory*. University Park: Pennsylvania State University Press, 1991.
Sharpe, Kevin. 'Private Conscience and Public Duty in the Writings of James VI and I.' In John Morrill, Paul Slack, and Daniel Woolf, eds, *Public Duty and Private Conscience in Seventeenth-century England: Essays Presented to G.E. Aylmer*. Toronto: Clarendon Press, 1993.

Spretnak, Charlene, ed. *The Politics of Women's Spirituality: Essays on the Rise of Spiritual Power within the Feminist Movement.* Garden City, NY: Anchor Press, 1982.

Students for a Democratic Society. 'SDS National Resolution on Women.' Boston: New England Free Press, 1968. New York University, Tamiment Library, Women's Liberation File 1968.

Thom, Mary. *Inside Ms.: 25 Years of the Magazine and the Feminist Movement.* New York: Henry Holt, 1997.

Walker, Barbara G. *The Woman's Dictionary of Myths and Secrets.* San Francisco: Harper & Row, 1983.

Zerilli, Linda. 'In the Beginning, Rape.' *The Women's Review of Books* 6:6 (March 1989).

Zuckoff, Aviva Cantor. 'The Lilith Question.' *Lilith* 1:1 (Fall 1976).

# Index

Aboriginal Peoples, 20, 71–2, 75
Adam, 8, 32, 59, 63, 72–5, 85–8, 178n60. *See also* Genesis
Aeschylus, 41–3, 172n41
Alpert, Jane, 143–4, 146–7, 149–50, 152–4, 156–7, 199n76, 200nn94, 95, 99, 101, 105
Amazon myth, 75, 87, 89–93, 95, 102, 114, 120, 127, 131, 134–6, 147, 149, 151, 159, 184n46, 185nn51, 53, 54
Anderson, Bonnie S., 193n6
androgyny, 92. *See also under* women, masculine
anthropology, 151–2, 163
Antonelli, Judy, 152
anxious masculinity, 81–2, 85–6, 92, 95, 99, 120, 182n18
archaeology, 151, 153, 163
Arendt, Hannah, 10–11, 57
Aristotle: and consent, 62; and familial structure, 110; and gender hierarchy, 79, 82, 92, 96, 153; and public/private dichotomy, 45, 83; and reproduction, 42, 173n45; theory of lost matriarchy (E.G. Davis's), 137; and theory of motion, 67; and women, 38

Armstrong, Karen, 74
Atkinson, Ti-Grace, 134, 140, 152, 155
Atlantis, myth of, 25–6, 30, 36
Attica prison, 147
authority. *See* power
autochthony, 4, 6–7, 21, 54, 74

Bachofen, J.J., 118–19, 127, 130, 133–4, 136–7, 150, 193n3
Bacon, Francis, 91
Bailyn, Bernard, 12
Balme, D.M., 173n45
Barnard Center for Research on Women, 20?n128
Barry, Kathleen, 201n123
Barthes, Roland, 10, 17
Battigelli, Anna, 103, 89n100
Bedford, David, 166n20, 174n60
Being, 29–30, 37. *See also* essentialism
Bell, Shannon, 105
Binford, Sally, 151–2
biological determinism, 19, 47, 168n38
birth, 10, 18–19, 46, 115, 120, 155, 174n55, 184n40. *See also* reproduction
Black Power, 138–40

Blundell, Sue, 171n26
Breitenberg, Mark, 81, 182n18, 184n46
Briffault, Robert, 130
Brown, Judith, 197n59
Brown, Wendy, 51

Cagan, Leslie, 139
Cambridge approach, 13–14. *See also* Skinner, Quentin
Campbell, Joseph, 193n3
Carmichael, Stokely, 196–7n54
Cary, Mary (Rande), 97
Cavendish, Margaret, Duchess of Newcastle, 101–4, 189nn95–100
Chalker, Dawn, 132
Charles I, 63, 102, 186–7n70
Chesler, Phyllis, 134–5
Chidley, Katherine, 98–100, 188n86
citizenship: Athenian, 4, 38–41, 58; and consent, 124; and democracy, 50–1; and gender, 19, 39–40; and Hobbes, 21, 55; and men, 109; and myth of the metals, 4–5; and origin stories, 20, 22–3; script of, 57, 75, 124, 148, 151–2, 164; and social contract, 125; and subjection, 76; and women, 38, 109
civil rights movement, 137–9, 141–2, 196n49
civil society: and commonwealth, 66, 108; and gender hierarchy, 121; and Hobbes, 54, 66, 70, 74; and public/private dichotomy, 83, 109; and sexual contract, 105; and social contract, 57, 107; and state of nature, 58, 68–9, 109, 111, 113, 116; and women, 77, 111–12, 117
class distinction, 5–6, 10, 50, 53, 75–6, 155–6

Columbus, Christopher, 20
commonwealth, 61, 66, 86, 108, 181n11, 185n55, 189n95
conflict. *See* violence
conjugal right, 106, 112, 115–16
conquest. *See* violence
consent: and citizenship, 124; and civil society, 105; and class distinction, 5; and conquest, 124, 175n9, 191n22; and feminism, 124; and hierarchy, 62; and Hobbes, 58–60, 62–3; and Levellers, 62; and liberalism, 122; and marriage, 85; and origin myths, 5; political, 6, 63, 85; and power, 89–90, 92; and sexual relations, 123; and social contract, 85, 126; and sovereignty, 90; and state of nature, 115; and subordination, 111; and women, 85, 89, 187n72
constitution theory, ancient, 60–2
conventionalism, 89, 95
Copernicus, 67, 156
Cornford, Frances MacDonald, 170–1nn13, 18, 171n21
cosmogony: and birth metaphors, 46; Christian, 73, 75; as cultural narrative, 7; and Hobbes, 54; mythopoetic, 30; and patrogenesis, 49; and Plato, 24–9, 35, 50, 73
Crawford, Patricia, 96, 180n5, 185n54, 187n72
creationism, 26–7
creation myth. *See* cosmogony
Cromwell, Oliver, 60, 98
Culpepper, Emily Erwin, 200n109
cultural universalism, 47

Daly, Mary, 130, 192n62
Davies, Lady Eleanor, 97, 186–7n70

Davis, Elizabeth Gould, 130–1, 135–7, 142–3, 145, 147–50, 153–5, 195–6nn32–4, 38, 200n99, 202n128
de Beauvoir, Simone, 133
democracy, 50–3, 62–3, 123, 162, 176n22
de Pisan, Christine, 179n1
Descartes, René, 67
Diner, Helen, 134, 145, 199n86
Di Stefano, Christine, 119, 176n29, 178n68
divine right, 63, 86, 94
Dunbar, Roxanne, 201n116

Echols, Alice, 140, 157, 202n127
Ehrenreich, Barbara, 192n62
Eisler, Riane, 158
Elizabeth I, 90–1, 93, 150, 182n15, 185n57
embryology, 37, 41, 43, 45, 49, 171n23
Engels, Friedrich, 127, 130–3, 194nn10, 14
English, Deirdre, 192n62
envy-appropriation thesis, 17–19, 46, 52–3, 132, 134, 136, 154–5
epistemology, 52
equality. *See* gender hierarchy
essentialism, 9–12, 19, 36–7, 67–9, 178n67
Evans, Sara, 138, 141
Eve: biblical, 8, 32, 73, 86, 88, 165–6n10, 178n60 (*see also* Genesis); paleoanthropological, 153
*Everywoman*, 129, 131
evolution, 27

Fall, the, 32, 74–5, 85, 88–9. *See also* Genesis
femininity, 51
feminism: and citizenship, 148, 151; and civil rights movement, 196n49; and consent, 124; and envy-appropriation thesis, 17–18; and foundational oppression, 148; and gender symbolism, 30; and historical inquiry, 14–15, 150–3, 188n91; matriarchal, 153, 200n94; and nationalism, 155; and patriarchy, 4; politics of, 13, 123–4, 126, 141, 143, 147, 149; and primacy of women, 135; and primary contradiction of sex, 148; radical, 18–19, 60, 106, 115, 122–3, 125–58 *passim*, 161, 164, 193n4, 197n59, 202n127; and rejection of the left, 143; and reproduction, 17; and revolution, 147–8, 156; Second Wave, 4, 16, 121, 123, 125–58 *passim*, 161; and sexual contract, 105; and social contract, 16, 78, 179n3; and spirituality, 155, 157; and state of nature, 95; and theory of lost matriarchy, 143–4; and treatment of Hobbes, 15, 18, 76–9, 179n1; and treatment of Plato, 18–19, 36–7, 47, 169n2; and witch hunts, 192n62. *See also* Women's Liberation Movement
feminist origin theories: and Amazon myth, 159; and birth, 174n55; and citizenship, 22; and envy-appropriation thesis, 132; and historical inquiry, 14, 124–6, 152–3; and Hobbes, 55, 76; and liberalism, 142; and Lilith, 8; and matricide, 11; and parthenogenesis, 131; and patriarchy, 11, 17, 121–2; politics of, 147, 155; Second Wave, 161; and theory of lost matriarchy, 137; and violence, 163

feminocentricity, 40
fictional origin stories, 23
Filmer, Sir Robert, 59–60, 63, 72, 78–87, 119–20, 181nn7, 11
Firestone, Shulamith, 130, 140–2
Fletcher, Anthony, 186n59, 188n88
Forms, the, 27, 29, 33, 36, 48–50
Foucault, Michel, 9–10, 13
foundational oppression, 125–8, 131, 140–3, 145, 148, 154–8, 164
foundation myths, 20–1, 25
Fraser, Nancy, 105
Freedom Summer (1964), 138
Freeman, Jo, 140
Freud, Sigmund, 81, 115–16
Fromm, Erich, 127, 193n3

Galileo, 67
Garden of Eden, 72–3, 86, 165–6n10. *See also* Genesis
Geddes, Anne, 171n23
gender. *See* men; women
gendered power, 79–81, 100, 103, 121, 186n69
gender hierarchy: and Amazon myth, 90; and anxious masculinity, 81, 86; and Aristotle, 96; and citizenship, 19; and civil society, 121; and equality, 56, 95, 111, 117, 148; and feminism, 78–9; and historical inquiry, 13, 15, 128, 166n28; and Hobbes, 14, 56, 77–80, 83–4, 86, 96, 104, 121; inversion of, 80, 91–2, 95, 103; and James VI and I, 83; and matriarchy, 136, 153; natural, 53, 81, 91, 182n19; and origins, 8, 19, 23, 34; and patriarchy, 25, 56; and Plato, 6, 23, 35, 37, 77; and the public/private dichotomy, 38–40, 45, 79, 83–4; and reproduction, 44, 155; and sexual contract, 105; and state of nature, 56; and subjection, 111. *See also* men; women
genealogy, 9
Genesis, 8, 32, 72–4, 85, 88, 128, 162, 165–6n10, 178nn60, 62. *See also* Adam; Eve; Fall; Garden of Eden; Lilith
Genova, Judith, 170nn11, 12
Gert, Bernard, 179n71
Gitlin, Todd, 139, 156, 196n51, 197n58
Goddess worship, 146–7, 151, 156–7, 161, 196n45, 200n106
Goldhill, Simon, 172n34
Gowing, Laura, 96
Greek origin stories, 24
Green, Karen, 179n1, 185n55
Grimké, Sarah M., 128
*Guardian*, 141
Guthrie, W.K.C., 34–5, 169–70n6
gynocracy, 136–7, 143, 145, 147, 150, 155

*Haec Vir: Or The Womanish Man*, 92
Halperin, David M., 40–1, 174nn56, 62
Hanisch, Carol, 139
Hansen, Pat, 199n86
Harris, Pamela, 133
Hayden, Casey, 197n56
Hayden, Tom, 144, 154, 199n75
Hegel, G.W.F., 109
Held, Virginia, 174n55
Heraclitus, 28–30
Herodotus, 137
*her-self*, 129, 132, 200n105
Hesiod, 24, 137, 169–70n6
*Hic Mulier: Or, The Man-Woman*, 91, 185n51

Hill, Christopher, 74
Hippocrates, 43–5, 172n41
historical inquiry: and capitalism, 142; and feminism, 14–15, 150–3, 188n91; and feminist origin theories, 14, 124–6, 150, 152–3; and foundational oppression, 132; and gender hierarchy, 166n28; and myth, 129, 136, 152; and origins, 12, 163; and Plato, 14; and politics, 13; and sexual contract, 110, 122, 126; and social contract, 105; and theory of lost matriarchy, 133, 136, 150–1
Hobbes, Thomas:
– *Behemoth or The Long Parliament*, 69
– *De Cive*, 60, 65, 70, 88–9, 175n5, 177n50, 185n55
– *De Corpore Politico*, 65, 69, 120
– *Leviathan*: Amazon myth, 90; and citizenship, 55; and civil society, 73; and gender hierarchy, 77, 80; and inertia, 68; and natural philosophy, 102; and nature of man, 56; and nominalism, 70; and power, 60–1, 87; and sovereignty, 189n97; and state of nature, 57, 177n50; use of rhetoric in, 69–71, 75, 176–7n32; and women, 117
Hobsbawn, E.J., 20, 22
Homer, 137, 169–70n6
Honig, Bonnie, 11
Houston, Alan Craig, 62
Howard, Lady Frances, 184–5n49
Hughes, Ann, 187–8n79
human nature, 74–5

Ideas, the. *See* Forms
Ionians. *See* Presocratics
Ireton, Henry, 97
Irigaray, Luce, 36–7

James VI and I, 63, 78–80, 82–4, 86–7, 91, 108, 120, 181nn7, 11, 184–5n49
Jaquette, Jane, 179n3
Johnston, Jill, 195n32
Judeo-Christian mythology, 8, 178n60

Kahn, Robbie Pfeufer, 46
Kahn, Victoria, 175n9, 189nn96, 97
Kennedy Commission on Women, 142–3
King, Helen, 43, 197n56
King, Mary, 139
Kirk, G.S., 170n8
Knitting Circle of the New Left Caucus, 197–8n61
Knox, John, 93
Krell, David Farrell, 34, 170–1n18

Ladies' auxiliaries of the Left, 140
Lady Marchioness of Newcastle. *See* Cavendish, Margaret, Duchess of Newcastle
language. *See* nominalism
Laqueur, Thomas, 44–5
Lederer, Wolfgang, 130
Lenin, Vladimir, 132
Lerman, Rhoda, 137, 143
Leslie, Pat, 130–1
Levellers, 59, 62–3, 98, 100–1, 176nn22, 24, 187–8n79
liberalism, 107, 109–10, 122, 125–6, 142
Lilburne, John, 98
Lilburne, Elizabeth, 98
Lilith, 8, 32, 165n9. *See also* Genesis
Locke, John, 71, 85, 107, 109–10, 167n30, 180–1n7
Loraux, Nicole, 7
Lyon, Mary, 194n12

Machiavelli, Nicholo, 168n42
Mack, Phyllis, 186n68
marriage: and civil society, 111; and consent, 85; and contract, 110–12, 124, 172n36, 189n97; and Elizabeth I, 93; and James VI and I, 82–3; and Margaret Cavendish, 102–3; patriarchal, 59, 93–4, 103; and state of nature, 88
Marston, William Moulton, 134
Marx, Karl, 132, 162, 194n14
Mary, Queen of Scots, 93
Mary I, Tudor, 93, 150
Mary II, Stuart, 150
Mary of Guise, 93
masculine origin stories, 17, 19
masculine political birth, 118–20
masculinity, 36, 39, 46, 51–3, 119, 174n62. *See also* anxious masculinity
maternal dominion, 88, 94–5, 185n55
maternal receptacle, 32–3, 36–7, 41, 44, 48–9
matriarchy: and Amazon myth, 131, 134; and conventionalism, 95; and counter-revolution, 137; definition of, 136; and female identity, 149; and Goddess worship, 146; and historical inquiry, 22, 133, 151, 201n123; and men, 127, 156; original, 88, 94, 119, 121, 129, 133, 135–6, 158–9, 164, 193n3, 194n14, 199n86, 202n127; and origins, 143; and patriarchy, 136; and power, 156; and Second Wave feminism, 161; structure of, 147, 150; theory of lost, 9, 129, 131, 136–7, 144–5, 148, 150–2, 157
McEntee, Ann Marie, 188n91
mechanics, 65, 67–8
Melville, Sam, 147

men: and conjugal right, 106, 116; creative potency of, 49, 51, 53; and envy-appropriation thesis, 17–18, 132–3, 154; and equality with women, 88, 95, 111, 117; and fear of women, 133, 136; and matriarchy, 127, 154; and patrogenesis, 25, 42–3, 48, 86; and politics, 25, 79, 119; and power, 152; primacy of, 32, 34, 36, 43, 87, 93, 127, 132–3, 135, 153; public activism of, 138, 141; and public/private dichotomy, 38–40, 45, 109; reproductive significance of, 31–2, 119–20, 154; and segregation, 38–40; and sexism, 144; and subordination, 136. *See also* gender hierarchy
Mendelson, Sara, 96, 180n5, 185n54
Miles, Barbara, 131
Miles, Rosalind, 153, 158
Milesians, 24
Millet, Kate, 130
Mills, Charles W., 72
misogyny, 82, 84, 144, 173n45, 182n20
'Miss America,' 141, 145, 198n70
Morgan, Robin, 127, 142–6, 152, 156–7, 192n62, 199n84, 200nn94–5
mother-right, 111–15, 117, 119, 185n55. *See also* matriarchy
Mt Holyoke College, 194n12
*Ms.*, 134, 137, 143, 202n128
myth of the metals, 4–7, 9–10, 20–1, 24, 50. *See also* autochthony

National Conference for New Politics (NCNP, 1967), 140
nationalist narratives. *See* foundation myths
National Mobilization Committee to End the War in Vietnam, 139

National Organization for Women (NOW), 142
Neville, Henry, 91
New Left, 16, 131, 137, 139, 141–2, 144
New Left Caucus, 197–8n61
Newton, Esther, 195n33
New York Radical Women (NYRW), 130, 139, 145
*New York Times Magazine*, 144
New York University, 200n102
noble lie, 4–5. *See also* myth of the metals
nominalism, 66, 70, 178n67
Northern Student Movement, 139
Norton, Mary Beth, 79, 109, 191n26
Nussbaum, Martha C., 22–3, 161

O'Brien, Mary, 17, 19, 46, 119–20, 132, 154–5, 168n38, 174n55
*off our backs*, 129
Okin, Susan Moller, 171n23, 191–2n38
Ontario Institute for Studies in Education (OISE), 132
ontology: Aristotelian, 150; dualistic, 35, 49; feminist, 150, 154; and Genesis, 73; Hobbesian, 178n68; and origin stories, 52, 72; phallocentric, 154; Platonic, 27, 30–1, 35, 49, 52, 170n11; and women, 45
opportune falsehood. *See* noble lie
*Other Woman, The*, 129
Overbury, Sir Thomas, 184–5n49
Overton, Mary, 98
Overton, Richard, 98

Pagels, Elaine, 73
*Parliament of Ladies, A*, 91
Parmenides, 28–9

parthenogenesis, 131, 135, 154
Pateman, Carole, 15, 77–8, 104–26 *passim*, 132, 167n30, 178n68, 185n55, 190n7, 191n26; *The Problem of Political Obligation*, 122; *The Sexual Contract*, 15, 106, 121, 123, 180–1n7, 191–2n38
patriarchal protective confederacy, 112–13, 116, 119
patriarchy: and Amazon myth, 91; and anxious masculinity, 81–2; and consent, 60, 62, 89; and divine right, 86; and envy-appropriation thesis, 154; and family, 22, 94–5, 99, 112, 191n25; and feminism, 123, 156, 161; and gendered power, 80; and gynocracy, 155; and Hobbes, 56, 63–4, 75, 78, 84, 86, 94–5, 110, 117, 151; and James VI and I, 83, 87; in Judeo-Christian mythology, 8; and marriage, 59, 93–4, 103; and matriarchy, 10, 129, 136–7; modern, 110, 122, 126; and mother-right, 115, 117, 119; origins of, 19, 22, 128, 133–4, 142–3, 148, 158; and Plato, 47, 52, 171n23; and political theory, 63–4, 78, 82, 104, 162; and religion, 97, 146; and revolution, 130; and social contract, 105–6, 116, 121; and social relations, 17, 104, 118, 125, 158, 160–1, 193n3; and sovereignty, 63, 182n15; and state of nature, 85; theorists of, 78–9; and violence, 11; and women, 22, 96, 100, 149, 199n86, 201n123. *See also* patrogenesis; phallocentricity
patrimonial kingdoms, 113–14
patrogenesis, 31–3, 37, 41–2, 44–9, 52, 85–6, 88, 119, 173n45, 174n58. *See also* patriarchy

phallocentricity, 37, 43, 45, 49–50, 154, 169n2, 173n45. *See also* patriarchy
Plato:
- *Critias*, 25–6
- *Laws*, 34
- *Phaedo*, 34–5
- *Republic*, 4, 6, 25–6, 36, 52
- *Symposium*, 36, 48, 135, 174n56
- *Timaeus*: as a cosmogony, 21, 24, 27, 30, 34, 43–4, 170n14; and femininity, 51; gendered symbolism in, 24–5, 36, 47–51, 120–1, 171n21; and masculinity, 52, 118; and ontological dualism, 30, 49; and patriarchy, 4; and politics, 9, 50; and public/private dichotomy, 39; and Pythagorus, 29; and reproduction, 31; and scientific inquiry of origins, 28; as a script of citizenship, 51, 53; and segregation, 39. *See also* myth of the metals
political origin stories, 3, 8, 152
political society, 6, 54
Pomeroy, Sarah, 133–4, 150
Poole, Elizabeth, 80–2, 97
power: absolute, 56, 58, 63–4, 72, 76, 92, 109; and civil society, 57; and consent, 58, 63, 85, 87; and divine right, 63, 80, 85–7, 94, 175n9; and envy-appropriation theory, 46; and gender hierarchy, 86, 88, 94; and Hobbes, 54; and men, 51, 80, 85, 87–8, 94, 152; and origins, 3, 7–8, 23, 54, 59; and politics, 85, 148; relations of, 60–1, 80–1, 121, 123, 175n9; and women, 19, 46, 48–9, 89, 147, 151, 154–6. *See also* gendered power
Presocratics, 24, 28, 30, 41, 52, 170n11, 171n18
primordial truth. *See* essences

public/private dichotomy, 38–40, 45, 79, 82–4, 99, 106–10, 118, 123, 171–2n31, 180–1n7, 190n7
Purdy, Laura, 18
Purkiss, Diane, 125, 152
Pythagoras, 27–9, 34, 170n11, 171n18

*Quicksilver Times*, 127

Rainborough, Colonel, 62
rape, 115–16, 126, 152. *See also* violence
*Rat*, 144, 146
Raven, J.E., 170n8
Rawls, John, 177n44
Redstockings, 145, 157, 195n34, 200n102, 202n128
reductionism, 12, 46, 52, 150
Reed, Evelyn, 194n14
Reformation, the, 72, 156
religious creation stories, 3
religious inquiry, 7
reproduction: and feminism, 17, 154; and gender symbolism, 24–5, 30, 40, 46–7, 163; and Hobbes, 120; as intellectual process, 18–19, 155; men's contribution to, 118–20, 173n45; and patrogenesis, 31; as physical process, 18–19, 47, 155, 174n55; and Plato, 155; women's contribution to, 33, 41, 58, 119, 172n41, 173n45, 174n56. *See also* birth
Rich, Adrienne, 133
Rousseau, Rene, 107, 109–10
Rudd, Mark, 140
Rutherford, R.B., 26

Said, Edward, 3
Samuelson, Norbert, 169–70n6
Saxonhouse, Arlene W., 6, 51

Schochet, G.J., 59, 166n28, 184n40, 191n25
Schwarz, Kathryn, 91
scientific inquiry, 3, 7, 28, 55, 65, 69, 74, 163
scripts of citizenship. *See* citizenship
SDS. *See* Students for a Democratic Society
Seller, Mary J., 174n58
sex. *See* men; women
sexism, 144–5, 197n60, 198n67
sex-right. *See* conjugal right
sexual contract, 16, 77, 104–26 *passim*. *See also* Pateman, Carole
sexual relations, 115, 123, 125
Sharpe, Kevin, 108
Skinner, Quentin, 13–15, 175n12
Smith, Anthony D., 168n39
SNCC. *See* Student Nonviolent Coordinating Committee (SNCC)
social contract: and anxious masculinity, 82; and citizenship, 125; and conjugal right, 115; and consent, 58; and democracy, 62; and equality, 76; and feminism, 16, 77–8; and Hobbes, 4, 9, 54, 57; and masculine political birth, 118; and origins, 3; and patriarchy, 78, 112–13, 116, 121; and public/private dichotomy, 106–7, 180–1n7; and sexual contract, 105, 126; and sovereignty, 58, 68, 104; and women, 77, 106, 109, 111, 116–17
sophistry, 25, 51
sovereignty: and civil society, 107–8; and class distinction, 75–6; and conquest, 89–90, 114; and consent, 59, 63, 90, 114; and Margaret Cavendish, 189n98; and patriarchy, 63, 182n15; and power, 109, 175n9; and social contract, 58, 68; and subordination, 104; and women, 114
Spenser, Edmund, 185n51
Spinoza, Benedict De, 184n46
Stanton, Elizabeth Cady, 165–6n10
state of nature: and birth, 184n40; and civil society, 54–5, 57, 66, 68–71, 74, 109, 116; and commonwealth, 108; and consent, 88; and family, 110, 113; and feminism, 77–8, 95, 121; and Genesis, 89; and patriarchy, 56, 85, 113–14, 191n25; and power, 60, 64; and public/private dichotomy, 107; rhetoric of, 70, 86; and sexual contract, 116; and sexual relations, 115; and social contract, 9; and violence, 56–7, 115–16; and women, 106, 112, 114
Steinem, Gloria, 134, 202n128
Stone, Merlin, 151
Student Nonviolent Coordinating Committee (SNCC), 138, 196–7nn54, 56
Students for a Democratic Society (SDS), 139–43, 199n75
subjection, 76, 107, 111, 124. *See also* citizenship
Swetnam, Joseph, 182n20, 185n53

Table of Opposites, Pythagorean, 29, 34. *See also* Pythagoras
Taylor, A.E., 35, 170–1n18
teleology, 9, 67–8
*To the Supream authority of this Nation, the commons assembled in Parliament*, 188n81
*To the Supreme Authority of England. The Commons Assembled in Parliament*, 188nn82–3
Tower of London, 184n49, 187n70

Trigg, Roger, 178n67
tripartite theory of the soul, 6
*True Copie of the Petition of the Gentlewoman, and the Tradesmens-wives*, 100
Tuana, Nancy, 36
Tully, James, 71, 166n28

Vickery, Amanda, 180–1n7
*Village Voice, The*, 195n32
violence, 10–11, 56–7, 116, 124, 163. *See also* rape
*Voice of the Women's Liberation Movement*, 129
von Franz, Marie-Louise, 165n7

Walker, Barbara G., 159–62, 164
Walwyn, William, 98
war. *See* violence
Warrington, John, 169–70n6
Warrior, Betsy, 201n113
Weather Underground, The, 145, 147, 199n76, 200n95
Webb, Marilyn, 141
Webster, Paula, 195n33
Western origin narratives, 23
Westfall, Richard S., 177n37
Wildman, John, 62
Williams, Brooke, 202n127
Willis, Ellen, 148
WITCH. *See* Women's International Terrorist Conspiracy from Hell (WITCH)
witch hunts, 83–4, 146, 183nn24, 27, 192n62
Wolin, Sheldon S., 70
women: and autochthony, 6; and citizenship, 109; and civil society, 112, 117; and consent, 85, 187n72; and equality with men, 88, 95, 111; fear of, 133, 136; and Hobbes, 106, 120; and identity, 92, 149, 158; inferiority of, 32, 34, 79, 88–9, 133, 137, 184n46; masculine, 91–2, 185n53; and patriarchy, 22, 96, 149, 199n86, 201n123; persecution of, 83–4, 145, 183n24, 192n62; and Plato, 34; and power, 19, 147, 154; primacy of, 9, 135–6, 153–5, 185n53; public activism of, 59, 95–101, 138, 141, 176n22, 180–1n7, 187n79, 188n91, 196–7n54; and public/private dichotomy, 38–40, 45, 79, 82–4, 99, 171–2n31; religious activity of, 82, 96–7, 100–1, 104, 180–1n7, 187n73; reproductive significance of, 6, 17–18, 31, 41–2, 119, 127, 133, 147, 154–5; roles of, 6, 40, 79, 83–4; as secondary creation, 30, 32, 36, 43, 45, 49, 85, 171n23; and segregation, 38–40, 46; and sexual contract, 105; and social contract, 16, 77, 106, 111, 116–17, 179n3; and state of nature, 88–9, 106, 114; and subordination, 32, 46, 52, 77–8, 88, 96, 111–12, 123 (*see also* foundational oppression). *See also* gender hierarchy
Women's International Terrorist Conspiracy from Hell (WITCH), 145–6
women's liberation, 140–1, 143–4, 152, 168n38
Women's Liberation Movement, 16, 22, 127–30, 132–3, 141, 143, 150, 158, 193n4, 198n70, 200n102, 202n128. *See also* feminism
Workman, Thom, 166n20, 174n60

Zahler, Leah, 151
Zarka, Yves Charles, 177n42
Zinsser, Judith P., 193n6